Ancient Mesopotamia at
the Dawn of Civilization

Ancient Mesopotamia at the Dawn of Civilization

The Evolution of an Urban Landscape

GUILLERMO ALGAZE

THE UNIVERSITY OF CHICAGO PRESS   CHICAGO AND LONDON

GUILLERMO ALGAZE is professor of anthropology at the University of California, San Diego, and author of *The Uruk World System: The Dynamics of Expansion of Early Mesopotamian Civilization*, now in its second edition from the University of Chicago Press.

The University of Chicago Press, Chicago 60637
The University of Chicago Press, Ltd., London
© 2008 by The University of Chicago
All rights reserved. Published 2008
Printed in the United States of America

17 16 15 14 13 12 11 10 09 08   1 2 3 4 5

ISBN-13: 978-0-226-01377-0 (cloth)
ISBN-10: 0-226-01377-4 (cloth)

Library of Congress Cataloging-in-Publication Data
Algaze, Guillermo, 1954–
   Ancient Mesopotamia at the dawn of civilization : the evolution of an urban landscape / Guillermo Algaze.
       p. cm.
   Includes bibliographical references and index.
   ISBN-13: 978-0-226-01377-0 (cloth : alk. paper)
   ISBN-10: 0-226-01377-4 (cloth : alk. paper)   1. Cities and towns, Ancient—Iraq.
2. City planning—Iraq. 3. Commerce, Prehistoric—Iraq. 4. Iraq—Civilization—To 634.
I. Title.
   HT114.A524   2008
   307.760935—dc22   2008015337

FOR MY WIFE, SUSAN, AND DAUGHTER, ARIELLE,
WHO EVERY MORNING GIVE ME A REASON TO LIVE

Contents

List of Illustrations ix
Acknowledgments xi
Prologue xiii

CHAPTER 1. The Sumerian Takeoff 1

      Natural and Created Landscapes 1
      A Reversal of Fortune 3
      Forthcoming Discussions 6

CHAPTER 2. Factors Hindering Our Understanding of the Sumerian Takeoff 11

      The Material Limits of the Evidence 11
      Conceptual Problems 14
      Methodological Problems 24

CHAPTER 3. Modeling the Dynamics of Urban Growth 28

      Growth As Diversification 30
      Growth As Specialization 33
      Growth Situated 36
      Growth Institutionalized 37

CHAPTER 4. Early Mesopotamian Urbanism: Why? 40

      Environmental Advantages 40
      Geographical Advantages 50
      Comparative and Competitive Advantage 63

CHAPTER 5.   Early Mesopotamian Urbanism: How? 64

The Growth of Early Mesopotamian Urban Economies 64
The Uruk Expansion 68
Multiplier Effects 73

CHAPTER 6.   The Evidence for Trade 93

CHAPTER 7.   Early Mesopotamian Urbanism in Comparative
Perspective 100

Evidentiary Biases 100
Florescent Urbanism in Alluvial Mesopotamia 102
The Primacy of Warka: Location, Location, Location 109
Aborted Urbanism in Upper Mesopotamia 117

CHAPTER 8.   The Synergies of Civilization 123

Propinquity and Its Consequences 123
Technologies of the Intellect 127
The Urban Revolution Revisited 140

CHAPTER 9.   Conclusion: The Mesopotamian Conjuncture 143

EPILOGUE   Early Sumerian Civilization: A Research Agenda 151

Agency 152
Paleoenvironment 154
Trade 155
Households and Property 157
Excavation and Survey 159
Paleozoology 161
Mortuary Evidence 162
Chronology 163
The Early Uruk Problem 164

APPENDIX 1.   Surveyed Early/Middle Uruk Sites in the Mesopotamian
Alluvium Organized by Size and Presumed Functional
Category 167

APPENDIX 2.   Surveyed Late Uruk Sites in the Mesopotamian Alluvium
Organized by Size and Presumed Functional Category 173

Notes 177   Reference List 193
Source List 221   Index 225

Illustrations

Figures

1.   Map of the ancient Near East in the fourth millennium BC   4

2.   Plan of excavated Late Uruk structures in Anu Ziggurat (Kullaba) area of Uruk/Warka   13

3.   Plan of excavated Late Uruk structures in Eanna area of Uruk/ Warka (phases V–IV)   13

4.   Uruk cylinder seal impressions   42

5.   The ancient Mesopotamian alluvium during the late fifth and fourth millennia BC   45

6.   Arched reed hut (Arabic: *madhaif*) typical for Iraqi marsh environments   47

7.   Uruk period *madhaif* representations   47

8.   Uruk cylinder seal impressions depicting various types of canoes and boats   52

9.   Loaded donkey being led to market, Iraq   57

10. Sail barge being towed along river canal in southern Iraq (ca. 1950s)   60

11. Excavated areas of Late Uruk colonies at Jebel Aruda and Habuba Kabira-süd   71

12. Imported flint and obsidian blades   75

13. Locally manufactured clay sickle   75

14. Uruk cylinder seal impressions depicting various stages in the textile production process 83

15. Uruk sealing portraying scribes keeping track of various categories of agricultural production 91

16. Early–Middle Uruk period (ca. 3900/3800–3400 BC) settlement patterns in Nippur-Adab and Warka (Uruk) survey areas of the Mesopotamian alluvium 104

17. Late Uruk period (ca. 3400–3200/3100 BC) settlement patterns in Nippur-Adab and Warka (Uruk) survey areas of the Mesopotamian alluvium 105

18. Approximate outline of the Late Uruk occupation of Uruk/Warka (interior perimeter) 107

19. Fourth-millennium demographic trends 110

20. The High Mound at Tell Brak, as seen from the surrounding plain 119

21. Location of Late Uruk period sites and principal waterways of the time in Warka survey area 125

22. Uruk seal impressions depicting labor scenes 130

23. Uruk beveled rim bowl from Chogha Mish, Iran 132

24. Middle/Late Uruk period impressed ball from Chogha Mish, Iran 134

25. Seal impressed Late Uruk period numerical notation tablet 136

26. Late Chalcolithic numerical mnemonic device from Arslan Tepe VIA 137

Table

1. Reworking of Adams's data for Late Uruk period settlement in the Nippur-Adab and Warka regions 113

Acknowledgments

This book is an attempt at synthesis. By definition, it is based on the accumulated knowledge of a community of scholars. Over the years, however, no scholar has had more influence on my intellectual outlook than Robert McCormick Adams, whose fundamental work surveying vast portions of the ancient Mesopotamian alluvium forms the point of departure for any and all attempts to delineate the evolutionary trajectory of succeeding social formations in southern Iraq from prehistoric times onwards. Adams kindly read various iterations of this book in draft form, and each time provided insightful—and much needed—criticism (Adams 2005). Equally important, throughout the process he continually suggested new research directions that significantly altered the book and expanded its scope.

Others helped greatly as well. I am grateful to Mr. Clint Ballinger (2001), who graciously shared with me his master's thesis written at the Department of Political Science of the University of North Carolina. In so doing, he introduced me to the concept of "competitive" advantage (chap. 3), an idea central to this book. Much greater is the intellectual debt I owe to Jennifer Pournelle, my first doctoral student at the University of California, San Diego (UCSD). Many of the ideas presented in chapter 4 are based directly on numerous—and always illuminating—conversations with Jennifer, as well as on a close reading of her brilliant dissertation, which used remote sensing imagery to reassess the environmental context of the Mesopotamian alluvium in the fourth millennium BC.

In addition, I am also greatly obliged to friends and colleagues who read early drafts of this book and offered valuable criticism, numerous editorial comments, and suggested crucial missing references—particularly Robert Drennan (University of Pittsburgh), Joyce Marcus (University of Michigan), Joy McCorriston (Ohio State University), Michael Rosenberg (University of Delaware), the late Donald Tuzin (UCSD), Douglas White (University of California, Irvine), and two anonymous reviewers contacted by the University of Chicago Press. Without a doubt, the contributions that these scholars made to my work are quite substantial, although occasionally, no doubt to my detriment, I chose to ignore portions of their advice. Accordingly, remaining errors of omission and interpretation are entirely my own. In its final form, the manuscript also owes much to editorial comments and grammatical corrections suggested by my wife, Susan Becker Algaze. Those I dared not disregard!

Last, but most assuredly not least, this book would not have been possible without the generous support of the MacArthur Foundation, which, in naming me a fellow, provided me the luxury of time for research and peace of mind for reflection. Its assistance is acknowledged with gratitude.

Prologue

In *Big Structures, Large Processes, Huge Comparisons,* Charles Tilly (1984, 60–65) distinguishes four possible (and complementary) levels of analysis that social scientists can use to understand social change. In decreasing order of breadth, these levels are world-historical, world-systemic, macrohistorical, and microhistorical. According to Tilly, the broadest level, world-historical analysis, is concerned primarily with comparative studies across deep time, for instance, "schemes of human evolution, of the rise and fall of empires, and of successive modes of production." At this level, "the relevant processes for analysis ... are the transformation, contact, and succession of world systems." One level down in breadth are world-systemic studies, a term that Tilly borrows from the work of I. Wallerstein (1974) and his followers. Such studies are concerned with "big networks ... of geographically segregated and ... strongly interdependent social structures" that exist in any given historical era. In contrast, the third level—macrohistorical research—focuses on individual societies forming part of larger world systems and seeks "to account for particular big structures and large processes and to chart their alternate forms." This is the level of "history as historians ordinarily treat it." It is also the level in which "processes [such] as proletarianization, urbanization, capital accumulation, statemaking, and bureaucratization lend themselves to effective analyses." The final—and most narrowly focused—level within Tilly's analytical perspective is the microhistorical level, in which "we trace the encounters of individuals and groups with those [macrohistorical] structures and processes."

I find Tilly's analytical scheme quite useful in conceptualizing various aspects of my ongoing research interests in the emergence of early Sumerian civilization—widely acknowledged as the world's earliest—along the alluvial lowlands of the Tigris-Euphrates rivers during the second half of the fourth millennium BC.[1] My earlier publications on this subject (e.g., Algaze 1989, 1993 [rev. 2005], 2001b) focused on processes of external expansion that accompanied that emergence and are largely written from the perspective of the periphery. They are explicitly world-systemic in their outlook. The present book, in contrast, is written from the perspective of the Mesopotamian core and focuses instead on forces at work in southern Mesopotamia that allowed early alluvial societies to surpass their contemporary rivals and to become expansive in the first place. Its focus thus falls squarely within the purview of Tilly's macrohistorical perspective. To my mind, the world-systemic and macrohistorical analytical perspectives are entirely complementary and when used in tandem enable us to better understand the rise of early Sumerian civilization. To appreciate why this is so, it is necessary to briefly recapitulate the main lines of argument proffered in my earlier work and explain how the ideas presented here fit into and expand upon it.

Earlier, I had argued that during the Uruk period (ca. 3900/3800 to 3200/3100 BC) the alluvial lowlands of southern Mesopotamia became host to multiple politically balkanized but culturally homogeneous city-states, which, as a group, had no peers in southwest Asia at the time. For reasons that we do not entirely understand but that may well be related to the dynamics of internal competition between these states, some Uruk populations colonized the neighboring Susiana plain of Khuzestan, in southwestern Iran, while others established colonial settlements at locations of transportational significance for trade across the Mesopotamian periphery, usually at the juncture of the north-to-south–flowing rivers draining the surrounding highlands and east-west–oriented overland routes across the rolling plains of Upper Mesopotamia. I interpreted the strategic location of these settlements at many of the natural convergence points of intraregional (overland) and interregional (waterborne) routes to mean that their primary function was to redirect a portion of the commodities that flowed through Upper Mesopotamian and highland trade routes toward southern polities that, because of their privileged position astride transport choke points, must have enjoyed particularly favorable terms of trade.

Finally, I suggested that exchange between Mesopotamia and peripheral polities was inherently asymmetrical in its impact because, with the exception of metals, it was characterized by the exchange of largely raw or lightly processed commodities from the periphery for processed prestige goods crafted in southern Mesopotamian cities. This allowed Uruk city-states to accumulate resources drawn from a vast periphery over which, as a whole, they did not exercise direct political control. For this reason, the Uruk colonial settlements across the Mesopotamian periphery may be conceptualized as unwittingly creating the world's earliest world system: they united previously independent regions and polities into an overarching system of asymmetrical relationships of interdependency that were principally, but not solely, economic in nature.

These ideas have been scrutinized from various perspectives (e.g., Rothman 2001), and reviewers and critics have offered numerous variant interpretations of the Uruk world system model.[2] Of these, two lines of criticism stand out as particularly substantive and require further elaboration. Both are addressed in this book.

The first criticism is that I overestimated the degree of asymmetry existing in the system of interregional interactions between southern Mesopotamia and its neighbors during the fourth millennium. Underpinning this argument is the presumption that southern Mesopotamian societies of the fourth millennium BC did not enjoy any obvious technological advantages over societies in neighboring regions, and that this lack precluded the creation of a truly asymmetrical overarching system of regional interaction such as I had postulated to exist during the Uruk period (Kohl 2001; Stein 1990, 1999a).

Arguments about the technological parity of Mesopotamian and peripheral polities in the fourth millennium are problematic on several accounts. First, they implicitly presume that "technology" refers only to innovations that allow humans to manipulate, transform, and extract material gain from the world in which they live. This fails to acknowledge what the anthropologist Jack Goody (2000) and the sociologist Michael Mann (1986), each in his own distinctive voice, have cogently argued for many years, namely, that innovations in how power is conceptualized and materialized, in how labor is controlled and organized, and in how information is gathered, processed, and used are as capable of creating significant developmental asymmetries between different societies as imbalances in material technology (Goody 2000). Second, parity arguments gloss over the fact that the two types of technologies, material and social (organizational), cannot be understood except in reference to each other. As economists often remind us, the two types always exist in a matrix of mutual determinations: advances in the ability to manipulate the material world make possible innovations in social technologies that, in turn, provide a framework in which new material technologies can arise, etc. (Beinhocker 2006, 14–15). Third, early Mesopotamian technological parity arguments fail to consider that the impact of a new technology (whether material or social) in any given economy will always depend on exactly when that technology is introduced within the cybernetic feedback cycle that always exists between production, consumption, increasing returns to scale, market size, population growth, and innovation (chaps. 3 and 8 below). Accordingly, otherwise identical technologies will often lead to dramatically different results when adopted by societies with varying histories of development (Krugman 1991, 487).

The second substantive criticism of my earlier work is that I underestimated the degree of social complexity that existed in portions of the Mesopotamian periphery during parts of the fourth millennium and that this error mars my assessment of the nature of the "Uruk world system" as a whole (e.g., Emberling et al. 1999; Frangipane 1997, 2001a, 2001b, 2002; Oates 2001; Stein 1999a, 1999b, 2001; G. Schwartz 2001; Wilkinson 2001). Recent work in northern Iraq conducted just before the First Gulf War and ongoing work in northern Syria clearly shows that this criticism is well founded. In fact, as Henry Wright (2001 and personal communication, 2006) presciently noted, parts of the Khabur triangle region in Upper Mesopotamia appear to have been as poised for an urban takeoff at the start of the fourth millennium BC as the southern Mesopotamian alluvium itself. While this is a necessary—and welcome—correction to my earlier characterization of the nature of Late Chalcolithic societies in the periphery of alluvial Mesopotamia, the new data present us with a new research question: if polities in the alluvium hardly differed in nature and scale from those developing in other areas of southwest Asia by the beginning of the fourth millennium, as now appears to have been the case, how does one explain the sharp divergence that can be observed in the historical trajectories of southern Mesopotamia and the rest of southwest Asia through the second half of the fourth millennium, when the protourban systems of Upper Mesopotamia, so promising only centuries earlier, started to contract and disintegrate while the expansive city-states of southern Mesopotamia continued to grow in both scale and complexity?

To answer this key question, it is necessary to temporarily set aside the peripheral focus of my earlier work and pay greater attention instead on processes at work in the Mesopotamian alluvium itself. This book is an effort to do just that—within, of course, the limits of the evidence available at this time. It elaborates on arguments that first appeared in more limited and provisional form in articles published in the journals *Current Anthropology* and *Structure and Dynamics* (Algaze 2001a and 2005b, respectively). Because the pertinent evidence is largely archaeological in nature and therefore is entirely insufficient to the task of reconstructing details of the historical context at the time of the inception of Mesopotamian civilization, my effort is primarily—and necessarily—deductive in nature. Throughout this book, I explicitly assume that processes of urban and regional development in the modern world are similar in essence, although certainly not in detail or intensity, to pertinent processes in antiquity. Accordingly, by studying modern understandings of how cities form, grow, and shape their hinterlands we can better conceptualize the processes giving rise to the world's first cities as well as the forces underlying the formation of the world's earliest regional asymmetries. This presumption allows me to address, however clumsily, what I now perceive to be the most serious failing of my earlier research: while that work describes the main outlines of the asymmetrical system of interaction with southern Mesopotamia at its core that had emerged by the second half of the fourth millennium, it did not postulate a coherent set of mechanisms or processes to account for how that supraregional system evolved in the first place.

In attempting to grapple with this failing, in what follows I argue that the ecological and geographical conditions that existed across the alluvial lowlands of the Tigris-Euphrates fluvial system during the fifth and fourth millennia BC created regional imbalances in the availability and cost of various resources, which, in turn, made it likely that early southern Mesopotamian elites would use trade as one of their most important tools in their quest to acquire status and power.[3] In so doing, I contend that long-term import-export patterns were created that inadvertently, differentially favored the economic and demographic development of southern polities over neighboring societies throughout the fourth millennium.

To explain how this may have taken place, I present a hypothetical (but ultimately testable!) scenario in which, as the exchange unfolded over time, multiplier effects of trade fueled substantial increases in the density and propinquity of populations in the Mesopotamian alluvium, as compared to those prevalent in competing areas. In turn, this allowed for the number of possible interactions between individuals and factions within early Sumerian centers to multiply, and so too did the number of possible interactions between the growing centers themselves, which were commonly located within short distances and easy reach of each other via water transport. By the second half of the fourth millennium, this had set the stage for important organizational innovations to emerge within early Sumerian polities that, by then, had become increasingly diversified and populous. Most salient among these innovations were new, and more efficient, ways of organizing labor, as well as new ways of collecting, processing, and transmitting information. More than any other set of factors, these innovations ultimately explain why complex, regionally organized, and expansive city-states evolved earlier in southern Iraq than elsewhere in southwest Asia or the world.

CHAPTER ONE

The Sumerian Takeoff

Natural and Created Landscapes

E conomic geographers seeking to understand how substantial variations in population concentration and economic activity are created
across the landscape correctly note that, except in cases of colonial im-
position, such variations are always the result of cumulative processes
whereby initial natural advantages of particular sites or areas are extended and compounded by socially created technologies and institutions delivering increasing returns to scale. In this manner, they argue,
self-reinforcing processes of accumulation, exchange, agglomeration,
and innovation are created that ultimately determine the varying developmental trajectories of different regions and the location, number, and
rate of growth of cities within them (Krugman 1991, 1995, 1998a; Pred
1966).

The historian William Cronon (1991) vividly illustrates this process
in reference to the expansion of Chicago in the nineteenth century, as
outlined in his book *Nature's Metropolis: Chicago and the Great West.*
Cronon insightfully distinguishes between two settings in which the evolution of the city took place. The first was its "natural landscape," entirely determined by geography and environment. The second was what
he terms the "created landscape," which results from human innovations
and institutions that substantially alter and reshape a city's natural setting

and significantly expand the advantages of its location for human settlement. Cronon argues that in the modern world the created landscape has become more important than the natural landscape as a determinant of urban location and regional developmental rates. Specifically, he sees Chicago's initial role as a Great Lakes port, a role entirely determined by geography of the Great Lakes area, as eventually overshadowed by its later role as a railroad hub, a secondary but economically more important role that emerged as part of the "created landscape." Chicago became the early economic center of its region because it was a port. Railroads later used Chicago as a hub precisely because it already was the early economic center of its region, and thereby helped make its initial centrality that much greater. In so doing, Chicago surpassed its regional rival, Saint Louis, and became the undisputed commercial and cultural center serving as the "gateway" to the American West (see also Kruman 1996a).

New York City presents us with a similar case, according to the economist Paul Krugman (Fujita and Krugman 2004, 141). Its initial growth stems from its natural location at the juncture of the Hudson River and the Atlantic Ocean, which positioned the city early on as one of several important hubs of transatlantic trade along the Eastern Seaboard (together with Boston, Baltimore, and Philadelphia). Because it already was a hub of maritime trade in the first quarter of the nineteenth century, commercial interests in New York City were in an ideal position to lobby the New York state legislature to construct the Erie Canal, a 363-mile-long series of interlocking artificial waterways built within the relatively short span of eight years that linked the cities of Buffalo on the shores of Lake Erie and Albany on the Upper Hudson River (Cornog 2000). Upon its completion in 1825, the canal allowed unimpeded barge traffic between New York City and the Great Lakes via the Hudson River.

The benefits of the canal to the city were immediate: its barges and boats exponentially lowered transport cost of agricultural and other commodities to the city's merchants (chap. 4) and, in so doing, provided them with important advantages vis-à-vis competing commercial interests in Boston, Baltimore, and Philadelphia. Indeed, within fifteen years of the opening of the canal, New York City had eclipsed all of its competitors on the Eastern Seaboard, becoming the busiest seaport in all of the United States; and within thirty years of the opening of the canal the population of the city had quadrupled, as New York became the largest and most populous urban center in the country—exactly what the canal builders and financiers had intended.[1] As New York City achieved front-rank status in the mid-nineteenth century, in large part because of its increasingly disproportionate share of the inland and maritime trade at the time, economies of scale resulting from the city's larger size made many of its other related industries (notably finance and communication) more competitive than those of its by then smaller rivals, further accentuating the city's centrality and further accelerating its growth.

A Reversal of Fortune

The insights of Cronon and Krugman about the ways in which natural and created landscapes determine, reinforce, and compound each other in modern cities and their surrounding areas are applicable to earlier cases of urban transformation. A case in point appears to be the crystallization of early Sumerian civilization in the alluvial lowlands of the Tigris-Euphrates rivers of southern Mesopotamia during the Uruk period, which is radiocarbon-dated ca. 3900/3800 to ca. 3200/3100 BC (Wright and Rupley 2001; Rupley 2003). As Tony Wilkinson (2001) and Joan Oates (2001) have recently noted, this emergence took place after centuries, if not millennia, in which the developmental trajectory of polities in the southern Mesopotamian alluvium had hardly differed from that of neighboring societies across the ancient Near East. This becomes clear when we compare data pertinent for the fifth and fourth millennia BC produced by disparate surveys and excavations across northern and southern Mesopotamia, southwestern Iran, and the Levant.

Briefly summarized, these data indicate that during the second half of the fifth millennium, Late Ubaid settlements in southern Mesopotamia (Oates 1983) were entirely comparable in terms of both scale (roughly measured by settlement extent) and level of intrasite differentiation to those of contemporary (Middle Susiana 3–Late Susiana) societies in the Susiana plain of Khuzestan (Delougaz and Kantor 1996; H. Wright 1984; Wright and Johnson 1975) and also appear to have also been similar in scale to contemporary settlements in the Upper Euphrates, Upper Khabur, and Upper Tigris basins of Upper Mesopotamia (Kouchoukos and Hole 2003; Wilkinson 2000b, 2003a). Moreover, the Late Ubaid settlements of southern Iraq are comparable in scale to contemporary Ghassulian phase Chalcolithic settlements in the Jordan Valley (Bourke 2001, 111–16).

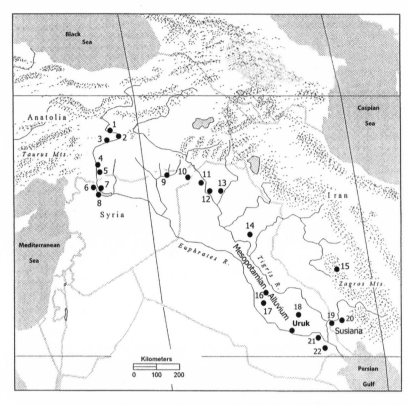

FIGURE I. Map of the ancient Near East in the fourth millennium BC illustrating the main geographical features, areas, and sites noted throughout the text. Key to sites: 1. Arslan Tepe; 2. Hassek Höyük; 3. Samsat; 4. Hacınebi; 5. Zeytinbahçe; 6. Jebel Aruda; 7. Sheikh Hassan; 8. Habuba Kabira-süd; 9. Tell Brak; 10. Hamoukar; 11. Tell el-Hawa; 12. Nineveh; 13. Tepe Gawra; 14. Rubeidah; 15. Godin Tepe; 16. Abu Salabikh; 17. Nippur; 18. Umma; 19. Susa; 20. Chogha Mish; 21. Ur; 22. Eridu.

A degree of differentiation in regional developmental rates starts to become apparent in some portions of southwest Asia at the transition from the fifth to the fourth millennia but this is mostly due to collapse of the indigenous societies in the Levant at the end of the Chalcolithic period, a process that is still not well understood (Levy 1998, 241–43). Elsewhere in southwest Asia, however, development continued unabated at this time. This is certainly the case in portions of "Greater Mesopotamia," where "protourban" polities of considerable extent and complexity were beginning to arise, first, in the parts of the Upper Khabur plains of northern Syria and, soon thereafter, within the alluvial lowlands of the Tigris and Euphrates rivers in southern Iraq, and, to a lesser extent, in Susiana (Adams 1981; Kouchoukos and Hole 2003; Nissen 1993; Oates 2001; Ur, Kaarsgard, and Oates 2007; Wilkinson 2000b, 2003a; H. Wright 1984, 2001).

Yet, only a few centuries later, by the second half of the fourth millennium, Upper and Lower Mesopotamia were no longer developing largely in tandem or at comparable rates. The available evidence clearly shows that by this time polities in the Tigris-Euphrates alluvial delta had surpassed their immediate neighbors and potential competitors across the Near East (and the world) in terms of scale, degree of internal differentiation, and extent of hierarchy present in surrounding settlement grids (Adams 1981). By the third quarter of the fourth millennium, if not earlier, southern Mesopotamia became a dynamic hub of interaction, where multiple thriving and competing city-states were forged into a politically balkanized but culturally homogeneous and expansive civilization that extended at this point into southwestern Iran and parts of Upper Mesopotamia (Algaze 2005a, 144–45; but see H. Wright 1998 for a contrary opinion).

In contrast, the early indigenous protourban sites of Upper Mesopotamia, such as Tell Brak, were in decline throughout the second half of the fourth millennium (Emberling 2002), just as a number of colonies of Uruk settlers of southern origin were established at strategic locations across the northern plains (Algaze 1993, 2001b; Gibson et al. 2002; G. Schwartz 2001; Stein 1999a, 1999b, 2001). While indigenous societies continued to flourish across the north at this time (Frangipane 2002), including in areas surrounding the intrusive southern settlements, the remaining Late Chalcolithic polities of Upper Mesopotamia as a group were no longer comparable in either scale or complexity to the much more developed polities of southern Mesopotamia, where by then a veritable revolution in human spatial, social, political, and economic organization had taken place.

Early southern Mesopotamian (Sumerian) civilization thus represents a dramatic "takeoff"—a decisive shift in favor of southern Mesopotamia of the balance of urbanization, sociopolitical complexity, and economic differentiation that had existed across the ancient Near East until the onset of the fourth millennium. Why did this shift take place? Could a comparable shift have occurred anywhere in the ancient Near East, or were there factors specific to southern Mesopotamia alone that made it more probable that the shift would occur there rather than elsewhere? If the latter, what processes help account for the emergence of civilization in the south? And, finally, why did this emergence take place when it did, in the second half of the fourth millennium, and not before?

Forthcoming Discussions

In the chapters that follow I attempt to answer some of these questions by focusing on aspects of how wealth was produced and distributed in the earliest Sumerian city-states. To be sure, as Lamberg-Karlovsky (1995, 2001), Henry Wright (2001), and others (e.g., Collins 2000) have repeatedly warned us, phenomena as complex as the emergence of early cities and the institutionalization of the first despotic governments cannot be fully explained by changes in economic factors alone. This admonition wholly applies to the Sumerian case: unquestionably, the initial growth of early Mesopotamian civilization also entailed equally important, but more difficult to document, concurrent transformations in conceptions of the social order prevalent until then. At a minimum, these must have included new understandings about the nature of rank, the duties owed by the ruled to their rulers, and possibly, new conceptualizations about the nature of property as well (North and Thomas 1973).

In addition, as any student of Max Weber will readily appreciate, social transformations of any consequence are also structured by culturally bound forms of perceiving and comprehending the world, which determine whether individuals and institutions recognize (or not) opportunities for gain in their natural and social environments, and whether they act (or not) on those opportunities. Accordingly, culture helps explain why some societies grow (or not) at an accelerated rate compared to their neighbors, or at their expense. For this reason, cultural factors are often seen, correctly, as having as key a role as economic forces in structuring asymmetrical rates of urban development across the world (Dymski 1996; Martin 1999), and without a doubt culture also plays a central role in structuring the location, form, and layout of early cities wherever they appeared (e.g., Wheatley 1971; Kolata 1983; Marcus 1983; Cowgill 2000), including the ancient Near East.

Finally, if the available ethnohistoric record documenting the transition from chiefdoms to states across the world teaches us anything pertinent about the emergence of early Near Eastern civilizations it is that however crucial economic factors may be in determining the locations where states may (or may not) emerge, in the ultimate analysis what determines whether states actually do arise at those favored locales is the will of particular self-aggrandizing leaders to conquer their neighbors, often while cloaked in the mantle of an expansive religious ideology (Flannery 1999; Wright 2006). Again, early Mesopotamia was no exception to this pattern, as shown by the fact that much of the iconography of the nascent Uruk city-states focuses on a larger-than-life male figure who is repeatedly depicted as a leader in both battle and ritual (Bahrani 2002; Schmandt-Besserat 1993, 2007; Winter 2007).

However, documenting either the political or military strategies taken by individual actors in their quest for power or the weight of ideological and cultural factors in the crystallization of early pristine civilizations is always inherently difficult because of the nature of the evidence at our disposal, which is commonly insufficient to the task (chap. 2 and epilogue). This is indeed the case when we turn to fourth-millennium Mesopotamia, where available evidence allows us to make inferences about broadly defined categories of people and institutions but precludes us from reconstructing in any detail the actions of specific individuals, the historical context of early cities in the area, or even the "weltanschauung" of the first urban populations. Accordingly, the perspective of this book is much narrower: taking advantage of the natural strengths of archaeological data, I focus on economic change in fourth-millennium Sumerian cities as a proxy for the wider set of transformations entailed by the rise of early Mesopotamian civilization. More specifically, I seek to elucidate the economic variables underlying the processes of urban growth and socioeconomic differentiation in southern Mesopotamia of the Middle and Late Uruk periods (ca. 3600–3200/3100 BC) and to shed light on why developmental processes of comparable scale and resilience appear to have been absent in neighboring societies at the time.

Chapter 2 details available evidence that bears on the initial emergence of urban civilization in the Mesopotamian alluvium and outlines important conceptual and methodological problems that, in my opinion, hinder our understanding of the role of economic processes leading to that emergence and that, if left uncorrected, may well limit the kinds of future research that are needed to fully understand the Sumerian takeoff. Without a doubt, these limitations will ultimately only be circumvented by a substantial amount of imaginative and carefully designed new research, and some possible avenues of investigation toward this end are suggested in the epilogue. However, it may be possible to look at existing data with new eyes by framing them in the context of pertinent models of modern urban growth derived from the work of economists and economic geographers. Outlined in chapter 3, these models are intended only as testable propositions, allowing us, at the same time, to speculate about the meaning of current evidence and structure future research designs to better understand the conjuncture of environmental forces, social institutions, and economic mechanisms that made it likely that the earliest urban civilization of southwest Asia would arise first in southern Mesopotamia and not elsewhere.

Chapter 4 focuses on the environmental side of this conjuncture. It explores the unique ecology and geography of the alluvial lowlands of the Tigris-Euphrates rivers during the fifth and fourth millennia BC. The former gave early polities in the area important advantages in agricultural productivity and subsistence resource resilience not possessed by potential rivals on their periphery, while the latter gave them enduring cost advantages in the accumulation and distribution of resources, both local and foreign, as a result of water transport. Derived entirely from what Cronon refers to as the "natural landscape," these advantages created opportunities and incentives that made it both possible and probable that early Mesopotamian elites would see trade as a particularly viable way to legitimize and expand their unequal access to resources and power.

Chapter 5, in turn, presents a speculative scenario to account for how the Sumerian takeoff could have resulted, in part, out of evolving, long-term trade patterns that ultimately favored the development of societies in the alluvial lowlands of Mesopotamia over that of polities in neighboring regions. This trade was, at first, largely internal and took place principally between individual southern polities exploiting rich but localized ecological niches within the Mesopotamian alluvium during the Late Ubaid and Early Uruk periods. By the Middle and Late Uruk periods, however, external trade between growing southern cities and societies at their periphery in control of coveted resources gained more prominence. As the exchange unfolded over time and as its scale and external scope increased, import substitution processes expanded economic activity in growing Uruk centers and fueled large-scale immigration to those centers and their immediate dependencies.

My argument thus far is entirely predicated on the existence of substantial intra- and interregional trade in fourth-millennium southwest Asia and presumes that Uruk polities, in the aggregate, became a key hub for that trade by the second half of the fourth millennium. However, not all early Mesopotamian specialists agree that trade was a significant factor in the Sumerian takeoff. Chapter 6 addresses these concerns by reviewing what evidence there is for imports and exports to and from southern Mesopotamian cities in the fourth millennium, and discusses existing evidentiary biases that need to be resolved before a true accounting can be made of the role of trade in the emergence of early Sumerian civilization.

Chapter 7 is a comparative review of urban phenomena across Greater Mesopotamia in the fourth millennium. Existing data for protourban settlements in the rolling plains of Upper Mesopotamia are contrasted against comparable evidence from the Mesopotamian alluvium, the two areas of southwest Asia that were further along the developmental path to urbanism at the time. Both areas developed more or less in tandem during the first half of the fourth millennium; however, by the second half of the millennium southern polities had far outstripped their northern competitors in scale and complexity.

Chapter 8 addresses the root causes of the divergence. My main contention is that the environmental and geographical advantages accruing to southern Mesopotamian societies (outlined in chap. 4) and the increases in the density and agglomeration of populations in the alluvium throughout the Uruk period that were selected for by those natural advantages (outlined in chap. 7) represent necessary but not sufficient conditions for the Sumerian takeoff. The sufficient conditions, in my view, were organizational innovations within the nascent city-states of southern Mesopotamian that fall entirely within the realm of Cronon's "created landscape." Most important among these were (1) new forms of organizing labor that delivered economies of scale in the production of subsistence and industrial commodities to southern societies, and (2) new forms of record keeping that were much more capable of conveying information across time and space than the simpler reckoning systems used by contemporary polities elsewhere. These innovations furnished early Sumerian leaders and polities of the fourth millennium with what turned out to be their most important competitive advantages over neighboring societies.

Chapter 9 recapitulates the conjuncture of natural and created landscapes that underpinned the Sumerian takeoff. Additionally, the chapter also briefly addresses two important logical research corollaries of the takeoff not previously dealt with: why did the precocious protourban experiments of early fourth-millennium Upper Mesopotamia eventually prove unsuccessful? And, why did full-fledged urbanism not arise in the plains of northern Mesopotamia until the middle of the third millennium, eight hundred years or so after comparable phenomena in the southern Mesopotamian alluvium?

The final chapter is presented in the form of an epilogue. It attempts to summarize major evidentiary problems that hinder our comprehension of the full range of factors at play at the time of the emergence of early Mesopotamian civilization, and that will continue to do so in the future until they are resolved. Toward that goal, the epilogue offers suggestions for future research geared to obtaining the missing evidence, when such research becomes possible. This is imperative if a full evaluation is to be made of the main hypothesis advanced in this book, that of the centrality of the ramifications of trade to the evolution of early civilizations in general and to early Mesopotamian urban process in particular. Until the missing evidence can be acquired, however, what we can do is to reassess some conceptual and methodological problems that, in my opinion, still mar our understanding of the evidence bearing on the Sumerian takeoff that we do have at hand. It is to that reassessment that we now turn.

CHAPTER TWO

Factors Hindering Our Understanding of the Sumerian Takeoff

The Material Limits of the Evidence

Existing evidence for the emergence and growth of early cities in the alluvial environment of southern Mesopotamia throughout the various phases of the Uruk period is of varying reliability, resolution, and scope. The formative phases of the process remain shrouded in the mist of the so-called Early Uruk period (ca. 3900–3600 BC), a phase that for all practical purposes is known only through survey evidence (Nissen 1993). The lack of excavation and stratigraphic data for the initial phase of the Uruk period immediately presents us with a significant obstacle to interpretation because by their very nature long-term historical processes can only be studied diachronically.

Later phases of the Uruk period, the Middle and Late Uruk periods (ca. 3600–3200/3100 BC), are better understood, since pertinent data are provided by settlement pattern surveys, excavations at a small number of sites, a fairly extensive corpus of iconographic representations, and by some textual documentation. However, even with this extended evidentiary base there are still substantial problems. Although existing excavations can be hugely informative for individual sites such as the ancient Sumerian city of Uruk (modern Warka, biblical Erech), because of its extraordinary size Warka is certainly not representative of the alluvium as a whole, for which the number of excavated Uruk period sites remains small and the extent of exposures at those sites smaller still. Moreover, even at Warka there are substantial problems of interpretation, as noted recently by Hans Nissen (2001, 2002). One is that existing exposures remain entirely unrepresentative outside of the intensively studied Kullaba (Anu; fig. 2) and Eanna (fig. 3) precincts, which are situated at the core of the city and appear entirely religious/administrative in nature. Another is that for the most part what is known of the city in those areas pertains only to the final phase of the Uruk period at the site (i.e., Eanna V–IV levels).

Likewise, available textual evidence is also problematic. To begin with, complex reckoning systems combining numbers and images and the later protocuneiform tablets (referred to as "Archaic Texts") exist only for the final stages of the urbanization process in the alluvium, dated to the Middle and Late Uruk periods, and shed no light whatsoever on the beginnings of the urban revolution in the area, which began already in the Early Uruk period (chap. 7). To be sure, the Late Uruk proto-cuneiform tablets (i.e., those written in Uruk IV–type script) help us identify various categories of individuals and resources listed in them, and they can be used to make general inferences about the cognitive idiosyncrasies of the scribes who produced them. However, these early tablets remain quite difficult to interpret in detail (Englund 1998) and are generally devoid of meaningful archaeological context (Nissen 2001, 2002). Lastly, by definition, neither the reckoning devices nor the tablets are likely to deal with activities beyond the immediate purview of the urban institutions for which they were produced. Assyriologists openly acknowledge that even the relatively large cuneiform archives that are available for some later periods of Mesopotamian history still exclude a substantial proportion of the economic activity that existed in those periods (Van De Mieroop 2000, 42). Why should we believe that the more meager protocuneiform archives currently at our disposal for the Uruk period are any different? Taken together, these drawbacks mean that the relevant texts are of little use in answering questions involving either the quantification of economic processes in the Uruk period, such as the procurement or distribution of resources and labor, or the study of how those processes evolved at the time.

Contemporary pictorial representations in a variety of media (cylinder seals, statuettes, carved stelae, and vases) offer an entry into the social ideologies and cosmography of the Uruk world and can be quite informative about the ritual and mundane activities of the elite individuals

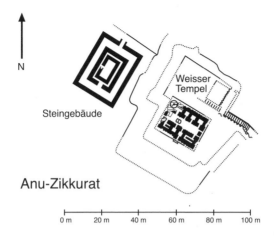

FIGURE 2. Plan of excavated Late Uruk structures in Anu Ziggurat (Kullaba) area of Uruk/ Warka.

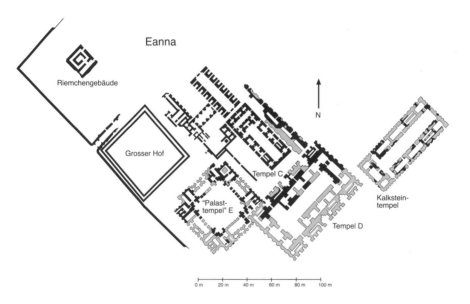

FIGURE 3. Plan of excavated Late Uruk structures in Eanna area of Uruk/Warka (phases V–IV).

depicted repeatedly (Schmandt-Besserat 1993) in Uruk art. Once again, however, the images we possess are restricted to the later half of the Uruk period, and their meanings are not always self-evident. Finally, even when the images can be interpreted by specialists (e.g., Bahrani 2002; Dittmann 1986; Schmandt-Besserat 2007; Winter 2007), we have to assume that they reflect only the ideological concerns of a small subset of individuals and institutions at the very top of early Sumerian society in the second half of the fourth millennium.

Conceptual Problems

It should be clear from the foregoing discussions that the archaeological, textual, and art historical data that currently exist from Mesopotamia during the fourth millennium are insufficient by themselves to clarify the details of either the institutions that structured social relations in early Sumerian cities or the circumstances of their evolution. Culturally idiosyncratic by nature, such institutions are likely to remain outside the purview of what researchers can reconstruct with the fragmentary and unrepresentative data at hand for fourth-millennium Mesopotamia. The assyriologist Marc Van De Mieroop (2004, 62) correctly diagnosed our predicament when he noted that "[t]he study of history shows that each society has its own characteristics and that all elements we observe need to be placed in their local context. The challenge is to find such a context, and [in ancient Mesopotamia] this can be impossible." Sadly, there is much truth to Van De Mieroop's remark. That said, however, there is still much that we can profitably accomplish with the evidence we have, which does allow us to focus our attention on clarifying the general outlines of the processes at work as early Sumerian civilization formed. These processes are amenable to reconstruction provided we presume the existence of some broad regularities in processes of urban formation and growth across the world.

Accordingly, this book invokes the work of economic geographers and developmental economists who seek to understand why, where, and how cities emerge in the modern world and how they grow, in order to generate testable propositions that will help us better interpret what evidence we do have for the much earlier processes of urban emergence and growth in Uruk period Mesopotamia. These scholars commonly acknowledge the key ideological and administrative roles that cities often play in the areas in which they arise, but take it as a given that trade is a crucial factor in their initial evolution and that, cross-culturally, they serve as the most efficient way to manage regional and interregional exchange in situations marked by asymmetries in resource endowments, commodity production, and access to transportation across the landscape (e.g., Hicks 1969; O'Sullivan 1996; Fujita, Krugman, and Venables 1999; chap. 3). In fact, economic historians and, to a lesser degree, some archaeologists have long argued for the primacy of trade in explaining, for instance, phenomena as diverse as the establishment of colonial cities across the Mediterranean coast of Europe in the Iron Age (Wells 1980) and the growth of urban centers across Europe throughout the medieval period (e.g., Pirenne 1936; Fox 1971, 1991; McCormick 2001).

In contrast, discussions in ancient Near Eastern studies about early urbanism have, in my opinion, paid insufficient attention to the work of classical economists regarding the social ramifications of trade and the conditions that gave rise to it. While work focusing on the effects of population growth and the impact of regional and interregional trade on the formation of early cities and states in the ancient Near East (e.g., Adams 1981; Service 1975; Smith and Young 1972; Wright and Johnson 1975) did take place during the 1970s, these subjects have received comparatively little attention of late. Moreover, other topics of equal or greater importance for understanding early urban processes have never been given the weight they deserve by scholars of the ancient Near East. Prominent among these neglected topics are how geographically determined differences in resource endowments and access to transport may have contributed to the formation of early cities in the area, and how differences in technologies of communication may have contributed to the further growth of such centers after they crystallized. These oversights are particularly surprising because resource variability has been recognized as central to spurring economic activity at least since the work of David Ricardo ([1817] 1971), and improvements in technologies of transportation and communication were understood to increase the specialization of labor already by Adam Smith ([1776] 1976, 13–15 [I.i.1–3]). Moreover, transportation and communication have been identified as crucial to processes of urbanization and sociopolitical evolution by social scientists in various disciplines, both in the abstract (e.g., Bairoch 1988; Fox 1980; Fujita, Krugman, and Venables 1999; Hawley 1986; McNeill 2000; Shennan 1999) and in myriad specific case studies (e.g., Spufford 2002; Vance 1970, 1986).

Even more troubling is the fact that, with the notable exception of Hans Nissen (1976, 2000), ancient Near Eastern scholars have yet to fully address the role that organizational efficiencies yielding significant economies of scale (increasing returns) in the production and distribution of commodities may have had in the development of early Mesopotamian cities. The continuing paucity of such research is particularly regrettable because economists have long known that the adoption of practices that systematically lower transaction costs and promote high rates of innovation can, like differences in resource endowments and access to transportation, be a critical factor in the emergence of sharply unequal developmental rates between regions and in determining how long such divergent rates of growth can be sustained (North 1991).

Given the importance of trade, transport, communication, and economies of scale to the study of urban processes across the world, why have these subjects been so consistently neglected in current inquiries into ancient Near Eastern urban origins? In great part, this failing is a direct consequence of the fragmentary nature of the archaeological and textual data at hand for early cities in the area, which are certainly unrepresentative, often difficult to characterize, and cannot be reliably quantified. This handicap may never be fully overcome due to the vagaries of archaeological discovery, but new and carefully targeted research could certainly do much to fill some of the existing evidentiary gaps (epilogue). To some degree, however, the present analytical problems are also derived from several conceptual and methodological misapprehensions that hinder our ability to interpret the data we do have.

On the conceptual front, one problem is that in rejecting the well-documented excesses of early twentieth-century diffusionism, many anthropologically oriented Near Eastern archaeologists, mostly in the United States, have striven instead to explain past cultural changes largely in terms of factors internal to the societies they study or tend to view them too narrowly as mere adaptive reactions to local ecological transformations. In so doing, their work fails to give proper consideration to a slew of other potential factors, which are also crucial to the explanation of pre- and protohistoric social change, including long-distance exchange and the cross-cultural interactions engendered by that exchange (Kohl 1987b). The same failing is also present in the work of many archaeologists and ancient Near Eastern specialists who are influenced, either implicitly or explicitly, by Marxian concepts of historical processes. With few notable exceptions (e.g., Zagarell 1986), in their analyses of ancient

Near Eastern urban process, such scholars commonly place undue emphasis on changes in how commodities were produced and distributed within a society to the detriment of complementary studies focusing on the role of trade as both trigger and ongoing spur for those changes. Underlying this perspective is a belief that only bulk trade in essential commodities and staples can act as a spur to social evolution and that more episodic exchange in luxury goods for elite consumption (generally dismissed as "preciosities") is necessarily of little consequence (e.g., Frangipane 2001b, 415, compare, for instance, Wallerstein 1974, 20–1).

This perspective is flawed on several counts, both general and specific. First, as noted by many who have studied what are often termed "prestige goods economies" (e.g., Eckholm 1977), it ignores the fact that political advantage gained through monopoly control and distribution of status-validating imports is often central to efforts by individual rulers to achieve legitimacy (Helms 1988, 1993) and to gain and maintain the loyalty of subordinate local and regional lineages. In so doing, such imports thereby contribute to rulers' successes in expanding the boundaries of the territories under their control and of the economic resources available to them. Second, when applied specifically to early Mesopotamian urbanism, this perspective disregards the fact that imports into the alluvium historically consisted not only of "luxuries" but also commodities such as timber and metals that, by any account, must be considered "essential" to the maintenance of complex social organizations in the resource-impoverished alluvial environment of southern Iraq (below).

A related conceptual problem is the implicit assumption shared by many in our field that ancient socioeconomic phenomena were of an *essentially* different nature from modern ones. This assumption is ultimately derived, again, from Marxian conceptions of history, which see capitalism as a uniquely modern historical phenomenon based on behaviors, institutions, and technologies that did not exist prior to the end of the Middle Ages (Polanyi 1944), the sixteenth century AD (Wallerstein 1974), or the Industrial Revolution (Landes 1998). Scholars who subscribe to this position consider the wealth-maximizing behavioral postulate typically assumed by most modern economists to be entirely inappropriate for the study of both non-Western (Sahlins 1972) and premodern societies (Polanyi 1957b, 1977; Finley 1985; Wallerstein 1991). Logically, they naturally also assume that the forces underlying the emergence and growth of early cities in antiquity must have also been quite different from those at work in more recent historical periods.

But is this really the case? I suspect that it is in some cases but not others, and that the existence of important continuities in economic processes between antiquity and today would be quite clear if only we had the ability to accurately characterize and precisely quantify the types of economic activity that took place in many urban societies of the premodern era. To be sure, Karl Polanyi's (1957b) admonition to the effect that economic behavior in early preindustrial societies is always embedded in broader sociopolitical and ideological systems is patently correct, as is Finley's (1985) insistence on the centrality of status as a determinant of economic interactions in antiquity. However, these peculiarities are hardly limited to the ancient world, and substantial continuities in economic processes can, in fact, be shown to exist across otherwise very different geographical spaces and historical eras (Gunder Frank 1993; North 1977, 709; Shennan 1999; Silver 1995, 2004; Warburton 2003)—at least since the rise of the earliest cities and states.

Early Mesopotamian civilization is a case in point. No scholar familiar with the vast literature on how early Mesopotamian states used dependent labor receiving fixed rations to extract resources from the countryside can deny the importance of redistribution, repeatedly highlighted by Polanyi (1957a), as a central organizing principle of ancient Mesopotamian economic life. In addition, as Polanyi also argued, there is substantial evidence for the existence of institutionally administered exchange funneled through and sponsored by early Mesopotamian urban temples and palaces of the third and second millennia BC. No doubt, again exactly as Polanyi claimed, the bulk of this exchange was geared toward satisfying the ideological rather than the economic needs of early Mesopotamian religious and political elites. That said, however, other contentions central to Polanyi's characterization of early Mesopotamian economies are now widely regarded by many specialists as untenable (Adams 1974; Foster 1977; Garfinkle 2005; Hudson 2004, 2005; Monroe 2005; Powell 1977), even as economic historians at large often continue to uncritically accept them (e.g., North 1981, 92). Two such contentions are Polanyi's insistence on (1) the irrelevance of wealth-maximizing goals and behaviors to the analysis of early Mesopotamian trade, and (2) the absence from early Mesopotamian cities of price-making markets able to respond flexibly to shifts in supply and demand.

Turning first to the issue of motivation, in many cases we find that the very same institutions that are at the center of early Mesopotamian centrally managed economies also engaged in what can only be described as wealth-maximizing behaviors that are incompatible with Polanyi's characterization of those economies. Most commonly this took the form of urban temples that used silver derived from the conversion of accumulated agricultural surpluses into usable capital (Powell 1996) to finance risky trading ventures in order to acquire nonlocal resources for profit, whether alone or in conjunction with palaces (Leemans 1960; Postgate 1972). Such ventures were led by merchants who, at times, were clearly subordinates of the sponsoring institutions and, at times, appear to have been wholly or partially independent of them (Powell 1977).[1] More rarely attested in surviving documentation of the time, but possibly also common, were independent merchant colonies sent by individual city-states that operated in lands outside southern Mesopotamia proper but were under Mesopotamian imperial administration. At least one such colony from Umma is known to have operated at Susa during the time that the Akkadian Empire occupied southwestern Iran (Foster 1993).

Even more relevant to the issue of motivations underlying ancient Near Eastern exchange is recent work by assyriologists clarifying the entrepreneurial and profit-seeking nature of Old Babylonian trade in the Persian Gulf (Leemans 1960) and Old Assyrian trade with Anatolia (i.e., Turkey). The latter example is particularly illustrative because it is unusually well documented. Moreover, it was the case study that Polanyi (1957a) himself used as evidence for what he termed "marketless trade," by which he meant centrally managed exchange between state institutions on the basis of arbitrary mutually agreed upon value equivalences (i.e., equivalences that disregard actual production costs). It is now generally accepted that Old Assyrian trade was nothing of the sort. Rather, it involved Assyrian middlemen operating largely outside the bounds of the Assyrian state that imported tin from Afghan sources and woven woolen textiles acquired from southern Mesopotamian cities into Anatolia in exchange for Anatolian silver and, to a lesser extent, gold (Adams 1974; Dercksen 2004; Larsen 1976). The texts leave no room for equivocation as to the issue of motivation: the goal of the enterprise was not obtaining needed resources for government institutions at Assur, but rather turning a profit in the form of fungible capital for the family-run firms and individuals that sponsored the trade caravans in the first place. To further this goal, Assyrian traders even managed to interpose themselves in internal trade in copper within Anatolia, purchasing and selling that metal purely for profit as they traveled between Assur in northern Iraq and the Assyrian colony of Kanesh (modern Kültepe) in central Turkey (Dercksen 1996).

Also refuted by current assyriological work are Polanyi's assumptions about the absence of price-making markets in ancient Mesopotamian cities. Even the most inveterate defenders of Polanyi's characterization of the nature of early Mesopotamian economies (e.g., Renger 1984) now acknowledge the parallel existence of what they reluctantly term "market elements" beyond the control of early Mesopotamian central urban institutions and through which many essential commodities, both imports and local products, flowed into alluvial cities.

It is clear, for instance, that markets existed through which some imported commodities reached southern cities already in the third millennium. This is underscored by Foster's (1977, 37) analysis of trade at the Sumerian city of Umma during the Akkadian period (twenty-third–twenty-first centuries BC). He found that whole categories of imports into the city were entirely absent from surviving cuneiform archives of the period, including various types of precious and semiprecious stones, woods, and even crucial commodities such as copper and silver—all of which are otherwise well attested in the archaeological record of contemporary sites. Given that state bureaucracies prepared available cuneiform documentation, Foster reasonably concluded that individuals or kin groups wholly outside their purview were primarily responsible for the importation of many needed commodities and resources into the city during the Akkadian period.

In addition, it is also clear that some locally produced agricultural commodities were being acquired through markets outside the control of the public sector at Umma during the Akkadian period. This can be inferred from the fact that silver was more than just an idealized value measurement used when bartering other commodities in the texts analyzed by Foster. In some cases, merchants actually exchanged silver for bulk agricultural goods (Foster 1977, 35), and this necessarily implies the existence of a market for those goods, whether at Umma itself or in neighboring alluvial cities.

To be sure, it could be argued that while the fungibility of silver implies the existence of a market it need not imply the existence of a dynamic market economy operating on principles of comparative advantage and able to respond flexibly to shifts in supply and demand (e.g., Renger 1984). However, we do have evidence for precisely such an economic structure in Mesopotamian economic texts of the late third and early second millennia. One source of evidence is provided by the so-called Balanced Silver Accounts, which again stem from Umma and that date to the Ur III phase at the site (ca. 2114–2004 BC). Studied by both D. Snell (1977, 1991) and the late G. van Driel (2002a), these tablets represent summary accounts of merchants who used silver both as a standardized measure of value in bartering and as a form of "currency," enabling them to directly procure a variety of needed resources for the Umma state, both domestic and imported.[2] Suggestively, these accounts are detailed enough to show that at different times the same merchants paid different prices for the same commodities (Snell 1991, 135). Snell (1977, 50) conservatively interprets this to mean that the state agency for which the merchants worked was "not interested in maximizing return on the money spent; it was only interested in making sure that the bureaux were properly supplied." A more parsimonious explanation is that the prices of the commodities acquired by the Umma merchants varied depending on availability in markets beyond the control of Mesopotamian urban institutions.

Another, more definitive, line of evidence for price-making markets in ancient Mesopotamia is provided by a seminal study of commodity prices and wages in northern Babylonian cities during the Old Babylonian period (ca. 1894–1595 BC) published almost thirty years ago by H. Farber (1978). The implications of this study effectively demolish the arguments of Polanyi and his followers about the uniqueness of premodern and non-Western economies. Farber's analysis documents wages for hired labor, house rental prices, and prices (exchange ratios) of commodities as varied as slaves, barley, oxen, cows, oil, and wool throughout the three-hundred-year history of the Old Babylonian period. Interestingly, his data show that the price of wool remained stable across many generations, suggesting that it was being set by nonmarket mechanisms. However, wool appears to have been the only exception among the commodities examined, because the data show that wages, and prices for land rentals, slaves, oil, oxen, and cows did fluctuate widely over time.

Sticking close to his data, Farber was unwilling to speculate on the causes of these price fluctuations, correctly acknowledging that both political and nonpolitical factors may have been involved. He specifically cites progressive salinization and consequent declines in land productivity as a possible nonpolitical factor. This note of caution is undoubtedly well taken. However, it stands to reason that to a significant degree the

fluctuations he documented also do reflect variations in supply and demand caused by the ebb and flow of political and military fortunes of
individual Old Babylonian kings.

This can be inferred from the fact that Farber's data generally show
prices falling and wages rising during the reign of kings known historically to have been politically powerful and militarily expansive, such as
Hammurabi and Samsuiluna, whereas one sees prices rising and wages
falling during the reigns of some of the weaker kings following Samsuiluna who reigned during times of political and military retrenchment
(Farber 1978, 38–40, graphs 12–14). This pattern makes perfect sense in
terms of supply and demand. Commodity prices fell in times of political
integration and military expansion, when the Babylonian crown was able
to extract resources from ever larger areas, and wages rose as the number
of available laborers diminished as a result of the military manpower demands of an expanding realm. Political and military contraction, in turn,
brought the reverse: fewer supplies of commodities, increased commodity prices, less demand for soldiers, and increased availability of labor,
which depressed wages.

In summary, earlier I had noted that many scholars consider the economic foundations of early civilizations to have been fundamentally different from those of modern "capitalist" societies, which, they argue, are
characterized by the "ceaseless" profit-spurred accumulation of capital
as their central principle of economic organization (Wallerstein 1991).
However, such clear lines of demarcation in the flow of history or in the
evolution of economic forms are belied by the Mesopotamian data. Indeed, the cumulative weight of available evidence discussed above suggests that, at least from the third millennium onward, Mesopotamian
cities were characterized by mixed public- and private-sector economies
(Garfinkle 2005; Hudson 2005; Wilcke 2007), in which the extraction
of local resources using encumbered labor, the procurement of imports
using state-controlled traders, and the acquisition of local and exotic
resources in markets affected by conditions of supply and demand, all
played important—though not easily quantifiable—roles. More specifically, existing evidence in Sumerian, Babylonian, and Assyrian cities
for (1) the wide and early fungibility of silver for other commodities,
(2) the profit-oriented nature of many personal, familial, and institutional trading ventures, and (3) correlations between commodity and
labor availability and price and salary fluctuations, effectively answers
in the affirmative the question of whether wealth-maximizing behaviors,

markets, and principles of comparative advantage are applicable to the study of early Mesopotamian urbanism as a whole.

It follows from this that Marx, Polanyi, and their intellectual successors were wrong in conceptualizing a clear line separating the economies of the modern (i.e., capitalist) and premodern (i.e., precapitalist) worlds, as Jack Goody (2006) has recently and eloquently argued. If such a line exists, it is far from as sharp a boundary as Marxian-derived modern economic theory would have it, and it is to be found, I would argue, at the dawn of history in various areas of the world—where it divides what we commonly refer to as prestate and state societies. Early Sumerian civilization is a case in point. Both in motive and mechanism, early Mesopotamian urban economies of the third and second millennia can justifiably be described as partly capitalist, as Andre Gunder Frank (1993) insightfully noted more than a decade ago. If this is correct, as I believe to be the case, then what requires further study are (1) the reasons why market mechanisms and profit motives acquired increased or diminished importance within the mixed economies of Mesopotamian cities in different historic times, (2) the processes whereby those changes were effected from period to period, and, (3) the degree to which, if any, comparable mechanisms and motives played a role in the emergence of the earliest Mesopotamian cities during the fourth millennium BC.

The first two questions are clearly beyond the scope of this book, but the third question is one to which we will return repeatedly—if obliquely—in the discussions that follow. To anticipate my conclusions in greatly abbreviated form: I argue that the principal outlines of forms of spatial, political, social, and economic relationships that would characterize Mesopotamian civilization for centuries—if not millennia—were initially forged at the time of the Sumerian takeoff. Evidence for this is admittedly circumstantial, as I discuss in forthcoming chapters, but there can be no doubt that substantial cultural and institutional continuities did in fact exist between the initial urban societies of Mesopotamia in the fourth millennium and those of the historic periods, as suggested principally by two disparate but complementary lines of evidence.

The first one is noted many years ago by the art historians Henri Frankfort (1951) and Helene Kantor (1984), who repeatedly drew our attention to the multiple ways in which the iconographic repertoire of Uruk art set the conventions of artistic representation in Mesopotamia until the demise of the neo-Assyrian and neo-Babylonian empires in the first millennium BC. The second consistss of a remarkably parallel phenomenon noted recently by the assyriologist Mario Liverani, who points out that the conventions of scribal administration that emerged at the end of the Uruk period and are represented in the Archaic Texts, in effect set the framework for how Mesopotamian urban scribes would continue to comprehend, categorize, and record their world until the end of the cuneiform tradition millennia later—save for minor improvements and adjustments (Liverani and Heimpel 1995, 134).

What is the meaning of these striking similarities in how Mesopotamian artists and scribes represented and manipulated their worlds over the millennia? While many interpretations are possible, I think it is safe to assume that they reflect essential continuities in the ideologies of the social order prevalent in early Mesopotamian cities of the Uruk and later periods. Following the Marxian notion of social totality wherein all aspects in society are embedded in a matrix of mutual determinations, I presume further that such ideologies would not—and did not— endure randomly or in a vacuum. Given this, would it then not be reasonable to see their continuity as a proxy for further homologies in the political and economic institutions in which the records were kept and for which the art was made? Further, and more specifically pertinent to the focus of this inquiry, might patterns of production, accumulation, distribution, and exchange typical for southern cities of the third and second millennia have existed in some form, however attenuated, already at the inception of Mesopotamian urbanism in the fourth millennium? These questions are central to many of the discussions that follow, which often employ data from well-documented periods in Mesopotamian history to shed light on less well-understood, but presumably related, phenomena taking place at the dawn of Mesopotamian civilization.

Methodological Problems

The evidentiary and conceptual problems reviewed in the preceding discussions that hinder an understanding of the processes leading to the Sumerian takeoff are compounded by a methodological error. Central place theory—the tool most commonly used by archaeologists approaching the issue of early Near Eastern urban origins (e.g., Johnson 1975)—is largely unsuited for the analysis of urban processes taking place under environmental and geographic conditions such as those that were prevalent in the alluvial lowlands of the Tigris-Euphrates fluvial system at the time early cities first emerged.

In essence, the locational theories put forth by twentieth-century successors of von Thünen, most notably Christaller ([1933] 1966) and Lösch ([1940] 1954), seek to understand the forces that spread economic activity *away* from a center as a result of the tradeoff between economies of scale (which provide an incentive to concentrate production) and transportation costs (which provide an incentive to disperse production and related managerial functions). These theories explicitly assume (1) that transportation costs increase steadily with distance, (2) that access to agricultural land is the most important economic variable affecting the location of premodern cities (and, therefore, that the movement of agricultural products is the main factor structuring the spatial relationship between settlements in any given region), (3) that production is directly proportional to scale (i.e., returns are constant), (4) that all settlements of comparable scale are equally competitive, (5) that commerce takes place only vertically within individual hierarchically organized settlement systems, (6) that settlements of the same order in different systems do not interact, and (7) that system expansion is due only to internal demand for staples, presumably as a result of population growth (Fujita and Krugman 2004; Vance 1970, 150).

While many of these assumptions are valid in some areas at particular historical junctures, as a group they fail to account for the complexity of the situation in southern Mesopotamia when Sumerian civilization first emerged. The first assumption, for instance, has always been largely irrelevant to conditions in southern Mesopotamia because transportation costs for bulky, locally produced, agricultural commodities would have not increased exponentially with distance within the alluvial delta of the Tigris-Euphrates system as presumed by central place models. Rather, historically, within the Mesopotamian alluvium such costs were kept partially in check by networks of natural and artificial canals surrounding early settlements, and transport costs would have been particularly low for settlements situated immediately near the enlarged marshes that characterized large portions of the Tigris-Euphrates Delta throughout the fourth millennium BC (chap. 4).

The second assumption, which privileges access to agricultural land as the key variable structuring urban location, also misses the mark in several crucial ways with respect to the Mesopotamian case. First, this

assumption fails to give proper consideration to nonagricultural industries that also powerfully contributed to early Mesopotamian urban
growth (chap. 5). Of these, the propulsive industry, at least from the
fourth millennium onward, was industrial-scale weaving of woolen textiles (chap. 5), which was based largely on the exploitation of otherwise
marginal lands eccentric to Mesopotamian cities. Second, the assumption underestimates evidence for the degree of ecological variability of
the southern alluvial plain in the fourth millennium BC and the economic importance of marsh and aquatic resources at the time (chap. 4).
Third, the assumption discounts the probability that resilience strategies
based on access to multiple resources (Adams 1978) within the alluvium
was a factor of equal—or, possibly, even greater—locational importance
for early Mesopotamian societies than maximizing access to agricultural
resources. Fourth, the assumption also discounts the probability that the
desire to maximize access to trade and communication routes in and out
of the alluvium was also a relevant factor determining, at least in some
cases, urban location within the alluvium. That this latter is a possibility
is suggested by the location of important Early Dynastic Mesopotamian
cities, such as Mari on the Euphrates and Assur on the Tigris, which
were situated in areas of the rivers that were marginal for cereal agriculture but ideally situated to control commodity flows within and along the
waterways. Such emplacements leave no doubt as to the importance of
mercantile agency as a determinant of early Mesopotamian urban process in the third millennium. Why should we believe that similar considerations would not have been pertinent a millennium earlier, at the onset
of Mesopotamian civilization?

Some of the other core assumptions of central place models are
equally problematic. For instance, assumptions of perfect competition
under conditions of constant returns to scale, and that sites within a
settlement system do not interact with peer polities outside of their own
system, may make sense as necessary analytical simplifications, but they
are patently inapplicable to any human society in the real world (chap.
3) and are, in any case, particularly unsuited to the Mesopotamian situation. Save for a few short-lived imperial bursts, southern Mesopotamia
was historically characterized by constellations of rival city-states engaged alternately in intense political competition and commerce, and a
similar situation almost certainly obtained as well at the onset of early
Sumerian civilization in the fourth millennium (chap. 7). Furthermore,
there is significant evidence of long-distance contacts between early

Mesopotamian polities and faraway societies well outside the Mesopotamian alluvium from the earliest phases of Mesopotamian prehistory onward. Enervated by multiple waterways that facilitated contacts across the Tigris-Euphrates watershed (chap. 4), the Mesopotamian alluvium never resembled the closed geographical system presumed by central place models (Adams 1981, 67).

Finally, and perhaps more crucially, central place theory is inherently incapable of addressing questions relating to how systems of cities evolve through time or—even less—how they originate. As John Marshall (1989) and Paul Krugman (1995) have insightfully noted, a common characteristic of all locational models based on central place theory is that they assume the a priori existence of a central urban market. Accordingly, even in cases where the key assumptions underlying central place models may be wholly or partly applicable, such models can never shed light on why population and economic activity become concentrated *in the first place*.[3] Issues relating to the origin and evolution of urban systems are the subjects of the chapter that follows.

CHAPTER THREE

Modeling the Dynamics of Urban Growth

This then is the crucial problem we face as economic historians of antiquity in general and the ancient Near East in particular: we cannot evaluate the individual data without some model; yet we cannot demonstrate the validity of the model without interpreting the data as supporting it. It is a hermeneutic circle . . . rarely acknowledged. It leads to the necessity that we state what model we use up front, before we do anything else. —Marc Van De Mieroop, review of *Privatization in the Ancient Near East and Classical World*

In a recent review of the relationship between scale and complexity of social organization in cases of pristine state formation, Gary Feinman (1998) argues that the form such states take at the outset is largely dependent on the specific combination of factors most central to their creation. If this is the case, then we should be able to make testable inferences about what the key formative factors may have been in the case of individual pristine civilizations by looking at the principal and most enduring characteristics they possessed at their floruit. Because city-states were the earliest (chap. 7), most typical, and most stable political formations in Mesopotamian civilization (Glassner 2000; Stone 1997; Yoffee 1995), what needs to be accounted for in the early Sumerian case is the origin of the city itself. In addition, we need to understand why, under conditions prevalent in fourth-millennium southern Mesopotamia, initial urban emergence did not take the form of a single city of considerable size controlling the whole of the Tigris-Euphrates alluvial delta (such as

Teotihuacan in the Valley of Mexico, for instance) but rather appears to have consisted of multiple contemporary, and no doubt competing, urban centers of varying size, each seemingly controlling only a portion of the southern Mesopotamian alluvium. The broader issue of origins is addressed here, while the nature of the earliest cities that emerged in Mesopotamia is treated in chapters 4, 5, and 7.

The emergence of large settlement agglomerations as an enduring phenomenon is particularly intriguing because of an apparent paradox inherent to premodern urbanism recently noted by the historian William McNeill (2000, 204): absent strict sanitation standards and recent advances in preventive medicine, early centers were almost certainly unable to demographically reproduce themselves without a constant stream of new population. Two reasons account for this, according to McNeill. The first and most crucial one is the fact that early cities must have been places of intensified mortality as a result of crowding and the consequent increase in the infection rates of a variety of diseases. The second is that a possibly substantial portion of the inhabitants of such cities lived lives of isolated dependency not conducive to forming families and raising numerous children.

While neither of these factors discouraging endogenous demographic growth in premodern times is easily quantifiable in the case of the earliest Mesopotamian cities (see the epilogue), McNeill's generalization does raise some important questions about how best to conceptualize early urban processes. Two of the most salient are (1) how to account for the formation of the initial cities that emerged in any given area given the demographic drawbacks of early urban life, and (2) how to explain the subsequent growth of those cities, once created? Phrased differently, if McNeill is essentially correct, as I believe he is, what mechanisms nurtured a continual flow of new inhabitants into early cities?

To answer these questions within the framework of analysis adopted in this book, we need to go back to ideas articulated by the great economist David Ricardo almost two centuries ago about the importance of trade for economic development and the role of comparative advantage between regions as a spur to trade. Further, we need to understand how Ricardo's seminal ideas have been modified and added to by modern scholars (Krugman 1998b). In fact, though Ricardo himself gave little thought to the implications of his ideas to processes of *initial* urban formation, those implications have been the focus of much work by modern scholars who focus precisely on the need to explain how spatial concentrations of population and economic activity come about. Particularly relevant in this context are (1) the ideas of Jane Jacobs on how trade spurs and sustains settlement growth; (2) the work of Paul Krugman and other adherents of the self-styled "new economic geography" explaining how unequal gains from trade structure differentially complex urban systems; and (3) the work of Gunnar Myrdal explaining the mechanisms that allow systems of cities to expand, once created, and thus become the primary motor of development in the regions they occupy. Their views, when combined, provide us with an explicitly evolutionary perspective on the origins and development of cities that adds much to the analytical schema that have characterized the study of early Near Eastern urban origins thus far, which, as noted in chapter 2, are largely descriptive in nature and devoid of a historical dimension.

Growth As Diversification

The central role of trade as the earliest and most basic spur to population clustering is explained by Jane Jacobs, the iconoclastic urban expert best known for her often controversial views about the future of the urban experience in America. Particularly relevant in this context are a number of Jacobs's more abstract contributions about the nature of urban economies (1969, 2000), which are, in my opinion, quite applicable to the study of urban growth in early civilizations (Kurtz 1987; Algaze 2001a, but for contrary opinions, see Van De Mieroop 1997, 25–26; and Santley n.d.). In the more theoretical aspects of her work, Jacobs is ultimately inspired by ideas first enunciated by the eminent sociologist Herbert Spencer well over a century ago. Spencer believed that a tendency toward increasing heterogeneity was inherent in all features of the universe. In this, he uncannily prefigured one of the principal tenets of modern "big bang"–related cosmologies. More pertinently, however, Spencer presumed that growing differentiation also characterized the evolutionary trajectory of human societies. Moreover, he recognized that the growth of differentiation in such societies was not strictly linear because, as polities became naturally more diverse through time, relations of interdependency were created among their increasingly more diverse social elements, resulting in emergent social properties that were not predictable a priori (Spencer [1876, 1882] 1967, 8).

In a similar vein but with a narrower focus, Jacobs sees economic differentiation as central to processes of urban growth. She argues that social differentiation results from economic differentiation and that social evolution and urban growth ultimately both depend on economic expansion. Jacobs is one of few economists who see human economies as sharing many characteristics with biological ecosystems (see also Mokyr 2000 and Ziman 2000).[1] The most salient of these similarities are that (1) the viability, stability, and resiliency of the two types of systems, as well as their ability to expand, are directly related to the degree of diversity present (Jacobs 2000, 22, 37); (2) expansion ultimately depends on capturing and using external energy, principally light in the case of ecosystems and exogenous resources in the case of human societies, and the more diverse means a system possesses for using, modifying, and passing around energy/resources, the larger the cumulative consequences to the system as a whole (Jacobs 2000, 47); and (3) development takes place as part of a larger web of codevelopments; the greater the internal diversity of the system, the more numerous and intricate the codevelopment relationships that will exist within it and the greater the number of emergent properties that will be spawned (Jacobs 2000, 19–22).

Given these similarities, for Jacobs the development of social and ecosystemic complexity is studied by exploring how diversity is created within the system, how resources external to the system are incorporated, and how developments that initially may have been independent join in inherently unpredictable and unforeseen ways to cause further differentiation. Jacobs explains that in both types of systems differentiation is an open-ended and self-amplifying process, since each new differentiation constitutes the basis from which further differentiation can eventually emerge.

What are the implications of these ideas for the study of early urban processes? Economists and anthropologists have long noted that, crossculturally, autonomous village societies practicing traditional agriculture are characterized by a Malthusian equilibrium in which they maintain relatively low rates of population growth over the long term, produce relatively little surplus, and tend to fission when population density increases beyond the coping ability of existing conflict resolution mechanisms. A key constraint retarding growth and limiting density in such societies is the one independently noted by both Ricardo and Malthus two hundred or so years ago (Clark 2007): when land is the principal factor of production and where its availability is limited (as for, example, by the inherent limits of premodern transport), per capita productivity necessarily diminishes in proportion to increases in labor (population). This means that simple agrarian societies can break the iron grip that their means of subsistence imposes on their demographic and economic growth only if they find a way to acquire resources external to themselves or, alternately, if they develop either new technologies or institutions that substantially boost their productivity or more efficient forms of transport that enlarge the territories from which they can extract resources.

To be sure, these different solutions to the so-called Malthusian trap are not mutually exclusive. On the contrary, more often than not, they complement and reinforce each other. However, if we follow Jacobs's ideas to their logical conclusion, the initial direction of causality in urban processes becomes clear: because, by definition, autonomous peasant societies are not diverse, have a small knowledge base, and possess little in the way of productivity-boosting material or labor capital to invest, trade represents the least expensive and most parsimonious way at their disposal to acquire exogenous resources in a predictable and systematic manner. Logically, for Jacobs, it is trade, therefore, that initially allows otherwise inherently homeostatic village societies to expand beyond the natural Malthusian constraints of their natural and created environments—at least temporarily until a new higher-level Malthusian equilibrium is formed. More specifically, she argues that what commonly determines a settlement's ability to urbanize is a positive feedback loop initiated by its capacity to generate exports by combining some of its resources and/or imports with existing human labor and capital. This generates economic diversity at the same time that it makes it possible for growing settlements to acquire more and different imports, some of which can again be used to generate further exports. This process creates codevelopments in the form of an every larger, more skilled, and more diverse workforce (i.e., human capital), and this, in turn, increases the potential for further economic diversification by adding new types of work and new ways of working and by making concurrent technological and organizational innovations more likely. As both work and diversity expand, so does population density within the affected settlements. This increase commonly takes place at the expense of nearby rural populations, which is why cities are always the economic and physical shapers of their hinterlands.

Growth As Specialization

Jacobs's main insight, namely, that urban growth is at its root a process of diversification, implicitly challenges two centuries of economic orthodoxy, which sees economies (and cities) as growing mainly through specializing in particular industries, through division of labor, and through standardization (Ellerman 2005, 50). At first sight, these models appear to be entirely antithetical since diversification sees expansion as emerging from the multiplication of epigenetically related activities, while specialization sees growth as arising from scale economies caused by concentration in an ever narrower range of activities.

Upon deeper reflection, however, the two models can be seen to describe sequential, overlapping, and iterative stages of economic (and demographic) growth. Trade-fueled diversification kick-starts the growth process, and remains a powerful—if unpredictable—force throughout every stage of economic development. Specialization then prunes down the bush, so to say, of possible alternative avenues of growth and selects those branches (industries) more likely to grow luxuriantly at any one time. Although historical contingency is largely what determines which branches those turn out to be in any particular case, what is common to all cases is that as the division of labor deepens in the selected industries the cycle starts anew because specialized techniques and processes that maximize efficiency in one industry often get adopted by related industries (e.g., the boring of cannon barrels leads eventually to the boring of piston engine cylinders [Landes 1998, 191–92]) or, more significantly, lead to totally new developments in unrelated fields (e.g., the spoke wheel [a means of transport] gets transformed into the waterwheel [a new source of energy]), thus creating new forms of diversification, and so on.[2] No doubt, the relative contributions of diversification and specialization to development have varied enormously through history, both between different societies and within a single society at different points in time. Nonetheless, by providing a substantial and predictable boost to productivity and employment that diversification alone can seldom match, specialization is considered by most researchers to be the key mechanism determining both overall social scale and which settlements will attain urban size at particular times.

The importance of specialization to urban development lies at the very core of the work of new economic geographers, and particularly that

of Paul Krugman and his colleagues, who model the impact of trade in
structuring uneven regional development in the modern world (Krugman 1991, 1995, 1998a; Krugman and Venables 1995; Fujita, Krugman,
and Venables 1999; Fujita and Krugman 2004). In trying to explain how
cities organize themselves within regions and how modern urban systems
evolve, these scholars start from a number of premises that likely are as
pertinent to researchers interested in understanding early civilizations as
they are to those interested in modern urban phenomena, and that, given
the right kind of data (see the epilogue), can be used to generate testable
hypotheses about urban processes in antiquity.[3]

The first premise is derived from Anglo-Saxon classical economics
and its long tradition of engagement with the principle of the division of
labor: specialization in production spurs trade between increasingly dif-
ferentiated settlements and regions and, in turn, is itself spurred further
by that trade. The second premise builds directly on the preceding: while
sustained economic growth is largely a consequence of specialization,
specialization can arise from a wider variety of advantages than those
typically specified by Ricardo, most importantly, from varying efficiencies in transport and from increasing returns to scale.

A third premise is one that follows logically from the traditional emphasis in Germanic location theory on the significance of transport costs
in structuring economic diversity across a landscape: because all economic activity takes place in space, economics simply cannot be understood in isolation from geography.[4] Like central place modelers before
them, new economic geographers see the number, size, and location of
cities in any one area at any one time as created by the interplay between
centripetal forces that tend to concentrate economic activity and population at a single location at low transport costs and centrifugal forces that
tend to disperse economic activity and population to multiple locations
when transport costs increase. However, whereas traditional location
theory presumes (at least for purposes of analytical simplicity) a perfect
competitive equilibrium at any given level of the settlement hierarchy
and constant returns to scale, new economic geographers instead presume instead that the rate of return on investments increases with scale,
as continual iterative processes between trade and specialization disproportionately amplify economic activity in centers where population,
production, and market size are already growing. Under this paradigm,
systems of cities are always dynamic and evolving, and are always capable of catastrophic change in their qualitative character as new technolo-

gies alter the equation between transport costs and settlement, and/or as culturally specific institutions either facilitate or hinder the operation of the cumulative economic processes that propel different cities and combinations of cities to the fore at different times.

Given these premises, Krugman and his colleagues see cities as the cross-culturally most efficient way to mediate sustained contacts and exchange between regions and polities with varying degrees of "competitive" advantage in the production of both necessary and desirable resources (Ballinger 2001). Such competitive advantage is by definition a dynamic and often transitory condition. Where and when it exists, it arises from three principal sources, which commonly compound and reinforce each other.

The first source is comparative advantage in its classical Ricardian sense. This is an idea so amply discussed in the literature that it requires little elaboration here. Its basic premises are that resources are unevenly distributed in the natural world and that labor does not move across political (or cultural) boundaries. Given this, polities will naturally specialize in the extraction and processing of resources close at hand and productivity differentials arising from such specialization will eventually lead to trade between polities and regions that have become differentially specialized.

A second source of competitive advantage of one region over another is caused by factors other than varying resource endowments that also create specialization—promoting differentials in the cost at which individual polities can produce specific commodities. This is also a type of comparative advantage, at least in the expanded sense that the term acquired in the work of neoclassical economists starting in the 1920s and 1930s. However, whereas they mostly focused on production factors such as differences in technology and/or labor costs as additional sources of comparative advantage, new economic geographers treat differences in the ease of or access to transportation across the landscape (chap. 4) as a further—and equally central—production factor capable of triggering imbalances in comparative advantage (Krugman and Venables 1995, 859). This matters because differences in transport cost can prompt trade even between regions nominally possessing comparable material or human resources, and even comparable technologies, something that neither Ricardian nor neoclassical comparative advantage can explain.

The third source of competitive advantage goes well beyond both classical and neoclassical economic principles and arises from what new economic geographers term "market effects." Simply stated, these result from the fact that production costs fall as the scale of output increases. Thus, as populations and markets grow in size, economies of scale in production create commodity cost differentials that can be as effective at triggering specialization and a transregional division of labor—and trade—as cost differentials arising from geographically determined differences in resources or in ease of transport. The underlying process at work here is that of agglomeration economies "in which spatial concentration itself creates the favorable economic environment that supports further or continued concentration" (Fujita, Krugman, and Venables 1999, 4).

Growth Situated

However different the schools of thought exemplified by Jacobs and Krugman may be concerning what each considers the key variable ultimately underpinning processes of urban growth and regional development (i.e., diversification versus specialization), both approaches share some fundamental premises. The most basic are that trade naturally develops whenever and wherever differentials exist in the cost of commodities over the landscape, that when trade occurs it ramifies into self-amplifying economic growth, that such growth has demographic and social consequences that are central to urbanism, and that trade between different regions and cultures that are urbanizing always involves partners that are initially unequal in some way. It follows from these assumptions that crosscultural trade does not lessen regional developmental asymmetries over time, as classical economists had long posited (Kaldor 1972; Myrdal 1970, 280), but rather leads instead to increasing regional disparities. Accordingly, for both schools, the study of how substantial developmental inequalities are created across the landscape, and how radically different historical trajectories come to be, ultimately boil down to the study of the differential rates at which urban systems form and grow (or not) in varying regions.

Equally important, because of the central points of agreement just noted, scholars in both camps also similarly conceptualize cities as nodes in wider regional and transregional transportation networks. In so doing, they hold a number of further premises in common, some explicit and some not, about the locations where cities will tend to emerge when they grow organically. The most salient are that they will form or preferentially grow in areas where resources involved in exchange naturally exist or, more likely, in areas along the trade routes through which such resources flow that possess the greatest positive productivity differential between the trading partners, thus ensuring larger amounts of surpluses usable for trade. In the latter case, in turn, they will tend to cluster at geographical passage points between contrasting regions involved in exchange, at the end points of natural transportation routes between such regions, or at critical nodes along such routes, such as bulk-breaking points and/or junctures where different types of transport come together (Bairoch 1990, 148, n. 26).[5]

Growth Institutionalized

The foregoing discussions explain the economic processes that create economic activity, concentrate it in particular locations, and propel population agglomeration at those locations beyond an urban threshold in the first place. But what are the mechanisms that allow urban systems to continue to expand once created, and, in so doing, to structure regional development patterns that naturally tend to become increasingly asymmetrical with time? The key concept here is "circular and cumulative causation." Situated at the very core of the new economic geography, this idea was first articulated as a coherent concept by the economist and social theorist Gunnar Myrdal and was later elaborated and formalized for economics by Allen Pred (1966).[6] The concept came to the attention of researchers interested in the rise of early civilizations through the early work of Jane Jacobs (1969). In its initial formulation during the 1930s and 1940s, and at its most complex, cumulative causation theory involved the recognition that economic, social, and cultural factors often reinforce each other, as Myrdal (1944) argued so eloquently in his path-breaking analysis of modern race relations in the United States. During the 1950s, Myrdal narrowed the focus of the concept to more specifically address the dual questions of specific concern here, urban process and regional development. In this context, cumulative causation implies that population growth, production, innovation, and urbanization are invariably interlocked in a circular process whereby change in one realm does "not call forth countervailing changes [in other realms] but, instead, supporting changes, which move the system in the same direction as the first change, but much further" (Myrdal 1957, 13). From the point of view of urban growth and the development of regional disparities, Myrdal (1970, 279–80) argued that the most important "supportive changes" were the creation of economies of scale in production and increases in the rate of innovation as a result of the expansion of knowledge. Both of these factors will figure prominently in later discussions of the Sumerian takeoff (chap. 8).

For the moment, suffice it to say that if we focus our attention on the economic side of the cumulative causation equation, the most important mechanism promoting differential regional growth is what economists often term "import substitution" (Jacobs 1969, 2000; Krugman 1995, 49). After a regional economy grows beyond a critical point by means of the iterative processes described by Jacobs and Krugman, it becomes profitable to replace imports of some commodities subject to scale economies with local production. This substitution creates a second burst of economic expansion that allows already growing centers to expand further by generating even greater diversity and employment, and thereby to draw in even more workers from the immediately surrounding countryside and possibly even from neighboring regions. The reasons for this have to do with the inevitable multiplier effects of increases in productive capacity. One is the creation of linked industries adding further value to semifinished goods produced by the initial industries (forward linkages). Another is the creation of new work in sectors providing services (backward linkages) to those industries (Pred 1966, 25–26). A final multiplier is provided by collateral employment in the managerial classes required to organize the larger number of workers created by these linkages, store and distribute their enhanced production, and keep records of these various activities. In turn, as managerial classes expand, new demands for internal consumption are created, and old demands for already existing products are intensified, adding further boosts to the economy of growing cities and regions.

In due course, the operation over time of these interrelated multipliers creates the enlarged population/market size necessary to induce even further rounds of import substitution processes. As this process is repeated on an ever larger scale, a circular (or, more precisely, spiral) relationship is created between population growth, market size, innovation, the range of productive activities that a region possesses, and the efficiency level of those activities: innovation is most likely and production is highest and most efficient where population and markets are larger, but markets are bigger where production and innovation are greater, so that city-led regional growth (or decline) always takes the form of a self-reinforcing snowball or cascade effect (Krugman 1995, 49).

The historical implications of processes of circular and cumulative causation are clear. Two such implications appear particularly salient for our understanding of early urban processes in ancient Mesopotamia. First, the impact of a new technology or innovation on a given society will always depend on when exactly that innovation is introduced in the cycle of mutual determinations that always exists between trade, production, population growth, commodity demand, market size, and increasing returns resulting from new economies of scale. Accordingly, depending on timing, the adoption of a new technology may lead to dramatically different parameters of an economy, and it follows from this that similar adoptions will differentially affect societies with varying developmental trajectories or with trajectories that are similar but of varying time depth. The importance of timing in determining how a society reacts to innovation is described by Krugman (1991, 487), who notes that "the details of the [human] geography that emerges—which regions end up with the population—depend sensitively on initial conditions. If one region has slightly more population than another when, say, transportation costs fall below some critical level, that region ends up gaining population at the other's expense; had the distribution of population at that critical moment been only slightly different, the roles of the regions might have been reversed."

Second, while an initial pattern of specialization in production may well arise from a variety of causes, once a pattern is established, that pattern is likely to become "locked in" by the cumulative gains from trade. Regional population growth rates and urban development are therefore highly historical (i.e., "path-dependent") processes, so that if a region gains an initial advantage, those processes will concentrate new growth and its multiplier effects in the already expanding region rather than elsewhere (Malecki 1997, 49–50). Processes of cumulative causation thus ultimately account for the division of the world into core and peripheral areas. We will now turn to the issue of how this self-amplifying chain of events may have gotten its start in early Mesopotamia.

Early Mesopotamian Urbanism: Why?

W hat can we learn from the modern economic models of urban process outlined in the preceding chapter that will help us better understand the forces at play at the onset of early Mesopotamian civilization? Two lessons come immediately to mind. First, trade and changes in commodity production and labor organization are as likely to have been fundamental agents of change in antiquity as they have proven to be in modern times. Second, processes of circular and cumulative causation are also likely to have been as consequential in antiquity as they are today. Given this, what needs to be elucidated are the forces that set the trade (and its multiplying ramifications) into motion in the first place. In the case of early Mesopotamian civilization, the trigger was provided by Cronon's "natural environment," referring, more specifically, to the combination of the unique environmental conditions that prevailed across the alluvial delta of the Tigris-Euphrates rivers at the time Mesopotamian civilization first crystallized, and the enduring geographical framework of human life in the area.

Environmental Advantages

Historically, societies in the alluvial lowlands of southern Mesopotamia enjoyed significant advantages over competitors elsewhere in southwest

Asia in terms of their ability to produce and accumulate surpluses of agricultural and subsistence resources. To a large degree, these advantages were derived from the environmental framework in which southern polities were embedded.

One such advantage was that the south possessed a greater variety of complementary ecosystems within exploitable distance than any other area in southwest Asia. As discussed below, this inherent advantage must have been particularly pronounced at the time of the initial urbanization processes in the Mesopotamian alluvium during the fourth millennium, when denser concentrations of usable resources would have been available in the various ecosystems comprising the area than was the case later on . Not surprisingly, many of these easily exploitable resources are depicted in Uruk period iconography (Winter 2007) or are mentioned in the known corpus of Archaic Texts from Warka (Englund 1998): (1) subsistence grain from the irrigable alluvial plain (e.g., Amiet 1961, pl. 44, no. 639); (2) fruits, vegetables and flax (used for textiles) from cultivated gardens and orchards near the rivers (e.g., Amiet 1961, pl. 16, no. 266); (3) extensive pasture for sheep, goats, and cattle created by fallow and recently harvested grain fields (Amiet 1961, pl. 41, no. 618); and (4) abundant fish (e.g., Amiet 1961, pl. 13bis, g, pl. 15, no. 260), fowl, wild animals (e.g., Amiet 1961, pl. 40, no. 609 [wild boar]), and various types of reed products, all obtainable in coastal and aquatic environments at the head of the Persian Gulf (Tengberg 2005; Tomé 2005; van Neer, Zohar, and Lernau 2005).

Of the enduring environmental advantages favoring southern Mesopotamian societies few were more important than the higher yields and reliability of the southern agricultural base as compared to neighboring areas. Modern agricultural data for cereal cultivation (summarized in Weiss 1986 and Wilkinson 1990a) and inferences from ancient cuneiform documents (Jacobsen 1982, but see the reservations of Powell 1985) show that, under conditions of controlled irrigation, the alluvial landscape of southern Mesopotamia could be, on average, about twice or thrice as productive per unit of land as the rain-fed agricultural regimes characteristic of neighboring societies. In addition, the reliability of that production was greater than that typical of dry-farmed areas at the periphery of Mesopotamia, which are subject to substantial and unpredictable spatial and temporal variations in rainfall (Perrin de Brichambaut and Wallen 1963, figs. 2–3; Turkes 1996).

FIGURE 4. Uruk cylinder seal impressions depicting resources available in various portions of the early Mesopotamian alluvium. Not to scale.

In fact, discrepancies in agricultural yield and reliability favoring southern societies would have been particularly pronounced at the time when cities first emerged in the Tigris-Euphrates alluvial lowlands. Available paleoenvironmental data suggest that increased winter rainfall prevailed across much of the Tigris-Euphrates watershed throughout the fifth and parts of the fourth millennia BC ("mid-Holocene climatic optimum"), as compared to present patterns in the same area (Algaze 2001a, 202–3; Hole 1994; Kuzucuoğlu 2007; Pournelle 2003b). Accordingly, the Tigris and Euphrates rivers would have carried increased late winter and spring flows at this time. This meant that when urbanism was first sprouting in southern Mesopotamia during the first half of the fourth millennium (i.e., the Early and Middle Uruk periods, see chap. 7), marginal areas of the alluvium that are today unproductive because of insufficient water or that lack of adequate drainage likely would have been integrated into fluvial networks draining into the sea (Hoelzmann et al. 1998, 47). This favorable situation was only reversed in the third or, more likely, the final quarter of the fourth millennium (i.e., at about the transition from the Middle to Late Uruk periods) with the onset of a cooler, drier, climatic spell that marked the transition to the less humid and more erratic climatic regime that has characterized southwest Asia until the present (Kuzucuoğlu 2007, 462–64; Stevens et al. 2006, 494; Staubwasser and Weiss 2006, 379).

Equally important, climatological models (e.g., De Noblet et al. 1996; Harrison et al. 1998) and sedimentological research in the Persian Gulf (e.g., el-Moslimany 1994; Sirocko et al. 1993) suggest that parts of the alluvium that today receive no summer precipitation whatsoever would have been affected by summer monsoonal rains of Indian Ocean origin that today skip the northern edge of the Persian Gulf but that had a more northerly track during the Ubaid and Early Uruk periods (Petit-Maire, Sanlaville, and Yan 1995). Summer precipitation must have had a variety of significant economic impacts on alluvial societies of the fifth and early fourth millennia. Basing herself on el-Moslimany's (1990, 348–49) analysis of changes in the distribution of nonarboreal pollen in now arid areas of the Arabian Peninsula throughout the Holocene, Joy McCorriston (personal communication 2001, 2007) suggests that the most important of these impacts would have been an expansion in the availability of animal forage at precisely the time of greatest need, particularly in the form of high temperatures and salinity-resistant C4 grasses (tropical, summer rainfall–adapted): *Panicum turgidum, Pennisetum divisum, Paspalum* sp., *Cymbopogon* sp., *Hyparrhenia* sp., *Heteropogon* sp., among others. A further consequence of summer precipitation at this time would have been an increase in the productivity of date palm cultivation throughout the southern portions of the Mesopotamian alluvium.

Also more abundant during the formative stages of Mesopotamian civilization as well as more accessible to societies of the time, would have been resources from freshwater marshes, brackish lagoons, and tidal flats, and estuaries at the intersection between the Tigris-Euphrates Delta and the Persian Gulf. This was so because mid-Holocene sea level rises taking place roughly between the seventh and fourth millennia BC resulted in a northward transgression of the head of the gulf and a concomitant shift northward of associated littoral resources (Hole 1994). Within Iraq itself, this transgression is attested directly in a series of sediment cores drilled by the Iraqi Geological Service during 1979–1980 at eight different locations within the roughly triangular area formed by the modern-day cities of Nasiriyya, Amara, and Basra (Aqrawi 2001). Though individual depositional strata in these cores are not amenable to precise dating, they document a complex succession of marine and brackish water environments across the sampled area through the mid-Holocene.

More precise evidence as to the chronology and, to a lesser degree, the extent of the transgression is provided by recent studies of relict beaches identified in Oman and various other points along the western end of the present coastline of the Persian Gulf (Berger et al. 2005) and by a new set of fifty-one shallow sediment cores taken by a joint Belgo-Iranian team along the eastern coast of the Persian Gulf in Iran (Baeteman, Dupin, and Heyvaert 2004, 2005). Radiocarbon dates associated with these data agree in placing the height of the transgression in the sixth and fifth millennia BC and show that it only started to recede in the second half of the fourth millennium (Pournelle 2003a, 2003b; Sanlaville 1989, 1992; Sanlaville and Dalongeville 2005). The Omani and Iranian studies exhibit some discrepancies, however, in the maximum height above present sea level that each indicates for the transgression, with slightly less than a meter above present levels being indicated by the Iranian data and up to two meters indicated by the Omani data. These discrepancies are almost certainly due to slight east-west–oriented variations in local tectonic subsidence and/or uplift since the mid-Holocene across the Persian Gulf, as well as to slight differences in soil compaction rates across the area.[1]

Taken as whole, however, the implications of the three available data sets (Iraqi, Omani, and Iranian) are clear. Absent evidence for substantial subsidence in the mid–late Holocene (Uchipi, Swift, and Russ 1999) and given the topography of the southern Mesopotamian delta region, at the peak of the transgression the head of the Persian Gulf would have been situated up to 200 km or so north of its present position and, particularly in soutern Iraq, extensive sweet water marshes and brackish lagoons rich in biomass would have existed well north of the intruding mid-Holocene coastline. Moreover, those marshes would have been particularly large because of two further compounding factors. The first was the relatively high water table that must have prevailed across much of the southern Mesopotamian delta region because of tidal forcing associated with the transgression (Hole 1994; Baeteman, Dupin, and Heyvaert 2005). The second was the already noted increase in rainfall in the Tigris-Euphrates headwaters during much of the fifth and fourth millennia, which increased the amount of water the rivers could contribute to marshes in their delta region at that time (Agrawi 2001). Accordingly, to a much greater degree than was the case in historic times, early Mesopotamian settlements would have been situated in close proximity to productive

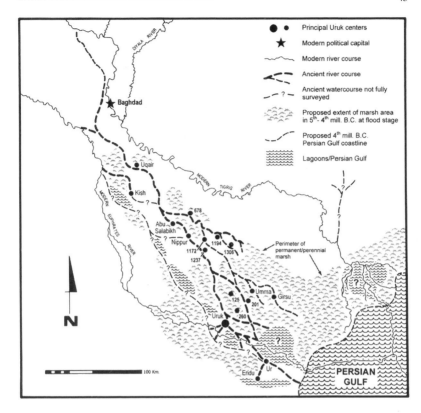

FIGURE 5. The ancient Mesopotamian alluvium during the late fifth and fourth millennia BC, showing the location of the principal Uruk centers, major watercourses of the time, and the probable location of mid-Holocene marshes and Persian Gulf coastline.

and easily exploitable aquatic resources throughout the Ubaid and Early Uruk periods. To a lesser but still significant degree, this continued to be the case even after the transgression slowly started to recede by the end of the Middle and Late Uruk periods.

In turn, the increase in both the extent of aquatic ecotones during the formative period of early Mesopotamian civilization and the ease of human access to the resources they contained were compounded by an increase in the relative productivity of those ecotones at the time. The reason for this is that the more northerly track of the Indian Ocean summer monsoon, noted above, must have increased the upwelling of nutrient-rich sediments and water oxygenation within the extensive marshes and lagoons surrounding Uruk population centers (Reichart et al. 1997),

thereby enhancing the biomass density of the enlarged southern Mesopotamian marsh ecosystem at precisely the critical time of initial urban
formation in the area.

This is relevant for two reasons. One is that it would have maximized
the availability of easily exploitable protein-rich fish, fowl, and wild animals within the engorged marshes of the time. Nutritionally, fish must
have been the most important of these resources. Dried fish was a significant source of protein for alluvial Mesopotamian societies in the historic
periods, and they figure prominently already in the Archaic Texts as part
of rations provided to laborers (Englund 1998, 134). Second, and equally
important, because the leaves of young reed shoots can be used as fodder
for domestic livestock (Pournelle 2003b; Ochsenschlager 2004, 193, 204),
the margins of the enlarged mid-Holocene marshes of southern Mesopotamia could have supported particularly large herds of sheep, goats, and
bovids.

It is difficult to quantify with any precision how much greater these
various resources would have been in the fifth and fourth millennia
than in later periods, as relevant archaeological data are either lacking
or, those that do exist, are wholly unreliable; nevertheless, available art
historical and textual evidence do provide useful glimpses. Herds of
livestock, for instance, are one of the most frequently depicted motifs
in the iconography of the Uruk period (Amiet 1961, 77; Kawami 2001;
see figs. 4e, 7a–7b, and 14a–14c), and the association between such herds
and marshy environments is quite clear in the art of the time. The large
arched reed huts (Arabic: *madhaif*) that have been shown ethnographi-
cally to be typical for marsh edges in southern Mesopotamia (e.g., Ochsenschlager 1992, 55–58, pls. IV–V) are commonly depicted in a variety
of media being used as sheep and cow barns during the Uruk period
(e.g., Kawami 2001, figs. 8A–B; Amiet 1961, pl. 42, nos. 629, 632 [seals],
and Amiet 1961, pl. 42, no. 623 [gypsum trough]).

Some indications as to the size of late fourth-millennium southern
Mesopotamian herds are provided by the Archaic Texts. Caprids are not
well represented in the earliest tablets in the corpus dated to the Late
Uruk Period (Uruk IV script), but they are commonly noted in later
texts dated to the immediately succeeding Jemdet Nasr period (Uruk
III script), when flocks averaging 75 sheep and goats are common and
flocks including up to 1,400 or so sheep are attested (Englund 1998, 148;
Green 1980, 11, n. 56). Bovids, in turn, are more clearly documented in
the earliest group of archaic tablets, which occasionally record numbers

FIGURE 6. Arched reed hut (Arabic: *madhaif*) typical for Iraqi marsh environments.

FIGURE 7. Uruk period *madhaif* representations. Not to scale.

of cows and calves assigned to specific overseers. Although most herds are smaller, herds of up to 50 animals are attested in the earlier texts (Englund 1995b, 33; 1998, 155). No doubt, the fact that bovids figure more prominently than caprids in the earliest group of Archaic Texts is due in no small part to accidents of preservation and discovery, since both species are amply documented in the iconography of the Late Uruk period (Amiet 1961, 82–85; Kawami 2001; Winter 2007). Nonetheless, it is also possible that herding cattle at the margins of marshes was an activity of greater economic potential in the Mesopotamian alluvium during the fifth and fourth millennia than was the case later on in historic times, after the mid-Holocene transgression started to recede.[2]

Be that as it may, in addition to providing an important activity creating economic and occupational differentiation (chap. 5), herds of sheep, goats, and cattle kept at the margins of the engorged mid-Holocene marshes must have generated a unique and ample supply of protein-rich dairy products easily exploitable by populations in growing nearby centers. On average, it should be remembered, the caloric yield of the dairy products that a lactating animal can produce over its productive life is about four times greater than the caloric yield of its meat if slaughtered as an adult (McNeill and McNeill 2003, 31), and this differential is much greater in the case of bovids. Early Mesopotamian urban dwellers of the fourth millennium surely understood this. In the Uruk period, scenes depicting cattle in marsh environments commonly do so in association with either the bundled reed standard used to represent the goddess Inanna, patron deity of Uruk (Amiet 1961, 78; see for instance figs. 14a–14b; Amiet 1961, pls. 42–43, nos. 623, 632), or the (bundled reed?) standard with three sets of paired rings, thought to be emblematic for the city of Eridu (Amiet 1961, 79; see, for example, fig. 7a; Kawami 2001, figs. 8a–8b), suggesting that religiously invested urban authorities directly intervened in the exploitation of marsh resources for milk production. The importance of milk products to early Sumerian city dwellers is confirmed by the Archaic Texts, which kept particularly close tabs on the production of cheese and various types of dairy fats, extracted principally from milking cows (Englund 1998, 155–69). In this light, it is almost certainly not accidental that the breed of cattle that becomes predominant in southern Mesopotamia at this time, to judge from artistic representations, is a short-horned variety that produces more milk per animal but requires more water per day, than the long-horned breeds that had until then prevailed over much of the Near East (Kawami 2001).

The various environmental advantages just discussed were compounded further by the nature of the Tigris-Euphrates fluvial system during the fifth and fourth millennia, which was very different from that typical for the two rivers during the historic periods. This realization has emerged only recently as a result of new work by Robert M. Adams (personal communication, 2002–5) and Jennifer Pournelle (2003a, 2003b, 2006) using newly declassified satellite images (CORONA) to correlate the location of previously surveyed fourth-millennium sites in southern Mesopotamia and relict watercourses visible in the images. They concluded that the two rivers formed a single dynamic network of anastomosing channels at the time of early urban emergence in the area, later separating to their historically known discrete courses after the fourth millennium (for tentative reconstructions of the fourth-millennium fluvial system, see fig. 5 above, and Wilkinson 2003b, 91, fig. 5.11). From this we may deduce that yield differences between alluvial Mesopotamia and its neighbors would have been greater during the Uruk period than was the case thereafter, because waters of the two rivers were likely to commingle at flood stage in the northern parts of the alluvium where their courses came closest, allowing not only for easier transport (below) but also for the creation of much larger areas than exist at present where various types of high-value vegetables and fruits could be produced in late spring and, possibly, early summer by means of simple flood-recession irrigation (Sanlaville 1989, 24).

In sum, the multiple highly favorable environmental conditions just described for the Mesopotamian alluvium throughout much of the fifth and early fourth millennia contrast sharply with the situation in the high plains on the periphery of the Mesopotamian lowlands at the same time. Those latter areas were unaffected by the monsoonal rains that fell on the south until the Early Uruk period, the formative phase of early Sumerian civilization, and they did not possess comparably varied, resilient, or dense concentrations of subsistence resources beyond a once-a-year crop of dry-farmed grain and ample pasture lands. Though northern and highland pasturelands were well suited for herding sheep and goats, they could not have supported herds of cattle as dense as those that could and apparently did thrive at the margins of the greatly enlarged mid-Holocene marshes of southern Mesopotamia.

Geographical Advantages

Greater variety, productivity, and resilience in subsistence resources were not the only material advantages that early southern Mesopotamian polities enjoyed over societies in neighboring areas. Of equal—if not greater—importance were transportational advantages that southern societies derived from the geographical framework in which they were embedded.

Geography was important because the absence from the southern Mesopotamian landscape of many materials necessary for the creation and maintenance of highly stratified social systems (most importantly, roofing-grade timber, wood, base and exotic metals, various types of semiprecious minerals and stones, and exotic intoxicants such as wine) made it probable that early southern elites would use trade as one of their most important tools to legitimize and extend their unequal access to power and privilege. At the same time, geography provided those societies an enduring and irrevocable advantage over their neighbors in the form of lower transportation costs based on water transport.

Throughout their history, the cities of the Tigris-Euphrates alluvial delta were situated, in effect, at the head of an enormous dendritic transportation system created by the north-to-south flowing rivers. This allowed them to procure information, labor, and commodities from areas within the vast Tigris-Euphrates watershed more efficiently than any potential upstream competitors or rivals away from the rivers. The crucial edge of southern cities lay in their ability to import needed commodities in bulk from faraway resource areas in the surrounding highlands at low cost, transported downstream on rivers by means of simple log rafts, rafts mounted on inflated animal skins, coracles, or bitumen-coated boats and canoes. Of equal importance, the network of canals surrounding Mesopotamian cities and connecting them with the main courses of the rivers allowed them to move bulky agricultural commodities across their immediate dependent hinterlands with great efficiency, either by using simple boats or barges towed by draught animals or human laborers.

There is no doubt that early Sumerian societies possessed the technologies they needed to exploit effectively the inherent transportational advantages of the environment in which they were embedded. The most important of these technologies were bitumen-caulked or covered boats and canoes made from reeds and/or wood planks, which were usable for hunting and fishing in the marshes and, more importantly, for the transport of both people and cargo. Because such vessels are capable of operating in relatively shallow water, they were particularly well suited for use in the expanded marshes that existed in southern Mesopotamia throughout the Ubaid and Uruk periods. Their use in such environment is, in fact, amply attested in the modern ethnographic record of southern Mesopotamia (Ochsenschlager 1992, 2004, 138–39, 176–85). Archaeological evidence indicates that reed and/or wood plank boats were widely used in the Tigris-Euphrates fluvial system and the Persian Gulf from very early on, at least from the sixth millennium onward.[3] In southern Mesopotamia itself, both larger boats with a characteristically upturned prow and stern raised high above the waterline and smaller canoes are commonly depicted in iconography of fourth- and third-millennium date (Potts 1997, 122–23, figs. V.1–2).[4] The vessels depicted appear almost identical to examples still in use in the area (e.g., Thesiger 1964, pls. 44, 56–57; Young 1977, 126–43). In addition, bitumen-caulked boats are also amply attested in cuneiform texts of the third and later millennia (Potts 1997, 122–37). Finally, wider sailboats capable, perhaps, of carrying heavier loads, and certainly able to travel longer distances, were also available to early southern Mesopotamian societies from relatively early on, as shown by a clay model boat of Late Ubaid date with a central shaft for a mast and sail found at Eridu (Safar, Mustafa, and Lloyd 1981, 231, fig. 111), a site that in the mid-Holocene must have stood near the then active coastline of the Persian Gulf.

As was the case with climate and environment, it turns out that advantages in ease of transport and communication accruing to southern Mesopotamian polities would have been more pronounced during the late fifth and fourth millennia than was the case later on in the historic periods. The reasons for this have already been discussed and have to do with the enlarged marsh ecosystem that existed in close proximity to many growing urban centers in the Mesopotamian alluvium throughout the fourth millennium. By allowing lateral movement, these marshes in effect created a single transport and communication network integrating many of the settlements across the alluvium at the time of initial urbanization in the area (Pournelle 2003b). Although this advantage would eventually be greatly reduced after the fourth millennium, once the head of the Persian Gulf started to recede and the main channels of the Tigris and Euphrates started to separate, the contrast in the overall efficiency of the transportation networks accessible to southern Mesopotamian societies of the Uruk period and those practicable in the rest of southwest

A

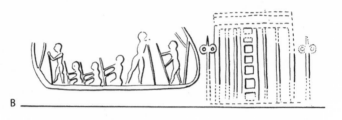

B

C

FIGURE 8. Uruk cylinder seal impressions depicting various types of canoes and boats. Not to scale.

Asia could not be greater. Outside of the Tigris-Euphrates Delta, reed boats benefited only polities that directly adjoined the rivers and would have been useful only for downstream navigation. Because the Tigris and Euphrates rivers and their tributaries are deeply incised as they cut across the Upper Mesopotamian plains and surrounding highlands, lateral movement via water was impossible anywhere within the Mesopotamian periphery. As a consequence, the land-locked polities of the area had to rely to a much greater extent than did southern societies on inherently less efficient modes of overland transport and communication, such as human portage, pack animals, or simple wheeled carts, both for their long-distance exchange needs and for the movement of subsistence resources across their immediate hinterlands.

We can use historic and ethnographic data for transport costs in traditional (preindustrial) societies to quantify, however crudely, the relative cost advantages accruing to southern Mesopotamian societies as a result of differences in the types of transport possible in the two areas. While these advantages would naturally vary with the bulk and value of the cargo transported, available data clearly show that transport by water across the south must have entailed substantial cost savings over any of the three main types of transport, noted above, possible for overland communication in regions at the periphery of southern Mesopotamia.

Take, for example, grain, a high-bulk, low-value commodity that must have constituted the most common shipment (in terms of both volume and weight) into all ancient cities, including the emerging protourban centers of both Upper and Lower Mesopotamia. Expressed in terms of grain equivalences and using raw data on transport costs prevalent in traditional third world societies compiled by Clark and Haswell (1970, 196–203), the historian Paul Bairoch (1990, 141) finds that under preindustrial conditions, the average cost to transport a ton of cereals was 8.8 kg of the cereals per kilometer if carried by human porters; 4.8 kg/km if transported by pack animals; and 3.9 kg/km for transport by simple carts pulled by draught animals. These costs compare unfavorably with transport by water. Bairoch's calculations show that dragging the same amount of grain on a barge alongside a canal, for instance, lowers costs to 0.9 kg/km. In other words, all other factors being equal, in the case of high-bulk, low-cost commodities, water transport proves to be four to five times more efficient than the most efficient types of possible overland transport.

These numbers are in line with results from pre-Hispanic Mesoamerica calculated by Robert Drennan (1984, 106–7, table 2) for the movement of maize and other high-bulk staples. Drennan found, on average, that canoes paddled upstream were about four times more efficient than human porters (Mesoamerica had no pack animals) and that increased to eight times the efficiency when being paddled downstream.

An even more substantial cost advantage for water transport over land portage/transport emerges when the value of the commodities being transported is higher. This is clear in the case of wood, for instance, a commodity that was of particular importance for southern Mesopotamian societies, which needed to import the overwhelming majority of their roofing timber. According to Bairoch (1993, 60), transporting timber over a distance of only 2 kilometers by cart doubled its price in

Europe prior to the Industrial Revolution. By inland waterway the distance was instead 10–16 kilometers, but in favorable conditions, namely, shipping wood downstream on a river, the price only doubled after 100 or so kilometers.

Another case in point is provided by the transport of coal extracted from British mines at the beginnings of the Industrial Revolution. This led to the construction of numerous artificial canals across the English landscape built expressly to transport the coal to both urban consumers and shipping ports. Simon Winchester (2001, 45) estimates that a single horse pulling a barge heavily laden with coal alongside these canals could haul eighty times more coal by weight than if it were leading a wagon down the muddy roads that characterized Britain at the time, and that the barge could in fact carry about 400 times as much as a single pack horse. Similarly, the binge of canal building in New York State in the nineteenth century also provides useful data as to the advantages of water transport. According to W. Langbein (1976), a team of four horses on a common nineteenth-century road in North America could haul 1 ton over 12 miles per day (5 degree grade max.). In contrast, a single horse could draw a 30-ton barge on a slackwater canal at a rate of 2 miles per hour. Conservatively presuming an eight-hour day, water transport in this case is 40 times more economical than carriage over land. These modern examples are pertinent to early Mesopotamia in that they leave no doubt that, on average, river transport can be many, many times more efficient than land carriage when transporting heavy loads.

If anything, the cost-effectiveness of water over land transport would be even greater in the case of high-value but low-bulk commodities, such as the exotic stones and semiprocessed metal ores and ingots that surely comprised an important proportion of imports into the emerging cities of fourth-millennium southern Mesopotamia (chap. 6). We can get a good idea of the potential savings by looking again to Mesoamerica, where pertinent data exist for the transport of obsidian cores. Lenore Santone (1997, 80), a Mesoamerican lithic specialist, for instance, has calculated that a single human porter could transport an average of 920 classic period obsidian cores, each weighing about 25 grams, over a distance of 29 kilometers per day. One canoe, in contrast, could have transported a load of 200,000 cores over the same distance—water transport in this case proves to be up to 220 times as efficient as land transport.

But how relevant are these parallels? It would seem that they are quite relevant, based on historic data from ancient Mesopotamia itself, which point to the existence of an exponential advantage in the efficiency of water transport over land carriage under Mesopotamian conditions. Two large bodies of data are particularly useful. The first is a corpus of upward of 20,000 cuneiform tablets, mostly plundered from the site of Kultepe near Kayseri (Turkey), which record the activities of Old Assyrian merchants operating between the Assyrian capital of Assur, on the Tigris in northern Iraq, and Kanesh, the capital of an indigenous kingdom in central Anatolia where an extramural Assyrian merchant diaspora settlement was allowed to operate.[5] Dating to the first two centuries of the second millennium BC, the tablets illuminate a wide variety of the economic transactions that involved Assyrian merchants and can be used to reconstruct the cost of travel using donkey caravans in the ancient Near East, the principal method of overland carriage for long distance trade in the area following the domestication of the donkey in the fourth millennium BC.

The second corpus of data consists of upward of 100,000 tablets from southern Mesopotamia stemming from provincial archives of the Ur III empire, dated to the last century of the third millennium BC. The great majority of these tablets were plundered from the sites of Drehem (ancient Puzrish-Dagan) and Tell Jokha (ancient Umma) or were haphazardly excavated by early French expeditions at Tello (ancient Girsu). Like the Old Assyrian archives, these tablets illuminate a variety of economic activities. They can be used to assess the cost of travel and transport between settlements in southern Mesopotamia by means of boats or barges towed by men along natural and artificial canals. Many of the pertinent texts have been the subject of two recent studies: one by the assyriologist Piotr Steinkeller (2001) on the hydrology and topology of Southern Mesopotamia in the Ur III period and the other by Steinkeller's student, Tonia Sharlach (2004), who looked in detail at the taxation system of the Ur III empire.

Regarding overland transport, Old Assyrian caravans headed to Kanesh from Assur normally included both tin and textiles, although more rarely loads consisting only of one or the other of the two commodities are also attested. By looking at data of specific shipments for which both the total weight of the items shipped and the number of donkeys used to carry the load are known, the assyriologist J. Dercksen (2004, 255, 260, 278) calculates that individual donkeys generally carried up to 75 kg of goods at a time. While the texts provide no clues for the speed of travel, Dercksen uses modern nineteenth- and twentieth-century

British Army records to infer that caravans covered an average distance of about 25 km per day—an estimate that appears warranted in light of other available ethnographic data from modern Iran (chap. 5, n. 3 below). Most caravans consisted of about 2 animals (Larsen 1976, 103). Single donkey caravans are not uncommon but, on occasion, small caravans led by different merchants traveled together for security and companionship. By the same token, many individual caravans larger than the average are also attested, at times consisting of 8 or more asses and, more rarely, of up to 14 animals. In one exceptional case, a caravan of up to 18 animals carrying only textiles is recorded (Larsen 1967, 146; Veenhof 1972, 69–76). In another unique instance, a caravan of 40 asses carrying mostly copper and some silver is noted (Dercksen 2004, 279). If we take these data to be representative of the nature of Old Assyrian trade as a whole, they mean that under Near Eastern conditions donkey caravans could transport anywhere between 75 (1 donkey) and 3,000 (40 donkeys) kilograms of cargo for a distance of 25 kilometers during one day—an efficiency rate that averaged 3,750 kg/km/day (2 donkeys) but, depending on the size of the caravan, could range from as low as 1,875 to as high as to 75,000 kg/km/day.

Turning now to water transport, we find that a sizable number of the extant Ur III texts deal with rotational tax obligations (Sumerian: *bala*) sent from the core provinces of the Ur III empire to either the imperial capital of Ur, the religious capital of Nippur, or imperial redistribution centers, such as Puzrish-Dagan, near Nippur (Steinkeller 1987; Sharlach 2004). A wide range of agricultural and processed commodities, and even, on occasion, manufactured goods were shipped as part of *bala*. Although a systematic quantification is still not at hand, grain (barley) was by far the most salient commodity being transported, followed by reeds and reed products.[6] The rate of resource extraction from the provinces appears to have been high in the Ur III period. In the case of the two provinces for which we have the most data, Umma and Lagash, grain shipments forming part of *bala* payments appear in the order of 43–48 percent of the total estimated cereal production in lands controlled by the crown in those provinces (Sharlach 2004, 160).

Because of their bulk and scale, these payments were commonly shipped on boats. In fact, texts from both Umma and Girsu (Lagash) show that, at times, grain was loaded into boats in the fields in which it was grown and shipped directly to royal storehouses at Ur or elsewhere (Sharlach 2004, 36, 82, 84). The amounts shipped were staggering. A few

FIGURE 9. Loaded donkey being led to market. Iraq, near modern Rania, ca. 1951.

examples will suffice to illustrate the point. Putting together extant texts detailing the shipment of reed bundles from Umma to Nippur, Sharlach (2004, 37) found that a total of 65,930 bundles were sent in the first regnal year of Amar-Sin, the third ruler of the III Dynasty of Ur—and this, of course (because of the way the tablets came to light), probably represents but a small random portion of the actual total, the size of which is entirely unknown. If we accept Waetzold's (1992, 128) estimate of a bundle of reeds as weighing between 1.5 to 3 kg, the known reed shipments in the one documented year of Amar-Sin's reign (Amar-Sin 1) work out to anywhere between 49.4 and 65.9 tons.

Another, more compelling illustration of the amounts of commodities that could be transported over water at any one time and of the efficiency of water transport in doing so is provided by a thus far unique document from Umma, which appears to represent a forecast written by provincial bureaucrats to estimate future allocations of commodities to be sent to the Ur III state, the number of workers needed to handle those payments, and the boats needed to carry them (Sharlach 2004, 32–33). The text is long and complex and lists large amounts of many different commodities. In its middle section, this tablet lists 8,700 gur of barley (2,610,000 liters) and the number of boats required to carry that volume of grain: 12. We can quantify the transportational implications of this text. We know that in the Ur III period a gur of grain was equivalent to 300 liters (Nissen, Damerow, and Englund 1993, 142). A liter of barley, in turn, weighs on average 0.7 kg.[7] Given this, in this text, Mesopotamian provincial bureaucrats of the late third millennium self-consciously asserted their ability to transport 1,827,000 kg or 913.5 tons of grain over water as part of one tax collection season. Each of the 12 boats needed to move this amount would have carried, on average, 76 tons of barley! It would be easy to dismiss this forecast of taxes to be collected and the transport capacity needed to convey those receipts as reflecting nothing but the wishful thinking of overoptimistic state administrators were it not for the fact that contemporary but independent texts from other southern sites, discussed below, show that shipments of the magnitude postulated for the Umma boats are not at all unusual.

Aside from this unique forecast, three different categories of *bala*-related texts together can be used to estimate the overall capacity and relative efficiency parameters of water transport within southern Mesopotamia in a way that can be compared with the measurements noted above for overland transport using donkeys, which would have prevailed elsewhere in ancient southwest Asia. Following Sharlach (2004), these categories may be labeled "boat," "cargo," and "labor" texts. Each is discussed in turn.

For reasons that probably reflect nothing but the randomly recovered nature of the archives available to us, boat texts (Sharlach 2004, 86–90, chart 3.13) are known only from Girsu. They represent attempts by provincial officials in Lagash province to summarize and keep track of the number and types of boats from that province carrying shipments to imperial storehouses at Ur or Nippur during the season of the year that their *bala* obligations became due. The extant texts only cover three years of the reign of Amar-Sin. During these years, the number of boats being tracked at any one time ranged from as few as 1 to as many as 98. While the larger number is exceptional, texts recording the movements of dozens of boats at a time are typical (Sharlach 2004, 87–89).

The size of boats tracked varied greatly, with boats ranging from 10- to 120-gur capacities recorded in the Girsu texts. Presumably, these boat sizes may have been appropriate for canals in Lagash province, but larger boats of up to 300-gur capacity are known to have been used at the imperial capital of Ur (Potts 1997, 128). There is no direct indication in the boat texts of the amounts of commodities actually loaded into the specific boats being tracked. Boats in the Ur III period were named according to their presumptive grain volume–handling capacity (e.g., 10, 20, 40, 60 gur, etc.), and it would stand to reason that these names are an indication of the nominal volume-handling capacities of the boats in question (i.e., a 60-gur boat would carry a 60-gur load of grain), but Sharlach (personal communication, 2005) notes that the texts habitually show boats being loaded with substantially more cargo than the nominal cargo capacity suggested by their names. This means that there is no easy way to correlate actual boat capacity with nominal vessel size (Sharlach 2004, 33, n. 38), although it still stands to reason that the larger the specified capacity of a boat, the greater its actual load capacity would have been.

Fortunately, the cargo and labor texts contain more specific information that can be used to shed light on the energetics of water transport in Ur III Mesopotamia. Cargo texts are attested at both Umma and Girsu and are concerned with the types of commodities that were shipped (i.e., Sumerian: *má-a si-ga* "loaded onto a boat"), their amounts, place of origin, and destination, when known (Sharlach 2004, 82). These texts do not, however, specify the number of days it took to travel between the two points or the number of men needed to tow the boats and load and unload their cargo. For the sake of brevity, only texts dealing with grain shipments, the most commonly transported and easily quantified commodity, are considered below.

The amounts of cargo shipped varied greatly. Sharlach's (2004, 329–31, charts 3.6–3.7) tabulations of grain "loaded onto a boat" in Lagash province and shipped to either Nippur or unspecified destinations, for instance, include 52 different texts and show that shipments could range in size from 1 to 3,581 gur.[8] By weight, this amounts to a range of 0.1 to 376 tons of grain. Considering all 52 texts, the average shipment would have been on the order of 474 gur or about 50 tons. Excluding the three smallest (1, 5, 10 gur) and three largest (1,740, 3,020 and 3,581 gur) shipments, however, the average comes to 355 gur or about 37 tons per shipment. These calculations appear broadly similar to estimates derived from Umma sources. Twenty-two texts detailing shipments of grain from Umma province to Nippur, Uruk, and Ur, for instance, range from 2 to 820 gur in size (ca. 0.2 to 86 tons), and average 262 gur or about 28 tons of grain per shipment (Sharlach 2004, 282–84, charts 2.5, 2.7).[9] Putting these data together, 32 tons appears to be a conservative estimate of the average amount of grain sent by boat from Umma and Lagash provinces to Ur III imperial centers in the late third millennium per shipping event.

FIGURE 10. Sail barge being towed along river canal in southern Iraq (ca. 1950s).

The labor texts are concerned precisely with issues not addressed in the cargo texts, namely, the labor needed to man and tow the boats and the number of days of travel. These texts are also attested at both Umma and Girsu. While they give no indication of the amounts of commodities involved, the labor texts can be used to estimate the average rate of travel per day. Pertinent data are provided by the analyses of both Steinkeller and Sharlach. Again, for purposes of comparison, only texts pertaining to grain are discussed here. A series of 11 texts recording the towing of boats between Umma and Nippur (upstream to a location named Kasahar, near Nippur, and downstream from there to Nippur) indicate that the trip took between 5 and 8 days. As the linear distance between Umma and Nippur is 81 kilometers—and one presumes that the actual distance between the two cities would have been greater because waterways were not always strictly linear—these texts indicate a daily rate of upstream travel that minimally ranged between 10 and 16 kilometers (Steinkeller 2001, 75, appendix A.5).[10] Other texts suggest a more modest speed when traveling upstream. One tablet from Girsu, for example, records the labor of 10 men who towed a boat for 15 days from Lagash province to Nippur (Sharlach 2004, 85), a distance of 107 kilometers as the crow flies. This text indicates a minimal average rate of 7.1 kilometers per day for upstream travel.

It stands to reason that downstream travel would have been significantly more efficient. Surprisingly, however, this is not borne out by the texts, possibly because even when heading downstream barges would have been towed across small lateral canals during much of the trip. In any event, one tablet records six men towing a boat for 15 days, first downstream from Girsu to Ur (a linear distance of ca. 65.5 km), and then upstream from Ur to Uruk (a further linear distance of 57.1 km). Mixing upstream towing and downstream travel, this text gives us an average speed of 8.1 km/day. Another trip involved only downstream travel and records one boatload of barley that was towed by 5 male workers from Idsalla, somewhere in Umma province, to Ur. The trip to Ur took 8 days. Once there, it took the workers 10 days to unload the boat and 8 additional days to tow the empty boat back to Idsalla (Sharlach 2004, 38). While the exact location of Idsalla is unknown, the linear distance between Umma and Ur was about 79 kilometers. This gives us an average rate of travel, minimally, of 10 km/day. Lest it be thought that these texts, which refer to the transport of grain, are unrepresentative, it is noteworthy that Steinkeller calculated an identical rate of daily travel for towed boats/barges in Umma province recording the transfer of reeds from the immediate environs of the city into Umma itself (Steinkeller 2001, 33, 48).

Because the Ur III cargo and labor texts from different sites yield results that are reasonably similar, it is likely that they reflect the true parameters of the energetics of water transport in the ancient Mesopotamian alluvium in the late third millennium. If we presume that the dozens of texts noted above are representative of the range of variance possible in each category, it turns out that in ancient southern Iraq shipments averaging 32 tons of cargo could be towed on a boat or barge over water for a distance that can be conservatively estimated at 10 km/day. This works out to an efficiency rate of 640,000 kg/km/day. As will be recalled, comparable statistics for donkey travel varied widely from 1,875 to 75,000 kg/km/day and averaged 3,750 kg/km/day. In other words, using watercraft technologies that almost certainly had not changed significantly since late prehistoric times, waterborne transport in ancient Mesopotamia could be about 170 times more efficient than the average donkey caravan.

A further difference between the two types of transport concerns the absolute capacity of each to move commodities over the landscape, and thereby the ability of societies employing each type of transport to accumulate surpluses. Here the discrepancies are even more glaring. The data summarized above indicate that whereas the average donkey caravan carried 0.07 tons of goods at a time, the average boat shipment carried 32 tons of goods. Put differently, and perhaps more strikingly, whereas the *largest* donkey caravans could carry about one-and-a-half tons of cargo at a time, the *average* Ur III waterborne shipment from Umma or Lagash was still 21 times greater. Indeed, it would appear that, on occasion, a *single* boat could carry fifty times as much as the *largest* donkey caravan (and 1,000 times more than the *average* donkey caravan!). Moreover, it should be remembered that boat and barge traffic in canals seldom consisted of a single vessel. As noted earlier, extant texts recording the movements of dozens of boats at a time are not uncommon.

To be sure, nobody in their right mind would argue that individual Uruk city states in the fourth millennium BC possessed anything close to either the surplus extraction capacity, military might, number of deployable workers, or shipping capabilities of the Ur III Empire a millennium or so later. Nonetheless, the Ur III data are still useful insofar as it allows us to gauge the general transport potential of the Tigris-Euphrates Delta, as compared to the friction of overland travel elsewhere in the ancient Near East. Moreover, in assessing the transport potential of the Mesopotamian alluvium at the time early Sumerian cities first arose, we need to remember that while Uruk polities did not enjoy the coercive powers of some of their successor states, they did have access to an enlarged marsh ecosystem that facilitated lateral traffic between the main branches of the rivers to a greater degree than was possible in the same area during later historic periods.

The substantial differences just outlined in the enduring transport capabilities of southern Mesopotamian societies versus those of neighboring polities matter. A recent cross-country review of development data from the modern world by Gallup, Sachs, and Mellinger (1999) found a very high inverse correlation between transport costs and growth rates: the lower the costs the higher the rates, and even small decreases in transport cost were found to have disproportionately positive effects on long-term growth rates. Not surprisingly, the study found a high correlation between economic growth and coastal societies or societies in close proximity to navigable rivers. Conversely, hinterlands devoid of navigable waterways were found to have sharply lower overall growth rates in the aggregate. The reason for these correlations is simple and has already been noted in an earlier chapter: as explained by Adam Smith, where transport costs are low, the division of labor is high, and vice versa.

Comparative and Competitive Advantages

Taken together, the various environmental and geographic advantages just noted had important consequences for processes leading to the Sumerian takeoff. On the one hand, advantages in productivity and resilience of their environmental framework meant that, in aggregate, elites in Uruk centers controlling the various ecotones that comprised the fourth-millennium alluvial landscape of southern Mesopotamia could extract larger (agricultural) surpluses per unit of labor than their counterparts elsewhere, and they could do so with greater reliability and predictability. On the other hand, the inherent advantages of water transport provided by their geographical framework meant that Uruk elites could concentrate and deploy the larger surpluses possible in their dependent hinterlands at much lower cost than their peripheral competitors. When combined, these parallel advantages meant that alluvial societies were subject to looser Malthusian constraints (chap. 3) than their rivals elsewhere. Of equal importance, water transport also allowed Uruk elites to procure nonlocal resources and information from a much vaster area, and again at much lower cost, than their landlocked contemporaries elsewhere. In addition, and equally crucially, ease of transport meant that the extent of the dependent hinterlands that Uruk elites could dominate would naturally be larger than those that rivals away from the river could control, and that the number of laborers that Uruk elites could command would be commensurably greater than the number deployable by contemporary rivals elsewhere.

Under conditions such as these, as Ricardo and his intellectual successors remind us, trade is the logical outcome. Specifically, I see imbalances in competitive advantage between southern Mesopotamia and neighboring polities as promoting evolving patterns of trade that are central to understanding the location of Uruk centers within the alluvial Mesopotamian ecosystem and the patterns of growth of those centers. We now turn to a discussion of those patterns.

CHAPTER FIVE

Early Mesopotamian Urbanism: How?

The concept of circular and cumulative causation discussed in chapter 3 allows us to visualize a still largely speculative, though ultimately testable, scenario to account for the urban takeoff of southern Mesopotamian societies in the fourth millennium. Following the insights of Jacobs, this scenario focuses on how economic differentiation could have evolved in the south. For heuristic purposes, this hypothetical process is divided here into a number of discrete stages, although substantial overlaps must be presumed to have existed between them.

The Growth of Early Mesopotamian Urban Economies

The initial stage of the growth of southern economies would have taken place during the late fifth and early fourth millennia (Late Ubaid and Early Uruk periods)—a time when the geographical and environmental framework of southern Mesopotamia created a mosaic of very different but easily exploited resource endowments across what is today the Mesopotamian alluvium. In its northern portions, gravity flow irrigation and increased water tables would have made grain cultivation and horticulture more profitable, whereas areas nearer the gulf were better situated to exploit its biomass-rich marshes, lagoons, and estuaries. Inadvertently, this setting provided the initial impetus for burgeoning trade between polities exploiting these varied economic resources. Each of these polities would have naturally specialized in the production of a small number of crops or commodities for which it had a comparative advantage, owing to its location within the alluvial ecosystem. Products traded in this initial stage would have included (1) raw wool, woven and dyed textiles, goat-hair products, leather goods, dairy fats, and other pastoral resources distributed by polities situated at the margins of the better-watered parts of the alluvium, where they would have enjoyed preferential access to pastoral and nomadic groups producing these various commodities; (2) flax-based textiles, garden crops, and grain produced by polities in the northern portion of the Mesopotamian alluvial plain, where the combined flow of the Tigris and the Euphrates made irrigation agriculture and horticulture both more likely and more profitable; and (3) dried, salted, and smoked fish, various types of fowl, reeds, and other marsh or littoral resources preferentially produced by polities near the Persian Gulf.

A second stage in the process may have started already by the middle of the fourth millennium (Middle Uruk period), and would have been marked by an emerging elite awareness of the social implications of the intraregional trade patterns in place until that point in time. In this stage, processes of competitive emulation would expedite the diffusion of technologies and practices that were initially developed by individual alluvial centers exploiting specialized niches but soon came to be perceived as highly advantageous by many of the centers in competition. This naturally would have decreased the level of regional specialization within the alluvium as each competing polity used the material surpluses and human skills acquired during the earlier stage to replace some imports from nearby centers, or possibly even from foreign areas, by creating their own productive capacities for those products, thus setting in motion the further growth spurt that accrues from the import-substitution mechanism discussed earlier.

The third stage of the process, datable to the second half of the fourth millennium (Middle and Late Uruk periods) would have been characterized by heightened competition between alluvial polities that had by now achieved broadly comparable productive capabilities. Since such polities no longer had much to offer each other in terms of exchange, I would expect this stage to include a significant expansion of external trade between individual alluvial cities and neighboring areas. Accordingly, ongoing import substitution processes in the south at this stage should have begun to focus primarily on the replacement of foreign commodities.

Enhanced foreign trade in this third stage would have been made possible by two interrelated factors, which can be thought of as necessary conditions for the Sumerian takeoff. The first was the early development and diffusion across the south of industries that were originally intended to satisfy local consumption requirements but which were easily adapted for export markets outside of the alluvium in later phases—a clear instance of "exaptation" in social evolutionary processes.[1] No doubt woolen textiles were the principal commodities fulfilling this double role in the fourth millennium, as they were later on in the historic periods. However, other indigenous southern industries that could be adapted for export at this time included animal hides, dried fruit, salted or smoked fish, and a variety of processed pastoral (animal and dairy fats) and agricultural (honey? unguents? aromatic oils? wine) products that likely constituted the contents of the various types of Uruk ceramic vessels (four-lugged, spouted, and pear-shaped jars) often found in indigenous Late Chalcolithic sites across the Mesopotamian periphery (Algaze 1993 [2005a], 63–74; Englund 1998, 161–69).[2]

The second factor was the domestication of the donkey sometime by the middle of the fourth millennium (H. Wright 2001, 127). This had interrelated conceptual and material consequences. Starting with the conceptual, the use of donkeys must have provided southern Mesopotamian polities with the enhanced geographical and "ethnographic" knowledge (Helms 1988) of neighboring regions and societies and of the resources available therein that are always a necessary precondition for the success of sustained efforts of cross-cultural trade and expansion. In studying the orientation of trade relations between different groups, economic geographers correctly observe that, historically, the trade of any polity expands (or contracts) in direct relationship with the limits of commercial intelligence available to its merchants and institutions (Vance 1970, 156). Such limits were substantially expanded by the use of donkeys in the Uruk period for overland travel.

Equally important would have been the material consequences of the introduction of domestic donkeys for southern polities: for the first time in their history they could export alluvial goods in bulk to foreign regions, something that was not practicable before, when all exports beyond the alluvial delta would have had to be carried on the backs of men. It is possible to use existing ethnographic and historic data for the ef-

ficiency of human versus donkey portage in traditional societies to assess the economic impact that the introduction of pack animals may have
had on early Sumerian economies, and the opportunities for growth (via
export) that would have been created by that introduction. Available
data show that the relative efficiency of the two modes of transport var-
ies greatly in different cultures and areas of the world, but equalized for
time and distance, at a minimum, donkeys can carry at least twice the
amount of cargo that humans can, and in many cases substantially more.[3]
These numbers appear to hold when we narrow our focus to ancient
Mesopotamia. The same Old Assyrian data noted above in connection
with the capabilities of donkey caravans indicate that individual porters
could carry standard loads of up to 30 kilograms (Dercksen 1996, 61–63),
while, as will be remembered, donkeys could carry two and a half times
this amount, up to 75 kilograms' worth of goods. We have no data for the
average distance that porters could cover in one day.

   The Old Assyrian evidence can also be used to obtain a rough idea
of the scale of the export activities that would have become possible in
southern societies as a result of the introduction of pack animals. While
most Old Assyrian caravan loads usually consisted of a combination
of metal (tin) and textiles, occasionally loads comprising only textiles
are attested. These are immediately pertinent to the Uruk case, since,
as noted above, finished textiles would likely have been one of the primary commodities exported from the alluvium at the time. When carrying only textiles, Old Assyrian donkeys were each packed with 20 to
30 bundles of cloth (depending on quality and weight). As noted earlier,
most caravans consisted of about 2 animals. However, larger individual
caravans of up to 5, 9, 14, and, in one case, 18 animals carrying solely
or primarily textiles are also known (Larsen 1967, 146; Veenhof 1972,
69–76). Presuming that the capabilities of the donkey breeds available
in the fourth millennium would have been similar to those available to
Old Assyrian traders,[4] and, further, that caravan procedures in the two
periods would also have been similar, the Old Assyrian data suggest that
the domestication of the donkey opened the door for individual alluvial
producers to export to distant consumers anywhere between 150 and
1350 kg of finished textiles per shipment (i.e., between 40–60 to 360–540
individual bundles of cloth).

   In the final analysis, however, the economic impact on early Sumerian
economies of the domestication of the donkey cannot be reduced to statistics. While human porters were used in ancient Mesopotamia to carry

loads within and, occasionally, between towns (Dercksen 1996, 61), there is no indication that porters were systematically used for long-distance trade, as we know donkeys were. In other words, the introduction of pack animals must have had a qualitative impact in the ability of southern societies to interact with faraway cultures that far surpassed quantitative differences in economic efficiency in carrying cargo. It allowed for cross-cultural contacts to be intensified to a level that hitherto simply had not been culturally feasible. We now turn to a discussion of how those contacts were operationalized.

The Uruk Expansion

Existing archaeological evidence substantiates parts of the third phase of the hypothetical developmental process just outlined. As bulk external trade became both possible and increasingly important in the Middle and Late Uruk periods, various types of southern outposts were established at strategic locations of significance for transport across the Mesopotamian periphery, principally, but not solely, at the intersection of the north-to-south flowing rivers and the principal east-west overland routes across the high plains of northern Mesopotamia. As these outposts have been the subjects of considerable discussion in recent literature (Algaze 1993, 2001b, 2005a, 128–155; Postgate 2002; Rothman 2001; Stein 1999a, 1999b, 2005), only a brief summary of the pertinent evidence is needed here.

Stated simply, intrusive Uruk settlements across the Mesopotamian periphery can be lumped into three principal types. The first two types are found in areas of the periphery where a local (Late Chalcolithic) settlement hierarchy was already in place. The earliest intrusions into such areas are best characterized as small trading diasporas, as Gil Stein (1999a) has aptly noted, and appear to have represented small groups of Uruk colonists living in the midst of preexisting indigenous centers already exploiting coveted resources or controlling access to those resources. In many areas of the Mesopotamian periphery, Uruk penetration never proceeded beyond this initial stage and outpost type. In some areas, however, a second stage followed in which important preexisting centers of substantial size, which by their very nature already served as nodes for interregional trade, were taken over by Uruk colonists, possibly by coercive means. The rationale for these two distinct but related strategies of Uruk contact with peripheral polities was succinctly summarized by Machiavelli ([1532] 1940, 8–9) almost five hundred years or so ago: "[W]hen dominions are acquired in a province differing in language, laws, and customs, the difficulties to be overcome are great and it requires great fortune as well as great industry to retain them . . . One of the best and most certain ways of doing so. . . . is to plant colonies in one or two of those places which form as it were the keys of the land."

The third type of intrusive settlement is found in areas in which no significant preexisting occupation had to be reckoned with. In those areas, from the very beginning, Uruk penetration was a process of urban implantation whereby Mesopotamian social and urban forms were reproduced in essentially virgin landscapes. Again, we can turn to one of the classics of modern thought to understand the rationale for this strategy. In reviewing the history of colonies in the classical and modern (European) worlds, Adam Smith ([1776] 1976, 564, IV.vii.b.1) insightfully concluded that "[t]he colony of a civilized nation which takes possession, either of waste country, or of one so thinly inhabited, that the natives easily give place to the new settlers, advances more rapidly to wealth and greatness than any other human society." Plus ça change, plus c'est la même chose . . .

In any event, the best-known examples of diaspora-type Uruk outposts are Hacınebi Tepe, located just north of modern Birecik in Turkey, astride one of the few natural fording areas of the Upper Euphrates in antiquity, and Godin Tepe, situated in the Kangavar Valley, a strategic node controlling the historical east-west overland route from southern Mesopotamia into the Iranian plateau (the Khorasan Road) as it cut across the Kermanshah region of the western Zagros mountains of Iran. In both cases, we appear to be dealing with a small group of resident southern Mesopotamian settlers/traders living in a segregated area or compound within a larger indigenous host community. This is clearest at Hacınebi, where Stein and his coworkers have shown through careful analyses that the Uruk colonists living at the eastern edge of the Late Chalcolithic site maintained their identity and some degree of economic autonomy for many generations, using typically southern administrative technologies, and producing crafts and cooking food in distinctive Mesopotamian styles throughout their stay (Stein 2002).[5]

Evidence for Uruk outposts implanted, possibly by violent means, on top of important preexisting centers is more ambiguous. My earlier suggestion (Algaze 1993) that Carchemish on the Euphrates and Nineveh on the Tigris may represent preexisting regional centers taken over by Uruk colonists remains impossible to evaluate, as no new work has taken place at either of the two locations. More promising, however, is new work at Tell Brak on the Jagh Jagh branch of the Upper Khabur in Syria, which was clearly the most important Late Chalcolithic center in the Upper Khabur area during the first half of the fourth millennium. As will be discussed in more detail in chapter 7, there is mounting evidence that by the end of the Uruk period Tell Brak became the locus of a southern Mesopotamian colony. While we still lack data that clarifies how that transformation was effected, military conquest cannot be excluded (Emberling 2002). This possibility is made all the more likely by the results of the 2005–2006 seasons of excavations at the smaller Late Chalcolithic site of Hamoukar in northeastern Syria, where clear evidence for warfare (a burnt destruction level and thousands of sling shots and other types of projectiles) was found in levels that immediately predate the apparent takeover of the settlement by Uruk populations (Lawler 2006; Clemens Reichel, personal communication, 2006).

More easily recognized are examples of the third type of Uruk outposts: massive, town-sized enclaves founded from scratch in areas of the periphery that were only minimally inhabited by local populations. Such sites have been identified principally along the Euphrates River in southeastern Turkey and northern Syria, and they were commonly surrounded by clusters of much smaller Uruk villages, which may have served to supply them with agricultural and pastoral products, as shown by recent excavations at the small site of Yarim Tepe in Turkey (Kozbe and Rothman 2005). The clearest example of an implanted Uruk urban complex is comprised by the excavated sites of Habuba Kabira-süd and the smaller nearby settlement of Jebel Aruda, which may represent an associated administrative quarter (Kohlmeyer 1996, 1997; Strommenger 1980; Vallet 1996, 1998; Van Driel and Van Driel Murray 1983). Both sites are situated in the immediate vicinity of a historical fording place of the Euphrates near Meskene, Syria.

The Uruk settlement at Jebel Aruda was founded on virgin soil on the summit of an easily defensible hill overlooking the Euphrates Valley. Its excavators were able to expose about 10,000 square meters of the settlement, representing about 30 percent of the total occupation (which covers slightly more than 3 hectares). Their exposures revealed several phases of construction and reconstruction, all dating to the Late Uruk period. Throughout these phases, however, the essential character of the

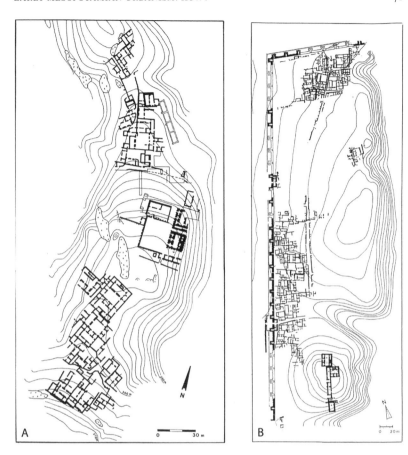

FIGURE II. Excavated areas of Late Uruk colonies at Jebel Aruda (*left*) and Habuba Kabira-süd (*right*). Scale indicated.

settlement remained unchanged and consisted of a number of large do-mestic structures, apparently representing elite housing, surrounding a central raised platform where first one and later two massive tripartite structures of presumed administrative/religious function stood.

Some 8 kilometers to the south and bordering directly on the ancient Euphrates floodplain was the larger, contemporaneous, and no doubt, associated urban settlement of Habuba Kabira-süd/Tell Qannas. As the site was largely unoccupied after the Uruk period, extensive horizontal exposures of Uruk levels were feasible, totaling well over 20,000 square meters. A recent reassessment of pertinent data by Regis Vallet (1996) indicates that the Habuba/Qannas settlement grew in three stages, all dated to the Late Uruk period. As was the case at Aruda, the earliest Uruk settlement at Habuba was founded on virgin soil. We know little about this initial settlement other than it was about 6 hectares in extent and appears to have lacked an external defensive wall. In any event, the Habuba/Qannas outpost soon doubled in size and became a fortified city with carefully laid-out streets and well-differentiated residential, industrial, and administrative quarters, all apparently constructed as part of a single master plan and coherent building effort. At a later date still, a further extramural area of habitations grew on the south side of the settlement, accounting for a contiguously occupied area totaling about 22 hectares at its floruit. In addition, less dense suburban occupations existed along the river directly north of the walled settlement.

The function of massive well-planned outposts such as Habuba-süd/Qannes/Aruda complex has been the subject of much discussion. Some argue that they served as outlets for displaced population from the south (Johnson 1988/89; Pollock 1999; H. Wright 2001; G. Schwartz 2001), and this is indeed quite likely. At the same time, however, their carefully selected locations near historical fording places in the Euphrates Bend suggests that they also served as focal nodes for the collection of intelligence and information about conditions across broad swaths of the Mesopotamian periphery, as collection and transshipment points for the increasing amounts of peripheral commodities imported into the alluvium in the later part of the Uruk period, and, possibly, as distribution points for alluvial exports (Algaze 1993 [2005a], 2001a).

The hypothesis that the outposts had an important role in mediating the external commerce of early Sumerian polities finds support in the outposts themselves, where a variety of metal ores, minerals, and raw exotic stones have been found. More importantly, several of the outposts have also provided evidence for installations and workshop areas where such resources were processed in situ, presumably for export to the growing cities of alluvial Mesopotamia. The pertinent evidence is detailed in greater detail below as part of separate discussions of, first, the social and economic ramifications that increased trade in the Middle and Later Uruk periods would have had on early Sumerian polities and, second, the scale of that trade.

Before proceeding to those discussions, however, two points must be made. First, irrespective of their type, there is no need to presume that the establishment of variously configured Uruk colonial outposts across

the Mesopotamian periphery was part of a centrally controlled and organized process. Rather, as I have argued elsewhere in detail (Algaze 1993
[2005a], 115–17), the Middle and Late Uruk colonial process is best conceived as part of an organic process of action and counteraction, wherein
individual Uruk city-states scrambled to found specific outposts tailored
to local conditions in varying areas in order to secure access to the critical lines of communication through which coveted resources were obtainable and, equally important, to deny their local southern rivals such
access. Second, there is also no need to presume that every Uruk outpost
was set up by public sector institutions in distant early Sumerian cities, or
that all Uruk trade was "official" exchange geared toward fulfilling the
strategic needs of controlling institutions in those cities. While it is clear
that massive coordinated building efforts such as evinced, for instance,
by the Habuba/Qannas/Aruda complex cannot be anything other than
the product of state-level organizations, it is entirely possible to interpret
smaller outposts, and particularly those embedded in host communities,
as the work of small groups of Uruk merchants in search of personal
or familial profit, acting much like their better-documented Old Assyrian successors would a millennium and a half later, as Piotr Steinkeller
(1993) has suggested.

Multiplier Effects

It is easy to visualize the role that the still partly hypothetical patterns of
internal and external trade described earlier would have had in the emergence of Sumerian civilization if we focus our attention on the long-term
multiplier effects of the associated import substitution processes. Some
of those processes can readily be documented in the archaeological record of Ubaid and Uruk period Mesopotamian societies, and their likely
impact can be gauged in reference to later historical documentation from
Mesopotamia itself and to pertinent ethnographic models, when available. Below we examine some of the relevant data.

Flint

The southern Mesopotamian alluvium is entirely devoid of flint sources,
and cutting tools and materials used for the manufacture of such tools
constitute the earliest imports yet attested in the archaeological record of

alluvial societies (G. Wright 1969). Accordingly, it is not surprising that perhaps the earliest example of import substitution in the archaeological record of southern Mesopotamia is the partial replacement of imported flint and obsidian blades (fig. 12) for less efficient but much more economical terracotta clay sickles manufactured locally (fig. 13). This replacement process starts already in the Late Ubaid period and continues through the various phases of the Uruk period (Benco 1992).

In addition, by the end of the Uruk period some imported flint also began to be replaced with flint implements manufactured by southern craftsmen. Not surprisingly, this took place in some of the Uruk outposts along the Upper Euphrates, many of which were conveniently situated near flint sources. Indeed, specialized workshops producing Canaanean blades, presumably both for local use and for export to Uruk centers elsewhere, have been found at Habuba Kabira-süd (Strommenger 1980, 55–56, fig. 45), in Syria, and at the much smaller Uruk outpost at Hassek Höyük (Otte and Behm-Blancke 1992) along the Upper Euphrates in Turkey some 200 kilometers or so upstream of Habuba. In addition, some evidence for the manufacture of flint tools has been identified in the Uruk quarter at Hacınebi. Careful analysis by the archaeologist Chris Edens (1999, 32–33) of the evidence from that sector reveals that Uruk knappers at that site produced tools in types that were, at times, indistinguishable from those used by their indigenous neighbors and, at times, made in distinctively southern Mesopotamian technological styles.

Metals

A much more important and enduring example of the import substitution process in southern Mesopotamia is provided by metals, which are first attested in the south by the end of the Ubaid period (Moorey 1994, 221, 255–58). Initially, metal goods must have been brought into southern centers as fully finished products imported from metal-producing highland regions of Iran and Anatolia where metallurgical technologies were first developed (Kohl 1987a, 16; Stein 1990). Finished metal implements continued to be imported into southern cities well into the later phases of the Uruk period, as Frangipane (2001a, 346, n. 14) has recently suggested on the basis of compositional analyses of a lance or harpoon head found in the Riemchengebäude at Warka (Müller-Karpe 1991, 109, fig. 3).[6] Nonetheless, the bulk of our evidence clearly indicates that, by the Middle and Late Uruk periods, southern societies were no longer mere

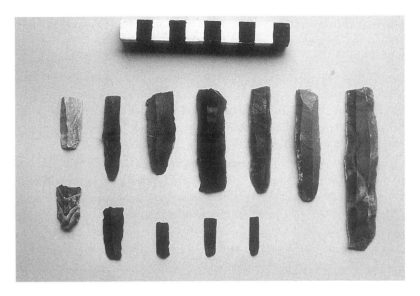

FIGURE 12. Imported flint and obsidian blades from site 765, a small Early and Middle Uruk period village in Adams's Nippur-Adab survey area. Scale indicated.

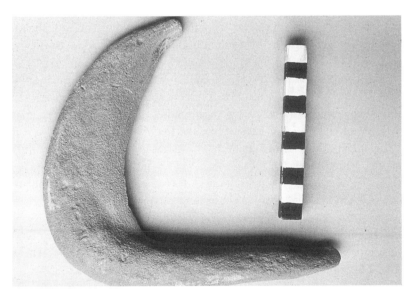

FIGURE 13. Locally manufactured clay sickle from site 765, a small Early and Middle Uruk period village in Adams's Nippur-Adab survey area. Scale indicated.

passive consumers of imported metal objects crafted in the highlands. Rather, by then they were well underway to creating their own value-added metal industries that relied instead on imports of only lightly processed ores and of ingots of smelted copper. Concrete evidence of this shift is provided by the remains of copper ores and ingots found in southern Mesopotamian Uruk cities and Uruk colonial emplacements in the Mesopotamian periphery, as well as by evidence for the processing of various types of metal ores at these sites.

At Warka, for instance, piles of copper ore dated to either the end of the Middle or the beginning of the Late Uruk period at the site were recovered in the basal layers of the Anu Ziggurat/White Temple Area (Algaze 1993 [2005a], 74–77; Moorey 1994, 242–77), and what has been described as a metal foundry of Late Uruk date was also found (Nissen 2000).[7] Recent excavations at intrusive Uruk outposts in the Upper Euphrates area have yielded both more extensive and clearer indications for metal processing. These activities are present even in the earliest phase of the Uruk intrusion into the area. At the already noted site of Hacınebi Tepe, for example, both polymetallic ores and crucibles were found in direct association with southern Mesopotamian materials (Özbal, Adriaens, and Earl 1999). Smelting crucibles are also reported in contemporary Middle Uruk levels at the small Uruk outpost of Tell Sheikh Hassan, further to the south on the Euphrates in Syria (Boese 1995, 175, pl. 13a).

Evidence for the processing of metals in Uruk outposts during the Late Uruk period is even stronger, possibly because pertinent exposures are much wider. From a storeroom at Jebel Aruda, for instance, comes a hoard of eight copper axes of varying size but roughly equal weight (Rouault and Massetti-Rouault 1993: fig. 115), which almost certainly served as ingots (Algaze 2001a, 208, n. 9).[8] Several metallurgical installations are reported at the nearby site of Habuba Kabira-süd (Kohlmeyer 1997), where detailed analyses have shown that an elaborate cupellation process was used to separate, extract, and refine lead and silver from polymetallic ores imported into the settlement (Pernicka, Rehren, and Schmitts-Streker 1998). Not coincidentally, a variety of lead and silver artifacts are known from contemporary Uruk period levels at Warka (e.g., Pedde 2000, nos. 1327–28, 1338–39), although the sorts of chemical characterization analyses needed to show correlation, if one existed, between the processing installation at Habuba Kabira and the Warka objects have not yet been done.

Although the bulk of available evidence comes from the Upper Euphrates, it is clear that Uruk outposts elsewhere across northern Mesopotamia were also engaged in metallurgical activities. Late Uruk period levels in Area TW at Tell Brak on the Upper Khabur, for instance, have yielded a positive impression in mud of a large pick-axe (23 cm in length). David Oates and Joan Oates (1997, 295, fig. 16) interpret this to represent the imprint of a decayed wooden form used to make clay moulds for the casting of comparably shaped copper pick-axes.

Finally, by the final phase of the Uruk period we also get textual corroboration for the partial shift in the south from consumers to producers of metal. One indirect clue is provided by the frequent mention of metals and metal objects in many of the earliest Uruk IV script economic tablets of the time, as well as in the much rarer, but critically important, contemporary lexical lists (Nissen 1986; Englund 1998). Another clue, this one more direct, is furnished by the fact that the pictogram for a smith is attested in the same tablets. The pictogram shows a smelting furnace with attached blowpipes (Moorey 1994, 243).

Textiles

However important the nascent metal industries of Uruk cities may have been, by far the most consequential case of early import substitution processes in those cities is provided by the adoption, probably sometime in the late fifth millennium, by the very end of the Ubaid period, of wool-bearing breeds of sheep initially developed in the highlands surrounding Mesopotamia (Davis 1984, 1993; Sherratt 1997, 539).[9] Because such sheep are not indigenous to the Mesopotamian lowlands, wool must have been initially introduced into the south as an import from the surrounding highlands. But wool and wooly sheep did not remain imports for long. As Joy McCorriston (1997) has convincingly argued, existing archaeobotanical, faunal, and textual data from various Uruk period sites leave no doubt that by the second half of the fourth millennium these imported commodities had been thoroughly integrated into the southern economy. This took the form of a fast-growing indigenous textile industry based on woven woolen cloth, which, for all practical purposes, replaced the flax-based textiles that had constituted the bulk of local production in the south until then.

The consequences of this new industry are not difficult to visualize. Copious textual documentation of third- and second-millennium date

(below) leaves little doubt that, once introduced, woven wool cloth became an indispensable component of rations given to dependent workers
in a variety of activities central to the economy of southern Mesopotamian cities and states. Elaborately crafted wool textiles, in turn, played
an equally central role at the time in the export economy of every southern center of any consequence (Potts 1997; Larsen 1987; McCorriston
1997; R. Wright 1996).

We can only speculate as to the reasons why, starting in the fourth
millennium, wool started to replace flax as the main source of textile
fiber in southern Mesopotamia, as we have no evidence about the prefer-
ences of the consumers of the new woolen textiles and the social obligations that those textiles fulfilled or about the institutions that oversaw
textile production in Uruk cities and their priorities (but see below for
inferences on process and administration derived from contemporary
iconography and later historical documentation). Nonetheless, it stands
to reason that, to varying degrees, four factors must have helped trigger
the shift from flax to wool in early Mesopotamian societies.

The first two factors operated at the level of the consumers of the textiles. Woolen cloth offered advantages in both functionality and appearance that cellulose-based fibers such as flax could not match. In terms of
functionality, one of the most important such advantages was that, when
wet, a wool garment keeps its wearer significantly drier and warmer than
linen clothing, and wool also provides much better protection against
outside temperature extremes, both cold and hot. This is explained in
part by how chemicals that naturally occur in wool react to water and in
part by the fact that pockets of air trapped in processed wool fibers act as
insulation (Butler 2006, 12).

No less important would have been the perceived advantages of wool
over flax in terms of appearance. Key here is the fact that wool lends itself
much more easily than linen to the creation of differently colored and
patterned textiles. Patterning is most easily accomplished by variations
in color within a single woven wool piece. To begin with, as opposed to
linen, which is generally white, wool grows naturally in different shades
of color (from black to brown to red to cream to white), which can be
mixed in a loom to achieve a distinctive effect. More importantly, as compared to linen, wool is much more easily dyed using natural dyes (Barber
1991, 223–43), and its fibers absorb such dyes much more deeply, resulting in saturated colors that are always more intense and more appealing than those achievable in cellulose-based textiles (Kriger 2006, 36).

This means that, unlike linen, wool threads dyed in different colors could be mixed within a single piece at the time of weaving to create appealing multicolored textiles. In addition, further patterning could also be achieved by weave structure, and here again wool is more malleable than plant-stem fibers. Accordingly, wool more easily allows for the mixing of weave patterns (based on how the warp is treated) in a single textile piece than linen-based cloth (Barber 1994, 103–4).

In practical terms, the greater malleability and visual appeal of wool over linen probably meant that woolen cloth lent itself particularly well, and in ways that less colorful linens could never match, to the expression of the multiple statuses arising from processes of internal differentiation, noted above, typical for urban processes across the world. At the same time, woolen textiles would have served as more versatile markers for the multiple local styles that surely accompanied the spread of urbanism across southern Mesopotamia in the fourth millennium, given the already noted polyglot and multiethnic nature of early Mesopotamian urbanism from its very inception (chap. 1, n. 1).

The final two factors that help explain the shift from flax to wool as the primary fiber of early Mesopotamian textile production involve economies of scale achievable by using wool as opposed to flax. One such economy is that noted by Joy McCorriston (1997), who points out that raising sheep instead of growing flax would have expanded the overall productive capacity and economies of early Mesopotamian societies, as textile production shifted away from the well-watered tracts that flax-growing requires to more marginal lands that could be profitably exploited for sheep/goat herding. This process, which McCorriston labels "extensification," allowed for the reallocation of prime agricultural land in the immediate vicinity of growing Uruk cities for new uses and alternative crops, while extant textile production could continue elsewhere at preexisting levels and could even have increased in scale.

That increase would have been due to a further economic gain derived from the shift from flax to wool in early Mesopotamia: efficiency. Although the production of wool fiber from sheep's fleece is quite labor-intensive (below), the production of an equivalent amount of linen fibers from flax was even more time-consuming and required still more effort. In terms of time, the key difference is the amount of preparation that each fiber requires before it can be woven into cloth using a loom. Ethnographic studies of traditional pastoral and agricultural practices show that, given enough labor, wool can be ready for weaving only a few hours

after being plucked or sheared, once it is washed, combed, and spun (below). In contrast, flax requires up to two weeks of retting (partially rot-
ting the fibers in standing water), as well as additional time for drying,
before it is ready for spinning and weaving (McCorriston 1997, 522–23).
The same studies also show substantial differences in the amount of labor required to produce equivalent amounts of the two fibers prior to
processing. A summary of pertinent evidence by McCorriston (1997,
524) suggests that an average of 9 days of labor per year would have been
required to produce 1 kilogram of wool ready to be woven.[10] In contrast,
up to 29 days of labor per year would be necessary for the production of
the same amount of ready-to-weave fiber extracted from flax.

   In spite of their late start, southern producers of woolen textiles soon
surpassed their highland predecessors in both scale and efficiency. Again,
we can try to speculate about some of the factors that help account for
this. One would have been that by pasturing sheep in previously under-
utilized marginal lands, by integrating them into the agricultural cycle of
grain (including fallow grazing and allowing sheep to graze on young barley in years when overplanting took place [Robert M. Adams, personal
communication, 2006]), and by exploiting marsh vegetation (chap. 4),
the south possessed as much fodder as the highlands, so that no dietary
disadvantages accrued to the sheep as a result of their introduction to
their new manmade habitat.

   A second factor would have been that the south had comparative advantage in access to pertinent natural dyes. This is a point recently raised
by McCorriston (1999, 2001, 222, and personal communication, 2001),
who notes that many of the dyes used in conjunction with wool in the
area in antiquity could be derived from desert or garden plants available
in or around southern Mesopotamia, such as *Chrozophora tinctoria, Ar-
nebia tinctoria, Papaver* sp., *Crocus* sp., *Salicornia* sp./*Cornulaca* sp, and
Punica granatum (pomegranate), from plants available in the high plains
of Syro-Mesopotamia and easily accessible by Uruk colonists in the area,
such as safflower, or from products that could only be obtained from the
Persian Gulf or through Gulf-related trade routes, such as various types
of marine gastropods and (much later) indigo. In contrast, the highlands
surrounding southern Mesopotamia were devoid of most plants from
which usable dyes could be extracted, save for walnut.

   The third—and most important—factor accounting for the takeoff of
woolen textile industries in alluvial Mesopotamia would have been that,
for reasons already explained, growing southern cities with burgeoning

populations arrayed around them possessed larger pools of labor available for textile work. From the beginning, these larger pools of workers appear to have been organized in ways that allowed for greater efficiency and superior craftsmanship in the production of textiles. This can be inferred from two distinct but complementary sources of evidence bearing on how textile production was organized in Uruk Mesopotamia.

The first of these sources is the Archaic Texts, many of which deal with the receipt of raw wool and disbursement of woolen garments and cloth (Nissen 1986; Englund 1998). While these tablets tell us little detail about the institutions that received and disbursed wool and wool products in Mesopotamian cities of the Late Uruk period, the texts are the product of central urban bureaucracies, and their very existence makes it clear that an important portion of southern Mesopotamian wool textile production must have been centrally organized from its very inception. The second source is provided by iconography from cylinder seals and sealings from the Middle and Late Uruk periods depicting various stages of the textile production process at the time. These early images are unique in the Mesopotamian cultural record insofar as they have no parallels in later periods, possibly in part because the information disseminated initially by iconographic means in the Uruk periods was later disseminated more efficiently and more precisely by writing.

Indeed, the gender-specific activities associated with the crafting of textiles portrayed in Uruk seals and sealings can be interpreted and organized in sequential order on the basis of later textual documentation of the Ur III period, a millennium or so later (below). This is so, minimally, in the case of Uruk images depicting (1) presumably male figures pasturing herds of small cattle under the control of fourth-millennium urban institutions (i.e., herds associated with the bundled reed symbol historically used to represent the goddess Inanna and her household [temple]: e.g., figs. 7 and 14a–b), (2) presumably male figures plucking sheep (fig. 14c), (3) presumably female workers ("pig-tailed" figures) spinning thread (e.g., figs. 14d–14e) and attending horizontal looms (figs. 14e–14f),[11] and (4) presumably male figures carrying bolts of cloth (figs. 14g–14h),[12] the latter most likely a depiction of the fulling of recently woven textiles. At a minimum, these images provide confirming evidence of state involvement in the textile production process already in the fourth millennium, as the seals and seal impressions from which they are derived were no doubt produced for and used by administrative institutions in Uruk cities. But the images also provide us with additional detail: in particular, the gendered spinning and weaving scenes suggest that from their very inception the state-sponsored weaving establishments of fourth-millennium Mesopotamia were staffed primarily by partly or fully dependent women (Zagarell 1986), as we know was the case in southern cities in historic times (Jacobsen [1953] 1970; Maekawa 1980; Waetzoldt 1972; R. Wright 1996).

The shift from linen to wool as the primary fiber used in textile manufacture in the south during the second half of the fourth millennium and the closely related development of state-sponsored weaving establishments at that time present us with a textbook case illustrating the many multiplier effects that commonly attend the introduction of new industries and increases in productive capacity, as noted above. Particularly noteworthy would have been the forward and backward linkages (chap. 3) created by the new wool-based textile industry. It may be possible to get a general idea of the nature, scale, and consequences of these linkages by using pertinent later historical data from Mesopotamia itself.

Particularly useful in this regard is the magisterial study by the assyriologist H. Waetzoldt (1972) of the textile industries of Ur III period Mesopotamia. His analysis shows the truly massive scale of the industry at the end of the third millennium. To briefly summarize: though the available cuneiform evidence is highly uneven, textile manufacturing appear to have taken place in at least seven individual cities at the time: Alsharraki, Guabba (the port city of Lagash province), Nippur, Puzrish-Dagan, Umma, Ur, and Uruk. These cities exploited millions of sheep for their wool—about 500,000 can be surmised to have been available to the imperial capital of Ur alone, to judge from records of the tonnage of wool received divided by estimates of yield per animal (Waetzoldt 1972, 14). With few exceptions (see below), labor was provided either by partly dependent women providing periodic service to state-organized weaving establishments or, most commonly, by fully dependent women and their children receiving rations, who labored year-round in state-organized establishments under the supervision of overseers. In either case, the number of workers involved was quite high. The texts studied by Waetzoldt allowed him to infer the existence of at least 15,000 workers at Lagash employed in various activities connected with processing wool and weaving (Waetzoldt 1972, 99), of which between 32 and 45 percent were weavers.[13] A further 13,200 weavers receiving rations are attested at Ur alone (Waetzoldt 1972, 106), implying a much larger number of textile production–related personnel at that city. While records from the

FIGURE 14. Uruk cylinder seal impressions depicting various stages in the textile production process. Not to scale.

other cities are too fragmentary to reconstruct employment, it does not take too much imagination to suggest that the number of workers employed in textile production in southern Mesopotamia during the Ur III period easily exceeded 50,000–60,000 people. Production totals appear as staggering as the number of workers. Based on a summary text from Ur, Waetzoldt estimates that the yearly production of wool textiles at that city alone was on the order of 24,000 individual pieces, weighing some 18,600 kilograms.[14]

Can fragmentary statistics derived from the records of a much larger imperial society that thrived in southern Mesopotamia a millennium after the Uruk period be relevant to an assessment of conditions operative in the same area during the fourth millennium? Indeed they can, provided that a number of defensible assumptions are explicitly made, that those assumptions are taken for what they are: analytical sleights of hand that allow us to conceptualize a problem, however tentatively, and that results inferred from later cuneiform sources are checked against pertinent ethnographic data where possible.

The first assumption, supported by the iconography of the Uruk textile production process noted above, is that there were no significant techno-logical differences in the ways wool was processed into finished cloth in ancient Mesopotamia between the Uruk and Ur III periods. The sec-ond is that, as argued earlier, the woolen textile industries that emerged in Uruk cities were organized along the same principles of gender spe-cialization, production clustering, and labor control as prevailed in their better-documented counterparts in the historic periods. Together, these assumptions allow us to use measurements of labor per unit of product derived from the better-documented later period to shed light on pre-sumably comparable activities in the earlier phase, provided some ad-justment is made for differences in productivity between the two phases arising from scale efficiencies (below).

The final set of assumptions is based on the observation that Adams's survey data show no significant differences in the *relative* proportion of people who lived in cities in the Mesopotamian alluvium during the Late Uruk and Ur III periods.[15] Taking this as a point of departure, we may as-sume further (1) that the mass production of textiles in both periods was essentially an urban phenomenon, one that took place either in cities and/or in their immediate dependencies; (2) that such production was entirely financed by urban elites and largely benefited only those elites; (3) that a similar proportion of elites lived in cities of each period; (4) that these elites consumed the finer grades of textiles at comparable rates, both for their own use and for export; and (5) that a similar proportion of workers would be needed to produce finished goods for elite consumers, workers who themselves would have consumed (coarse) wool rations.

These assumptions, in turn, permit us to use evidence relating to woolen textile production in the Ur III period to assess the economic impact of textile manufactures in the Uruk period, provided corrections are made for (1) differences in the size of the population of the alluvium between the two chronological stages and (2) differences arising from unique Ur III imperial institutions, such as the short-lived livestock col-lection facility of Puzrish-Dagan, which served as a collection point for sheep and wool obtained as taxes from internal provinces and as tribute from imperial allies outside the alluvium itself.

The relevant demographic differences are inferable from Adams's (1981, tables 3 and 13) survey data, which show that occupied hectarage (and hence population) in the Late Uruk phase was about 20 percent of analogous figures for the later period. Presuming similar processing technologies and comparable proportions of urbanites among them, it follows that the woolen textile industries of the Uruk period would have been about one-fifth of the size documented in the more easily quantifiable Ur III data. This estimate can be arbitrarily halved so as to account for the portion of sheep at Puzrish-Dagan in the later period derived from external tribute/taxes received at that site from outside the core areas of the Ur III state (Steinkeller 1987).[16] We may thus crudely estimate that Uruk textile industries would have employed about one-tenth of the workers documented in the later texts. If we, again arbitrarily, assume that the productivity of these workers was only, say, two-thirds that of their Ur III counterparts so as to account for efficiencies owing to scale in the later period and for efficiencies resulting from the greater elaboration of the writing and recording systems in the third millennium, Uruk workers would have required 33 percent more time than their later counterparts to accomplish the same tasks or, time being equal, required 33 percent more labor.

Mindful of these assumptions, we may now attempt to reconstruct, however crudely, some of the economic and demographic consequences of the new wool-based textile industries that emerged in southern cities during the Uruk period, which (conservatively) would have employed as many as 5,000 to 6,000 workers (i.e., 10 percent of pertinent Ur III numbers). Many of these workers would have labored in industries adding value to semifinished wool textiles (forward linkages). A case in point would have been the fulling of partially processed cloth so as to shrink and thicken the fabric and the dyeing of fulled cloth. Both practices are well attested in third-millennium texts (Waetzoldt 1972), and both existed already in the fourth millennium, since several colors of woolen cloth are noted in the Archaic Texts (R. Englund, personal communication, 2005). Both practices required a substantial input of value-adding labor and new resources.

While neither textual nor archaeological data bearing on the fulling and dyeing of wool textiles exist for the fourth millennium, the Ur III texts provide clues as to the procedures involved and the scale of the necessary postweaving inputs in both labor and resources. An examination of fulling is particularly instructive in this regard. In the late third millennium this involved repeatedly washing, rolling, pounding, and trampling the bolts of woven cloth, repeatedly treating them with oils and alkali, and repeatedly rinsing the treated bolts in water so to as to shrink and thicken the cloth in preparation for dyeing. Uniquely in the context of early Mesopotamian textile production, fullers were male, possibly because of the substantial weight of large bolts of cloth soaking in oils and other liquids (R. Wright 1996, 92–93; see fig. 14g–14h above, for a possible depiction of fulling in the Uruk period). Waetzoldt (1972, 92) was able to document that fullers at Girsu operated in groups of 2 to 11 individuals and each group required an overseer. He also found that the ratio of fullers to weavers in Lagash province varied between 1:45 to 1:18 through the Ur III period—proportions that, absent technological differences, are surely relevant for earlier periods as well (i.e., between 38 and 137 fullers in the Uruk period presuming comparable specialist proportions).[17]

The texts reveal substantial differences in the amounts of work and materials needed to full semifinished wool cloth, depending on the quality of the wool being processed. Again, the relevant data come largely from Girsu. In terms of new materials, for instance, Waetzoldt found that low-quality wool required approximately 0.09 liters of (sesame) oil and 0.37 liters of alkali per kilogram of fulled cloth. However, the comparable amounts of chemicals needed per kilogram of high-quality wool were much larger: 0.34 and 1.8 liters of oil and alkali, respectively. Equally variable, and much more substantial, were the amounts of additional postweaving labor involved in the fulling process. When dealing with low-quality wool, late third-millennium fullers at Lagash spent 6.6 workdays (computed at the rate of 12 hours per workday) to full each kilogram of finished cloth (i.e., the labor of one worker per 6.6 days; two workers, 3.3 days, etc.). However, when dealing with high-quality wool—wool to be used, no doubt, for the manufacture of elite garments—the same workers spent a staggering 71 to 81 workdays per kilogram of fulled cloth (Waetzoldt 1972, 159). Comparable inputs of new resources per kilo of finished product may be presumed to have obtained in the Uruk period, but the presumably less-efficient earlier fullers would have required a third more time (or labor) to process each kilo of finished cloth.

Examples of backward linkages created by the shift from flax to wool, in turn, are provided by a variety of labor-intensive activities that contributed necessary inputs to the weaving establishments but largely took place away from them. Minimally, these included (1) pasturing the sheep,

(2) plucking the wool, (3) washing the plucked wool to remove dirt and twigs as well as excess lanolin, (4) sorting and separating the cleaned wool by quality and color, (5) transporting the bales (or baskets) of raw wool to central storehouses, (6) combing (carding) the wool to remove knots and any remaining impurities and align all the fibers in a single direction in preparation for spinning, (7) spinning the wool, (8) dying the spun yarn (when applicable for the creation of embroidered multi-colored garments), and (9) delivering the yarn to the various locations where state-organized weavers labored.

The employment consequences of these various activities must have been quite considerable. A few examples should suffice to illustrate the point. Take pasturing, for instance, an activity well documented in Uruk iconography (e.g., fig. 4e). Further details are provided by the Archaic Texts, many of which attest to the existence of temple/state-controlled sheep herds (fig. 14a–14b; Green 1980; Englund 1998). As noted earlier, the tablets indicate that common sheep herd sizes at the time varied from approximately 22 to 140 animals and averaged 68 individuals. Much larger sheep herds are also attested, some comprising as many as 1,400 or so animals (Green 1980, 11; Englund 1998, 143–150). Unfortunately, while these texts are quite precise about the number, sex, and ages of sheep in individual herds and as to the individual functionaries responsible for the animals, they give us no indication of the actual number of herders required to, among other things, drive the animals to and from pastures, guard grazing flocks, water the animals, and attend to breeding. Regrettably, later cuneiform documentation is also inconclusive with regards to the full labor requirements of pasturing. Those requirements are linked, of course, to flock sizes, and these varied in different periods and areas (Green 1980, 11). Nonetheless, a study of twenty Old Babylonian herding contracts of early second millennium date analyzed by the assyriologist Nicholas Postgate is perhaps broadly representative. Flocks between 4 and 270 animals, including both sheep and goats, are documented by these contracts. A majority of the flocks consisted only of sheep. In turn, these latter varied in size from 4 to 185 animals (Postgate 1975, table 2). This suggests an average of 37 sheep per shepherd, which seems roughly in line with both the results derived from the Archaic Texts as well as with expectations derived from ethnography (below). Interestingly, some of these tablets show that shepherds entrusted with large flocks used "under-shepherds" (Akkadian: *kaparrum*), but such minor workers were not important enough to be formally recorded in the contracts.[18] No doubt the same was the case with the larger flocks noted in fourth-millennium documents.[19]

Ethnography helps us better assess the full labor requirements of sheep herding under ancient Mesopotamian conditions. Surveys of the pertinent literature by Ryder suggest 300 sheep as the maximum that can be handled by a single individual at any one time (Ryder 1993, 14) and flocks of between 20 to 100 animals as the norm in semiarid areas (Ryder 1983, 238). More detailed still is a survey of traditional pastoral practices in semiarid environments assembled by Kenneth Russell (1988), an archaeologist with substantial training in behavioral ecology. The data he marshals allow us to quantify the labor requirements of herding under complex strategies that take into account not only the normal pasturing of sheep herds but also the increased labor needs required to manage herds during breeding season and its immediate aftermath when immature animals must be continually taken care of prior to weaning. These data suggest that, under Near Eastern conditions, a herd of 100 animals would require the full-time work of one adult herder year-round (365 days) to take care of the mature herd, one full-time herder for 2 months (61 days) to take care of juveniles in the field, and one part-time herder for 2 months (31 days) to take care of infant animals, usually around encampments. The latter work is often entrusted to older children and adolescents. This amounts to 457 workdays per year (3 workmen) per 100 animals (Russell 1988, 83).

With these numbers in mind, we may return to pasturing sheep as a labor-creating backward linkage of industrial weaving in the fourth millennium. The cuneiform and ethnographic data just noted mean that the smallest herds attested in the Archaic Texts, averaging 68 sheep, would have required a minimum of 3 full-time and part-time herders per herd per year, while the largest flocks attested at the time needed a minimum each of 42 full and part-time workers. If we presume a very conservative total of 50,000 sheep under the control of urban institutions at the time (i.e., 10 percent of the absolute minimum number inferable from existing Ur III sources), 500 full-time and 1,000 part-time workers would have been required to attend to the myriad tasks associated with pasturing sheep prior to fleecing.

Also quite demanding in terms of labor must have been the collection of fleece from these herds. In the fourth millennium this had to be very carefully timed and required plucking each animal by hand (fig. 14c). This was so because, unlike modern sheep populations in the Near East, fourth-millennium sheep still molted their coats annually at the end of the spring, and their soft wooly undercoats were still covered by a layer of bristly kemp hairs. Plucking had to take place just after the undercoat was released from the skin but before the external hairs molted, so as to prevent the coarser hairs from contaminating the softer wool (Ryder 1993, 10–11). The Archaic Texts contain no clues as to the number of workers employed plucking sheep under these conditions. Modern ethnographies, likewise, are of little use, because sheep are now sheared and not plucked, save for dead animals (Ochsenschlager 1993, 36–37). However, we can get a general idea of the labor requirements of plucking from late third- and early second-millennium documentation, as hand plucking was still the primary method of wool fleece collection in the ancient Near East through the Iron Age.[20] While available data do not allow us to reconstruct the relative efficiency of the plucking process under ancient Mesopotamian conditions (Waetzoldt 1972, 14), it is clear that plucking sheep was quite labor-intensive: many hundreds of workers were employed by individual cities in the Ur III and Old Babylonian periods to pluck wool-bearing sheep during the molting season, which lasted roughly between April and July of each year (Waetzoldt 1972, 14). Even at 10 percent of these totals, we are dealing with scores of pluckers in the fourth millennium southern Mesopotamian cities and their immeidate dependencies.

After plucking, wool had to be sorted by quality and color and had to be transported (mostly by boat or barge, see above, chap. 4) to locations where more detailed processing could take place. Late third-millennium texts give us glimpses of these activities but do not allow us to estimate the number of workers involved in them (Waetzoldt 1972, 69), workers who no doubt were also involved in a variety of other agricultural employment. We are on firmer ground, however, estimating the employment consequences of combing the sorted wool. Like plucking, combing is also a highly labor-intensive manual procedure in premodern societies. Workers commonly use a variety of implements with closely set teeth to remove impurities from plucked wool and repeatedly comb the wool with ever finer variants of such implements so as to separate individual fibers by length and arrange them in parallel strands in preparation for spinning (Ryder 1992). Late third-millennium texts show that a woman needed four days to produce one mina (0.5 kg) of combed coarse wool. Up to 33 percent of the raw wool could be lost during the combing process (Waetzoldt 1972, 116). As with fulling, we may presume that higher grades of wool would have taken more time (and/or manpower) to comb. One set of tablets from Ur summarizes the wool plucked in one year (presumably from sheep brought into the nearby center of Puzrish-Dagan) as amounting to 13,900 talents (ca. 417,000 kg; Waetzoldt 1972, 69). If we presume total Uruk period production at about 10 percent of this total and factor in the maximum wastage ratio (33 percent), about 223,510 workdays would have been required to comb the yearly output of fourth-millennium Mesopotamian cities. However, because we must also presume a decreased efficiency rate in the earlier period, this already staggeringly high number must have been even higher still.

Once wool was combed, it could be spun into yarn. Of all the industries associated with weaving, spinning was one of the most time-consuming and was the industry requiring the greatest skill (fig. 14d–14e). Studies of textile production in traditional societies using simple whorls to spin yarn, such as are attested in the Uruk period (chap. 6, n. 4), show that it can take up to six years to teach an individual (usually a young girl) how to properly spin short fibers into yarn (Kriger 2006), and spinning can take well over half of the total time needed to produce a garment (Tiedemann and Jakes 2006, table 1). In addition, spinning was also one of the most labor-intensive manual activities associated with weaving. Ethnohistoric accounts of traditional West African weaving practices in the nineteenth century show that between 2 to 8 spinners were required to produce enough (cotton) yarn to keep a single weaver employed (Kriger 1993).

Ur III cuneiform evidence is consistent with these data and clearly shows how labor-intensive spinning must have been under ancient Mesopotamian conditions. Two different spinning techniques are attested at the time. According to Waetzoldt (1972, 120), one technique yielded, on average, approximately 8 grams (1 shekel) of spun yarn per worker per day while the second yielded approximately 63 grams (7.5 shekels). These averages can be used to arrive at a rough estimate of the labor involved in spinning yarn to produce ancient Mesopotamian garments. One Ur III text from Ur summarizing coarse cloth sent to fullers details 5,800 individual pieces weighing a total of 155 talents (4,650 kg; Potts 1997, 95). Each individual cloth piece in that batch would have thus weighed approximately 0.80 kg. If, for illustrative purposes, we take this weight to be representative for the cloth density of coarse Mesopotamian textiles over time, we may infer that the wool contained within a single piece would have required anywhere between 12.7 and 100 workdays of spinning work.

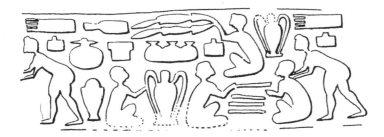

FIGURE 15. Uruk sealing portraying scribes keeping track of various categories of agricultural production, according to Pittman (1993). Note the depiction of tasseled bolts of cloth (*top*) as one the commodities being tracked.

As noted earlier, Waetzoldt (1972, 106) estimates that the yearly production of the city of Ur alone in the Ur III period was somewhere in the vicinity of 24,000 pieces. At the highest efficiency rate, this would have required 304,800 workdays of spinning and at the slowest rate it would have required as many as 2,400,000 workdays of labor—and, of course, as noted earlier, Ur may have been the most important center where textile manufactures took place in the late third millennium but it surely was not the only one. Even if Uruk period production only amounted to 10 percent or so of these calculations (i.e., between 30,480 and 240,000 workdays, average: 135,240 workdays), we are again dealing with breathtakingly high amounts of time and labor—even before factoring in the decreased productivity presumed to be typical for the earlier period.

No less important would have been a final backward linkage of the start of industrial-scale wool cloth production in Uruk societies. Under Mesopotamian conditions this would have required scores of bureaucrats to organize the work, oversee individual work gangs, supervise the distribution of subsistence rations to laborers, and record, store, and redistribute the output. Uruk iconography often portrays scribes keeping track of the productive processes and labor (Pittman 1993), and such scenes occasionally depict tasseled bolts of cloth as one of the commodities being tracked (fig. 15). Be that as it may, the Archaic Texts, many of which deal with the receipt and distribution of wool, are themselves the best and most direct evidence we have for the existence of this bureaucratic multiplier effect.

By now the point should be abundantly clear. Import substitution processes throughout the fourth millennium nurtured a continual flow of laborers into early Mesopotamian cities and their immediate dependencies.

Workers would have been drawn from the surrounding countryside and, almost certainly, from surrounding regions as well.[21] This centripetal flow explains why Uruk city-states grew in spite of the demographic paradox of early urbanism noted by McNeill. Of the emergent industries of the time, none would have contributed more to the growth of internal diversification, specialization, and overall employment than woolen textile manufacture, even if, as no doubt was the case, some of the skilled tasks involved in transforming wool fibers into garments (e.g., combing, spinning, and weaving) were sequentially performed year-round by many of the same laborers, or, even if, as is also likely, some portion of the intermediate stages in textile production (e.g., spinning yarn) may have been done by (female) labor in rural villages as part-time corvée service and sent in to urban weaving establishments as taxes.

The centrality of textiles to the early Mesopotamian urban process has been elegantly expressed by Robert McCormick Adams (1981, 11), who notes that "without the wool for textiles to be traded for natural resources that were wholly lacking in the alluvium, it is difficult to believe that Mesopotamian civilization could have arisen as early and flourished as prodigiously as it did." Adams's observation naturally brings us to an examination of the evidence for trade in fourth-millennium Mesopotamia.

The Evidence for Trade

The foregoing discussions follow the lead of economic geographers interested in the dynamics of urban growth and identify trade, both internal and external, as the engine of early Mesopotamian urban growth. There is, however, substantial disagreement about the importance of trade in general, and long-distance trade in particular, to the processes of urban and state formation in southern Mesopotamia.

Many scholars reviewing data for southern Mesopotamian economies of the fourth millennium properly highlight the importance of local tribute exaction and intraregional distribution of resources as key elements in that economy, but they either minimize the overall importance of long-distance trade to the socioeconomic processes at work at the time (e.g., Frangipane 2001b; Pollock 1999; G. Schwartz 2001, 256; Weiss 1989) or presume that rises in long-distance exchange were a consequence of urbanism rather than a cause (e.g., H. Wright 1981a, 2001).

Such views are flawed on two accounts. First, they do not fully consider the evidence for cumulatively valuable imports in both the textual and archaeological record of Uruk sites. Available cuneiform evidence is actually quite informative regarding the types of imported commodities brought into the alluvium at this time. Even the earliest economic records and lexical lists that form part of the Archaic Texts, for instance, already include numerous references, some noted above, to metals, including pure and alloyed copper and silver, which must have been imported into the south either as finished products or, most likely at this point, as ores and ingots. The same tablets also make reference to various types of wooden and stone objects, not all of which are immediately identifiable but which were clearly made from materials that were not local to southern Mesopotamia and must have been procured from peripheral sources in either partly processed or finished form (Englund 1998).

In addition, wool textiles also figure prominently in the Archaic Texts. It is generally presumed that the wool mentioned in them was locally produced and, no doubt, the bulk of it was. However, it is possible that some raw wool was also being imported in the Uruk period. Almost two decades ago, Rita Wright (1989) perspicaciously suggested that the location of Uruk outposts in areas of northern Mesopotamia propitious for extensive sheep and goat husbandry could be taken as prima facie evidence for a southern Mesopotamian interest in the acquisition of (additional!) wool to satisfy the requirements of their nascent textile production industries. I strongly suspect that Wright may be at least partially correct. Faunal data from at least three intrusive Uruk period sites along the Upper Euphrates in Turkey (Hassek Höyük, Hacınebi, and Zeytinlibahçe) published largely after Wright made her suggestion show that the Uruk presence in the Upper Euphrates is marked by an emphasis on sheep/ goat herding that marks a shift from the economic strategies practiced by immediately preceding (Late Chalcolithic) populations in the same area (Bigelow 1999; Wattenmaker and Stein 1986), which focused more on the exploitation of pigs. Tellingly, as soon as intrusive Uruk populations withdrew from the Upper Euphrates, remaining sites (Early Bronze I) reverted to the preceding pattern of animal exploitation (Boessneck 1992; Syracusano 2004).

Be that as it may, available archaeological evidence complements and expands what can be inferred from the textual data. As noted in the preceding chapter, some of the Middle and Late Uruk period southern colonial sites on the Euphrates have yielded ample evidence for the import and in situ processing of silver and copper ores (for specific references, see Algaze 2001b, 208–9). Those same colonial sites have produced evidence for lapidary workshops where various types of exotic stones were processed into luxury items (Kohlmeyer 1997, 447; Strommenger 1980), and several kilos worth of unprocessed lapis lazuli were found in a storeroom at Jebel Aruda, together with a variety of other precious stones

(Roualt and Massetti-Roualt 1993). It is likely that these re‹
intended for eventual transfer to larger Uruk centers in the
    Southern cities, in turn, have probably yielded more di
logical evidence for valuable imports than is generally ach
some of the relevant literature, and this has become particularly clear in
recent years as more and more of the final catalogs of finds from early
German excavations at Warka have appeared in print. Nowhere is the
wealth of imports into southern cities clearer than in the so-called Riemchengebäude structure found in the Eanna precinct at Warka (Late
Uruk: Eanna IVa), which may represent either a temple (Forest 1999)
or a storeroom associated with a nearby temple (Nissen 1988). Burnt in
antiquity and buried as it stood, this building was literally brimming with
objects made of imported woods, precious and semiprecious stones, and
metals (for a full inventory, see Forest 1999, 67–73).

In fact, the list of imports attested in Uruk period levels at Warka and
other Uruk sites is quite impressive. Leaving aside the issue of the import
of foreign captives used as labor, which will be the subject of discussions
in chapter 8, archaeologically attested imports include (1) pine used as
roofing timber; (2) copper, silver, lead, and gold for use as tools, weap-
ons, vessels, jewelry, and other objects of personal adornment and, more
rarely, as architectural accents in elite buildings; (3) precious stones such
as lapis, carnelian, agate, chalcedony, amazonite, amethyst, aragonite,
and jasper for use in jewelry, seal making and, occasionally, as architectural decoration in public buildings; (4) semiprecious stones such as
chlorite, obsidian, rock crystal, quartz, alabaster, gypsum, marble, dio-
rite, serpentine, and bituminous limestone used for statuary, ritual and
utilitarian vessels, and implements; (5) common stones such as basalt,
flint, and obsidian, used for agricultural and household implements, and
limestone, which, uniquely in the Uruk period, was occasionally used in
foundations of important buildings and platforms; (6) bitumen, which
was used as a general-purpose adhesive and waterproofing substance, for
caulking boats, and, again uniquely in Uruk times, for flooring and even
as brick mortar in some public buildings; and finally, (7) valuable liquids
such as wine.[1]

Second, views that deny or minimize the early importance of trade
consistently overestimate how representative the archaeological record
really is. Must we believe that the Riemchengebäude was an exceptional
find that bears no relationship to normal elite activities at the site? On

the contrary, it is more parsimonious to think that this is not a case of unusual wealth but rather one of unique preservation, since the very fire that destroyed it preserved the contents of the building. Most likely, one reason why wealth on the scale attested by the Riemchengebäude has not been found in other excavated structures at Warka, save for scattered buried hoards such as the Sammelfund, is that so many of the Uruk buildings cleared in the Eanna precinct at the site represent merely foundations that were carefully and purposefully cleaned and emptied in antiquity (Eichmann 1989).[2]

An equally important reason that accounts for the unrepresentative nature of available evidence for Uruk period exchange as a whole is that many of the exports from alluvial centers, either to peer centers or to neighboring areas, would have left few traces in the archaeological record. Prominent among these difficult-to-document export items would have been various types of dairy fats and, most importantly, elaborately crafted textiles.[3] The production processes for these exports also would have left few traces for us to find. Take, for instance, the production of cloth. Although both vertical warp-weighed and horizontal ground looms were in use in late fourth-millennium Mesopotamia (Delougaz and Kantor 1996, 107–8, n. 39), it is the latter that would most likely have been used in the mass production of textiles, at least to judge from later practice in the historic periods (Waetzoldt 1972, 132–37) and from the fact, noted above, that only horizontal looms are depicted in Uruk iconography (fig. 14e–14f). This affects our ability to identify industrial weaving archaeologically not only in the fourth millennium but in general because, unlike vertical looms, which require numerous easily identifiable weights, horizontal looms do not require weights, and the looms themselves would have been entirely built using wood and animal sinews (Barber 1991, 83–91), leaving no clues for the archaeologist to discover other than postholes on the ground.[4]

Archaeological visibility problems, albeit of an entirely different nature, also affect our understanding of the scale and variety of imports flowing into the Mesopotamian alluvium in the fourth millennium. Because of its historical use by Near Eastern elites as a status-legitimizing drink (Joffe 1998), it stands to reason that wine must surely have been one of the most important—at least ideologically—of the "invisible imports" (Crawford 1973) flowing into southern Mesopotamia in the Uruk period. Until recently, there was no reliable way to test this proposition as there was no way to recognize the decomposed traces of fermented grape beverages in the archaeological record. However, new chemical characterization analyses devised at the Museum Applied Science Center for Archaeology (MASCA) of the University of Pennsylvania Museum focusing on the identification of tartaric acid residues on ancient pottery have now solved this problem. These analyses reveal that wine was certainly produced at the small Uruk fort at Godin Tepe (McGovern 2003, 43–63). Since no attempts have been made to run comparable tests for tartaric acid at Uruk outposts elsewhere across the Mesopotamian periphery, we have no way of knowing how representative the Godin results truly are for the Uruk expansion as a whole.[5] Nonetheless, it is certain that wine was being imported by Uruk societies, even if the ultimate point(s) of origin of that wine remains unclear. In addition to their analysis of the Godin materials, the University of Pennsylvania Museum team tested at least three Uruk type jars with characteristically downward curving spouts that they believed could have served as wine-serving and -shipping containers in Uruk societies. The tested jars were excavated at Warka, Girsu, and Susa. Each produced chemical evidence for wine (McGovern 2003, 160–64).[6] As the jars in question are of a type that is quite common in Uruk assemblages, where they are sometimes found in direct association with drinking cups (e.g., at Jebel Aruda [Van Driel 2002b, 195, fig. 10]), we can expect that systematic testing of such jars will eventually allow us to get a better handle on the scale of wine imports into the Mesopotamian alluvium during the Uruk period. I suspect that wine might have been as significant an import into southern Mesopotamia already in the fourth millennium as it was in the historic periods, when it was imported by the boatload (Finet 1969).

Without a doubt, however, the most significant (by volume) invisible import into the southern Mesopotamian alluvium during the Uruk period would have been roofing timber (but see Weiss 1989 and 2003, 594–95 for a contrary opinion), which tends to disappear from the archaeological record save under exceptional conditions. Nonetheless, imports of timber at the time can be inferred indirectly from considerations of architectural needs. These needs would have been quite substantial indeed, as southern cities grew rapidly by absorbing populations from the surrounding countryside throughout the Uruk period (Adams 1981) and would have been particularly acute in the case of the large administrative and religious structures at the center of those cities, each requiring many long beams of imported timber for roofing. A single example will suffice to illustrate the point. Jean Claude Margueron (1992) has estimated that somewhere between 3,000 and 6,000 linear meters of timber would have been necessary to roof the Limestone Temple uncovered in Level V of the Eanna area at Warka, depending on, among other things, whether its courtyard was roofed, number of stories, or roofing beam placement interval. Extrapolating from these figures and presuming similar construction parameters, the impressive series of structures that stood in the Eanna and Kullaba (Anu) Precincts at the core of Warka during later phases of the Late Uruk period (Eanna IVb-a, see above, chap. 2, figs. 2–3) would have required somewhere between 16,800 and 33,600 linear meters of imported roofing timber.[7]

Other contemporary imports would have consisted largely of a variety of exotics and semiprecious commodities, principally metals, which are also unlikely to be preserved in representative amounts in the archaeological record of complex central sites, absent a destruction level. The reasons for this are explained by the late Andrew Sherratt (2004), who noted that in truly complex societies sumptuary goods and metals will be distributed more widely across social hierarchies than in simpler societies, as such commodities become a medium of exchange capable of being converted into a wide range of goods and services. This naturally increases the likelihood that such commodities will be kept longer in circulation, that they will be transformed more often when practicable (e.g., metals by melting), and that they will be passed on across generations more consistently.

Two consequences may be derived from this; both make it more likely that as a society becomes increasingly complex, its sumptuary goods, counterintuitively, may become less visible in its archaeological record. First, the longer things are in circulation, the less likely it is that excavations in any one level of any one site will be representative. Second, as commodities circulate more broadly across wider social networks, excavations at single central sites or, worse still, at the core of such sites, are increasingly unlikely to produce a representative sample of the scale and type of valuable commodities in circulation any one time. Regretfully, such excavations presently provide the bulk of the available excavated evidence for the Uruk period in the alluvium.

A related problem of interpretation is that in complex societies a high proportion of exotics would also naturally get withdrawn from circulation for use as burial gifts. One wonders what our views about the scale of imports of exotic stones and base and precious metals in Mesopotamia during the third millennium would be if extensive cemeteries and numerous intramural burials had not been discovered at Kish, Khafajah, Tell Asmar, Abu Salabikh, and, most spectacularly, at Ur? The point of this rhetorical question is to suggest that the still fairly common view that imports of sumptuary commodities into fourth-millennium Mesopotamia were relatively rare may, to a large degree, be illusory—a consequence of the still puzzling dearth of mortuary evidence from southern Mesopotamia for the Uruk period.

It may be possible to circumvent some of these evidentiary biases by shifting our focus away from individual sites and looking at the horizontal distribution of exotics throughout the alluvium as a whole for any given period. For the time of initial urban emergence, this can only be done by looking at existing surface reconnaissance data for sites occupied solely or primarily in one or more phases of the Uruk period. Existing tabulations of surface finds collected by Adams and his associates in pertinent sites show that metals and exotic stones in fact did occur in mounds of all sizes at the time, and were often found even in small hamlet- or village-sized settlements (Adams 1981, 117–18, 122, tables 8–9; Adams and Nissen 1972, 205–8).[8] Though these data tell us nothing about the mechanisms whereby the inhabitants of smaller sites gained access to imports, the presence of exotics at every level of the urban-rural continuum of the earliest Sumerian societies certainly highlights the importance of crosscultural trade in the fourth millennium. The developmental consequences of this trade are explored in the chapter that follows.

CHAPTER SEVEN

Early Mesopotamian Urbanism in Comparative Perspective

Evidentiary Biases

Where trade flows, its ramifications in the form of increasing social complexity and urbanism soon follow. Thus, the precocious development of southern Mesopotamia throughout the fourth millennium BC comes as no surprise. The uniqueness of the development in the south at this point becomes clear when we compare available survey and excavation data for the nature of both sites and patterns of settlement in the alluvium against comparable data from neighboring regions, and particularly from Upper Mesopotamia. Such comparisons are difficult, however, because of the very different archaeological recovery biases inherent to each of the two areas. These biases must be kept in mind when evaluating available evidence.

The first bias stems from the different archaeological methodologies used to survey parts of the two areas under comparison (Wilkinson 2000b). Though the quality and variety of surveys in Upper Mesopotamia vary widely, a large portion of pertinent results for that area stem from a small number of fairly recent and fairly systematic surveys that emphasized full coverage of the surveyed areas, included a significant walking component, and made considerable effort to map variations in the extent of the occupation of individual sites through time (e.g., Wilkinson 1990a, 2000a; Wilkinson and Tucker 1995; Wilkinson in Al-

gaze et al. 1992; Algaze et al. 1994; Sallaberger and Ur 2004; Stein and
Wattenmaker 1990; Ur 2002a; Ur, Karsgaard, and Oates 2007). In contrast, many of the pertinent surveys available for the south (e.g., Adams
1981; Adams and Nissen 1972; Gibson 1972; H. Wright 1981b), while
also systematic, were conducted well over thirty years ago and, because
of political uncertainties (Robert M. Adams, personal communication,
2006), were designed from the beginning to be extensive in nature, so
as to cover as large an area as practicable during the rare times when
regional fieldwork was possible in Iraq during the 1960s and 1970s. As
a consequence, those surveys generally did not include as substantial a
walking component as their more recent Upper Mesopotamian counterparts or made as detailed an effort to map the extent of occupation
of different periods in each of the sites surveyed. Thus, in the aggregate,
available surveys of southern Mesopotamia are more likely than existing Upper Mesopotamian surveys to have missed small shallow sites and
are more likely as well to misrepresent the extent of occupation in any
one period.

A second bias is perhaps more consequential and stems from the different historical trajectories of Upper and southern Mesopotamia throughout the fourth and third millennia. As will be outlined in greater detail
below, across Upper Mesopotamia there is a widespread discontinuity in
settlement patterns between the Late Chalcolithic (fourth millennium)
and Early Bronze Age (third millennium) periods. Accordingly, in many
cases, and particularly so in smaller sites, fourth-millennium layers are
not covered by later deposits and are clearly recognizable in survey. In
contrast, the reverse is true in southern Mesopotamia, where substantial
overall settlement continuity was the norm between the fourth and third
millennia, which often results in the masking of earlier Uruk materials
under later Early Dynastic deposits across a wide cross section of sites.

The third and final bias is probably the most important and is a consequence of the very different geomorphological processes operating in
Upper and southern Mesopotamia. Processes typical for the southern
lowlands include river meandering (particularly likely under the climatic
regime of the area in the fourth millennium), alluviation, and aeolian
sand deposition (Wilkinson 1990b, 2000b, 243–44), conditions that would
naturally tend to destroy or obscure a large proportion of the smaller
Uruk period sites in southern Mesopotamia. In contrast, the main geomorphologic factor affecting site recovery in the Upper Mesopotamian
plains is erosion caused by both episodic winter rains and the year-round

grazing of sheep. This would tend to enhance (rather than mask) site recognition.

Put together, these various biases mean that results from well-surveyed portions of the Upper Mesopotamian plains pertinent to the fourth millennium should be fairly representative of conditions in that area at the time while comparable results from southern Mesopotamia probably significantly understate the extent of contemporary Uruk period settlement. Keeping this important caveat in mind, we now turn to brief contrastive summaries of the relevant data from both regions.

Florescent Urbanism in Alluvial Mesopotamia

Available survey data for southern Mesopotamia are derived largely from systematic surveys of substantial portions of the Mesopotamian alluvium conducted in the decades between the 1950s and 1970s by Robert McCormick Adams and a group of his associates and students (Adams 1965, 1981; Adams and Nissen 1972; Gibson 1972; H. Wright 1981b; for a reworking of the data, see now Kouchoukos 1998, 230–49; Kouchoukos and Wilkinson 2007; Pollock 2001; and Wilkinson 2000b). While results from these surveys are not particularly fine-grained from a chronological standpoint, available evidence indicates that multiple interacting urban sites existed there throughout *every* phase of the Uruk period, all situated alongside water channels and within relatively short distances of each other, and each positioned at the apex of a variegated settlement structure.

This pattern was in place already by the first quarter of the fourth millennium, the Early Uruk period, when Warka is estimated to have been between 70 to 100 hectares in extent, and at least three other sites across the alluvium were 40 hectares or larger in size (Eridu, site 1237, and Tell al-Hayyad [site 1306]). Multiple other sites across the alluvium at this time were in the range of 15–25 hectares (Adams 1981; H. Wright 1981b), as detailed in figure 16 and appendix 1. These centers did not exist in isolation. When the relevant survey data are tallied, it appears that they anchored complex settlement grids minimally comprising four tiers in depth (Johnson 1980, 249). Indeed, available data indicate that the proportion of the population living in relatively large town-sized (ca. 10+ ha) or urban-sized (ca. 40+ ha) agglomerations in the alluvium in the early Uruk period was just under 50 percent according to Adams's

(1981, 75, table 4) original calculations. If Pollock's (2001, 216, table 6.7) recent reassessment of the same data, which tries to take into account the fact that not all sites assigned to a discrete period are likely to have been strictly contemporaneous, is preferred, that proportion rises to an astonishing 80 percent or so.[1]

Development in the southern alluvial lowlands reached its peak in the second half of the fourth millennium. This is clearest by the Late Uruk period. As in the earlier phases, multiple small and large towns (ca. 5–15 ha) and small (ca. 25 ha: Nippur, site 1172, site 125) and larger (50 ha: site 1306) cities existed across the surveyed portions of the alluvium at this time (fig. 17, appendix 2). What is new at this point, however, is the extraordinary development and demographic growth of the southern-most portion of the Mesopotamian alluvium surveyed by Adams, where Uruk/Warka situated on a major branch of the fourth-millennium Euphrates attained the unprecedented size of up to 250 hectares in extent, according to a detailed surface survey of the site conducted by a German expedition just before the onset of the First Gulf War (Finkbeiner 1991; fig. 18). Although there is no consensus on precisely how to correlate settlement extent and population in ancient Mesopotamian cities, there is general agreement that Nissen's (2001, 158) estimate of 20,000 or so people for Warka in the Late Uruk period, is probably a highly conservative approximation.[2]

Not surprisingly, the settlement grid that surrounded Warka at this time was exceptionally complex in terms of its density and hierarchy (four or more tiers depending on how the data are analyzed). It included numerous dependent towns, villages, and hamlets situated within a 15-kilometer range of the city, totaling a minimum of 280 or so hectares of further occupation (Adams and Nissen 1972). In other words, at a mini-mum, by the Late Uruk period, the regional polity centered at Warka had a population of well upward of 50,000 people—and this estimate neces-sarily excludes associated, but inherently difficult-to-trace, transhumant and marsh-dwelling populations.

While the multiurban nature of the settlement structure that had emerged in the Mesopotamian alluvium by the Early Uruk period re-mained essentially unchanged in the Late Uruk phase, important changes in the distribution of populations within the area did take place in the later period. Adams's surveys document a reduction in the number of villages and hamlets in the northernmost surveyed portion of the al-luvium, the Nippur-Adab area. However, all of the towns and cities that

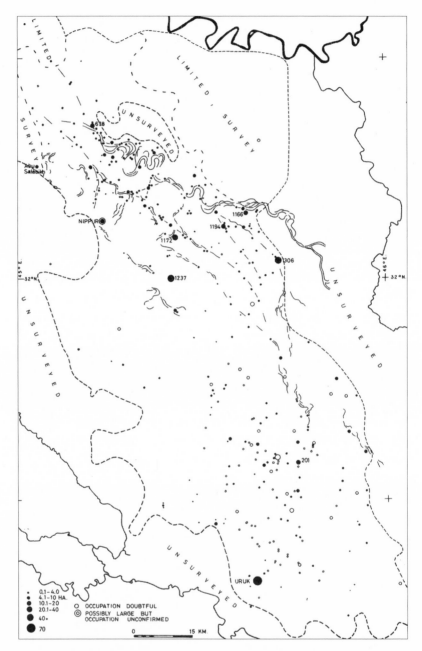

FIGURE 16. Early–Middle Uruk period (ca. 3900/3800–3400 BC) settlement patterns in Nippur-Adab and Warka (Uruk) survey areas of the Mesopotamian alluvium.

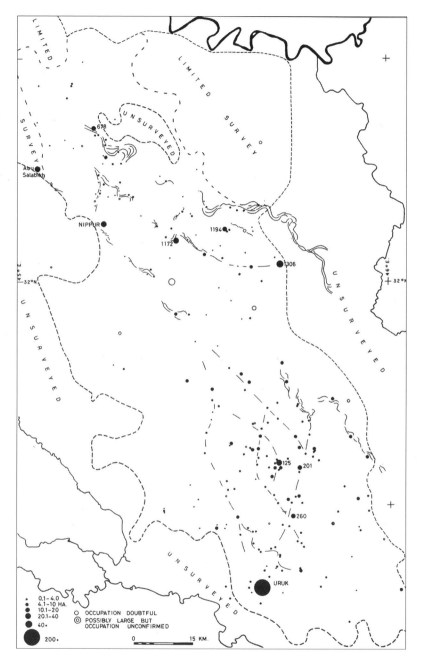

FIGURE 17. Late Uruk period (ca. 3400–3200/3100 BC) settlement patterns in Nippur-Adab and Warka (Uruk) survey areas of the Mesopotamian alluvium.

had existed in that area in the earlier part of the Uruk period remained inhabited into the Late Uruk phase (Adams 1981; Pollock 2001), so that the relative density of urban agglomeration in the Nippur-Adab area actually increased. Adams (1981, 70–71) plausibly suggests that many of the rural populations that abandoned the Nippur-Adab region at the end of what he calls the Early/Middle Uruk phase immigrated into the then fast-growing Uruk/Warka area. This is very likely, although it is also possible that a portion of the displaced rural populations became pastoral nomads or marsh dwellers and disappeared from the (easily traced) archaeological record.

Though smaller in scale, important changes were also taking place during the Late Uruk period in the southernmost portion of the alluvium, the Eridu-Ur basin surveyed by Henry Wright. Basing himself on the results of Anglo-Iraqi excavations at Eridu between 1948 and 1950 that show Early Uruk buildings at the top of the site filled with sand, Wright suggests that Eridu, one of the largest Early Uruk period sites in the alluvium, for the most part had been abandoned by the Late Uruk phase. This was accompanied by an expansion of Ur into a small town of approximately 10 or so hectares at this time and the foundation of a few small villages and hamlets in the northern part of the Eridu-Ur basin (H. Wright 1981b, 325–27, fig. 18). However, the extent of the growth at Ur and related rural foundations in the Late Uruk period hardly equals the population lost by Eridu in the Early Uruk phase (app. 2), so it is likely that some of the missing urban inhabitants of the Eridu-Ur basin also ended up fueling the explosive Late Uruk phase growth of Warka and its surroundings.

If anything, when considered in the aggregate, the proportion of the population of the Mesopotamian alluvium living in relatively large town-sized (ca. 10+ ha) or urban-sized (ca. 40+ ha) agglomerations during the Late Uruk period was even greater than that during the Early Uruk phase. Adams (1981, 75, table 4) originally estimated that up to 70 percent of the population in the Nippur-Adab region was "urban" in the Late Uruk period as opposed to about 40 percent in the Warka area, but the latter number must be revised sharply upward to about 60 percent to account for the greatly increased estimate for the size of Warka itself at the time (250 ha as opposed to Adams's initial estimate of 100 ha).[3] These estimates are quite similar to those arrived at by Pollock's (2001, 216, table 6.7) in her recent reassessment of the same data, which classified 70 percent of the population in the Nippur-Adab and 78 percent of the population of the Warka area as "urban."[4]

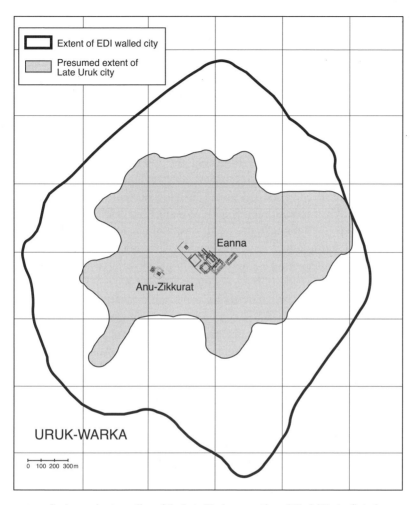

FIGURE 18. Approximate outline of the Late Uruk occupation of Uruk/Warka (interior perimeter) within the area enclosed by the ED I city wall (exterior perimeter). Also showing the location of the Eanna and Anu Precincts at the core of the city.

How do the patterns just described compare against those prevalent in neighboring areas of Greater Mesopotamia at the time? Until now it has been difficult to begin to tackle this question because of difficulties in correlating the developmental trajectories of the different areas involved as a result of chronological imprecision, the differences in the coverage of available surveys, and varying survey methodologies. However, these difficulties have now been smoothed to some extent by two methodological advances that, when combined, allow for comparisons of settlement processes across large areas and cultural boundaries. The first is improvements in our understanding of the absolute chronology of the fourth millennium across the various regions that composed Greater Mesopotamia in antiquity as a result of the collection of new radiocarbon dates from pertinent sites and the reanalsyis of previously collected ones (Wright and Rupley 2001). The second is the application to the Mesopotamian case of a probabilistic statistical model for the analysis of survey data elaborated by Robert Dewar (1991). First used on Mesopotamian data by Pollock (1999, 2001), Dewar's model corrects for the fact that not all sites assigned to a discrete period are likely to have been strictly contemporaneous and allows for comparisons to be made between survey data categorized in terms of chronological periods of disparate length.

These advances have made possible a recent comparative review of the available survey data from southern and northern Mesopotamia in the fourth millennium by Nicholas Kouchoukos and Tony Wilkinson (2007; see also Kouchoukos 1998 and Wilkinson 2000b). They make three important points that are particularly relevant here. The first is that settlement processes in Greater Mesopotamia throughout the Uruk period appear to have been causally articulated over vast regions. Indeed, Kouchoukos and Wilkinson persuasively show that, when recalculated using a single standard, demographic trends in the Mesopotamian alluvium and immediately neighboring areas appear to be inversely correlated at the time: growth in the Warka region took place not only at the expense of the Nippur-Adab and Eridu-Ur areas, as argued earlier, but seemingly at the expense of neighboring peripheral regions as well, where a monotonical decline in settled population can be observed throughout the fourth millennium. As charted in figure 19, which is abstracted directly from Kouchoukos and Wilkinson's work, this inverse regional correlation is clearest when we compare demographic trends in southern Mesopotamia and the Jazirah plains north of the Jebel Sinjar in northern Iraq. However, comparable demographic trends are also observable in other more remote areas at the periphery of alluvial Mesopotamia, such as Fars Plain in southwest Iran, where Sumner (1986, 200, 208, fig. 3) documented a steep decline (by a factor of 5) in settlement extent (and population) that correlates temporally with the demographic boom in the Mesopotamian lowlands through the Uruk period. To be sure, some of the settlers "missing" from Upper Mesopotamia and Fars may not be missing at all, but rather may have abandoned settled life to became pastoral nomads in response to growing alluvial demands for wool, as Kouchoukos and Wilkinson (2007, 18) have argued. While this is quite possible, it is also likely that immigration from peripheral areas losing settled population fueled—at least in part—the urbanization of the Mesopotamian alluvium through the Uruk period.

This brings us to the second and third noteworthy points that emerge from Kouchoukos and Wilkinson's work—that in absolute terms the population of the Mesopotamian alluvium throughout the various phases of the Uruk period was substantially greater than that of any one coherent area of the Mesopotamian periphery at the time, and that relative population densities in southern Mesopotamia during the Uruk period were also higher than those typical for contemporary polities in neighboring regions.[5] Starting with the former point, after recalibration under a single standard, the data marshaled by Kouchoukos and Wilkinson indicate that as many as 100,000 people lived within the main surveyed portions of the southern Mesopotamian alluvium during the final phase of the Uruk period (fig. 16). This contrasts sharply against the 6,000 or so people documented by Wilkinson as inhabiting the surveyed portions of the north Jazirah plains at this time. Presuming that Wilkinson's data is roughly representative for conditions in Upper Mesopotamia as a whole (an admittedly risky assumption that can only be tested once the results of the more recent surveys around Tell Brak are fully analyzed and published), and correcting for the overall 10:1 difference in survey extent between the two areas (roughly 5,000 square km for southern Iraq versus 500 square km for the north Jazirah plains), population density per square kilometer in the alluvium was just under double that prevalent in the Upper Mesopotamian plains. However, this estimate likely substantially understates the true difference in the demographic density between the two areas because of sharply depressed site counts in the south arising from the alluvial and aeolian deposition processes discussed earlier.

The Primacy of Warka: Location, Location, Location

The extraordinary growth of Warka and its immediate hinterland in the Late Uruk period demand explanation. Writing separately, Kent Flannery (1995) and Joyce Marcus (1998) both suggest that Warka would have been the capital of a territorial empire in the Late Uruk period, which

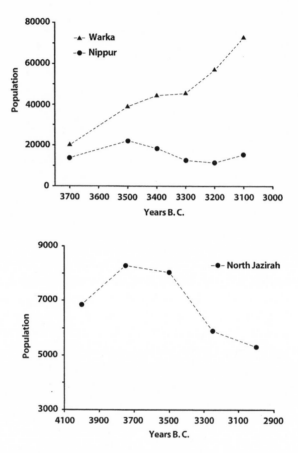

FIGURE 19. Fourth-millennium demographic trends in surveyed portions of the Warka and Nippur-Adab areas of southern Mesopotamia, and surveyed portions of the North Jazirah region in northern Iraq.

presumably would have encompassed not only the whole of the alluvium but also, at this time, colonized areas of southwestern Iran and, possibly, portions of northern Mesopotamia, such as the Euphrates Bend. Flannery and Marcus explicitly assume that all pristine states emerge from a crucible of conflict as earlier regional chiefdoms are consolidated by force into a single overarching polity, and they presume the same to have been the case at the onset of Mesopotamian civilization. As supporting evidence, they point to the four to fivefold size differential (below) that current data suggest existed between Warka and its nearest second-tier settlements in the alluvium during the Late Uruk period.

This is a plausible interpretation of the evidence we possess at this time, which, regretfully, aside from excavations at Warka, consists mostly of surface survey data. Equally possible at this point, however, are interpretations that acknowledge the importance of intraregional conflict as a mechanism promoting early Mesopotamian state formation and urban agglomeration but that see warfare as a consequence of more deeply rooted processes of asymmetrical growth initially set into motion by the already noted multiplier effects of trade. From this perspective, Warka and the various other cities that existed throughout the surveyed portions of the Mesopotamian alluvium and neighboring plains of southwestern Iran in the Uruk period developed in tandem and would represent the centers of independent polities of varying extent and power ancestral to the competing city-states that characterized the alluvium throughout much of its history.

Of these interpretations, I believe the latter (trade-fueled asymmetrical growth leading to coevolving polities of varying size) is the one that best fits available data for three principal reasons. The first is that existing size differentials between Warka (250 ha) and its nearest second-tier settlements (site 1306 at 50 ha) may well reflect nothing but an accident of discovery. Indeed, two facts raise the possibility that Warka and the other known Uruk urban sites in the surveyed portions of the alluvium represent only the visible tip, so to say, of the Uruk period settlement iceberg in southern Mesopotamia as a whole. First, as already noted, geomorphologic processes operating in the southern alluvial plains of Tigris and Euphrates rivers are particularly likely to obscure a large proportion of the smaller Uruk period sites in the south. In addition, in places, particularly dense Late Holocene alluvial deposits may even obscure some of the larger Uruk sites in the south. This possibility is raised by J. Pournelle (2003a, 2003b, 194, 247–48), who notes that, in some cases, satellite imagery shows that multiple small nearby Uruk period sites recorded by Adams as independent settlements could have been instead parts of much larger, contiguous shallow settlements partly covered by alluvial deposits (e.g., site 125; see Pournelle 2003b, fig. 80). Second, and more concretely, it should be remembered that much of the eastern portion of the Mesopotamian alluvium centered on the Tigris was never systematically surveyed because of the outbreak of the Iran-Iraq war (Robert M. Adams, personal communication, 2003). A number of sites exist in these still (systematically) unexplored areas that were occupied during one or more phases of the Uruk period. These sites are not considered in recent reviews of the nature of Uruk period settlement in southern Mesopotamia (e.g., Algaze 2001a; Pollock 2001; Wilkinson 2000b), but several are likely to have been quite substantial at the time.

Foremost among these are Umma and the nearby site of Umm al-Aqarib.[6] During a recent brief visit to Umma, McGuire Gibson (personal communication, 2001) reports Uruk period pottery spread widely over the surface of the site. More tellingly, numerous Archaic Texts recently plundered from either (or both) of those sites appear immediately comparable to the earliest examples from Warka (Englund 2004, 28, n. 7). At a minimum, these tablets attest to the economic importance of the Umma area in the Late Uruk period. However, since at Uruk these tablets are part of a wider urban assemblage of great extent and complexity, their presence in the Umma area argues for a similar context. Though circumstantial, this evidence suggests that Umma and its satellites may have been second only to Warka itself in terms of urban and social development in the Late Uruk period.

Buttressing this possibility is a glaring anomaly in the settlement data for Late Uruk southern Mesopotamia as presently known (table 1; app. 2): the largest site (Warka) is just over four times as large (i.e., populous) as second-tier settlements, which in the Late Uruk phase fall in the 50-hectare range (Tell al-Hayyad [site 1306]). This is anomalous because analyses of modern urban systems show that urban populations commonly arrange themselves in rank order by size in predictable ways ("Zipf's Law"), so that as the cumulative number of settlements falls by a given multiple, for example, by half, the site sizes typical for the immediately succeeding settlement tier increase roughly by that same multiple, for example, double (Krugman 1996b). In Zipf's terms a settlement at rank x is roughly $1/x$ the size of the largest settlement. If comparable rank-size behavior characterized the ancient Mesopotamian urban world, then existing 50-hectare-range second-tier sites would represent instead a third tier of Late Uruk settlement in southern Mesopotamia. By this logic, the second tier of that settlement system then would have been anchored by a site or sites roughly half the extent (i.e., population) of Warka, as can be observed in table 1. I expect that Umma and its immediate satellites will eventually be found to represent this missing tier and that further work at the site will eventually show it to have been somewhere in the range of 100–120 hectares in the Late Uruk period.[7]

Be that as it may, a variety of other important alluvial sites are further candidates for significant Uruk period sites or site complexes outside of

TABLE I. **Reworking of Adams's (1981, table 7, see appendix 2 below) data for Late Uruk period settlement in the Nippur-Adab and Warka regions according to Zipf-derived rank-size rules**

Category	Recorded Size Range (ha)	Average	Expected Number	Observed Number
"Hamlets"	0.1–2.4	1.56	52	69
"Villages"	2.5–4.9	3.125	26	31
"Small towns"	5–9	6.25	13	16
"Large towns"	10–14	12.5	6.5	6
"Small cities"	24–25	25	3.25	3
"Cities"	50	50	1.625	1
"Large cities"		100	0.81	0 (Umma?)
"Primate city"	200 +	200 +	0.4	1

Note: Douglas White (UC, Irvine) kindly helped in the preparation of this figure.

the present boundaries of systematic survey in the south. One such site is the Early Dynastic city of Adab, excavated by a U.S. expedition early in the twentieth century that was covered by sand dunes in the 1960s and 1970s, when the area surrounding the site was surveyed (Adams 1981, 63). While no archaeological evidence for the Uruk period is known from the haphazard excavations conducted at the site, it is certain that an important settlement existed here at that time, because Adab figures prominently among the toponyms found in the earliest group of Archaic Texts (Uruk IV date). In fact, of a total of 24 recognizable geographic names in those tablets, Adab is mentioned 8 times, or a full 33 percent of the references (for comparison, as Potts [1997, 29] notes, Uruk itself is mentioned ten times in the texts). Other candidates for significant Uruk settlements are Girsu, where French excavations in the late nineteenth and early twentieth centuries uncovered substantial Uruk period remains (Parrot 1948), and the smaller site of Surghul, downstream on the ancient Tigris, where Uruk deposits also exist (E. Carter, personal communication, 2001). Both times are situated entirely outside the areas systematic surveyed by Adams and his colleagues. Because both Girsu and Surghul were central settlements in the later third-millennium kingdom of Lagash, it is not farfetched to suggest that they formed parts of a smaller earlier polity of the Uruk period in the same region.

A second reason why political balkanization rather than centralization is a more likely description of conditions in the Mesopotamian alluvium and related areas in the Uruk period as a whole is that processes of urban growth throughout the period appear to have resulted in the creation of clear buffer zones between some of the emerging settlement centers of the time. The clearest instance of this pattern is that documented by Gregory Johnson for the Susiana Plain, an area not considered by Pollock in her proposal for the political structure of the early Sumerian world of the Uruk period but that, as noted in the prologue, appears to have been colonized by Mesopotamian populations relatively early in the Uruk period. Johnson's (1987, 124) surveys document the abandonment of all Middle Uruk period villages along a 15-kilometer-wide arc by the Late Uruk period, separating what by then appear to have been two rival early Sumerian statelets centered at Susa and Chogha Mish, respectively. This clear "buffer zone" indicates that these centers were independent from each other. More likely than not, they were independent from contemporary centers in the alluvium as well.

A further buffer area may perhaps be recognized in the widespread abandonment of villages along a broad arc between Abu Salabikh and Tell al-Hayyad at the transition between the earlier (Early/Middle) and later (Late) phases of the Uruk period as delineated by Adams (compare Adams 1981, figs. 13 and 12, respectively). This area of abandonment is situated between the northernmost (Nippur-Adab) and southernmost (Uruk) surveyed portions of the alluvium. Adams (1981, 66) has interpreted this arc as given over to pasture lands and foraging activities, and notes that important river course changes took place here that may have made the area uninhabitable by agriculturalists and thus contributed to the observed population shift. While this is almost certainly correct, it does not in any way exclude the possibility that the uninhabited arc between Abu Salabikh and Tell al-Hayyad could also reflect a political-military buffer between competing alluvial polities in the Late Uruk period.[8]

Finally, it is also possible that the primacy of Warka reflects a religious rather than a political paramountcy. This explanation, which is fully consistent with the reconstruction of the Mesopotamian alluvium in the fourth millennium as a politically fractious but culturally homogeneous landscape, was recently proposed by Steinkeller (1999), who argued that Uruk may have functioned as the religious capital of Sumer through the Uruk and the succeeding Jemdet Nasr periods. This assessment is based on a handful of Jemdet Nasr period tablets (Uruk III script) from Jemdet Nasr, Uqair, and Uruk that show that individual Sumerian cities were sending resources (including various types of foodstuffs and slave women) to Uruk as ritual offerings to Inanna, one of the city's chief deities. Steinkeller suggests, plausibly, that this situation reflects a continuation of conditions that must have started already in the Uruk period and that it represents, in turn, the precursor of the already noted *bala* taxation and distribution system that would later keep the religious institutions of Nippur and nearby cities supplied with necessary offerings and resources at the very end of the third millennium, during the Ur III period.

Steinkeller's hypothesis represents, in effect, an elaboration of a much earlier suggestion by Adams (1966), who argued that, whatever other factors may have been at work, early Mesopotamian cities also ultimately coalesced around preexisting centers of religious pilgrimage. Both views help account for the possibly quite unusual scale of religious architecture uncovered by German expeditions at the center of Warka, both in the Eanna Precinct (e.g., the "Stone Cone Mosaic" Temple [Eanna VI], the "Limestone" Temple [Eanna V], and "Temples C" and "D" [Eanna IVa]; fig. 3) and in the Anu Ziggurat area (e.g., the "White" Temple and the even larger "Stone Building," which Forest [1999] argues was also a temple; fig. 2). Both views also help to account for the wealth of precious imports found at the core of Uruk, many of which may have been brought in as votive offerings.

It should be noted, however, that even if Steinkeller and Adams are correct about the religious underpinnings of Uruk's centrality in the fourth millennium, their arguments need not necessarily be interpreted to mean that Warka was the political capital of a unified "national" state in the Uruk period. While in many early civilizations political control is often coterminous with religious paramountcy, this correlation is by no means absolute. Nowhere is this clearer than in Mesopotamia itself, where Nippur was the acknowledged religious capital of the alluvium throughout the third millennium without ever being the seat of a political dynasty.

Plausible as religious centrality may be as an explanation for Warka's preeminence through much of the Uruk period, the fact remains that available survey and excavation data from southern Mesopotamia remains entirely too ambiguous to allow for a detailed reconstruction of either the political or the religious landscape of southern societies at the time. Nor, given the nature of the evidence, is it within our power to reconstruct specific sequences of self-aggrandizing actions by particular individuals and institutions that may have contributed to that preeminence. What we can do, however, is outline the framework in which such actions would have been likely to take place and in which, once they did, they would have been likely to succeed. No doubt, that framework owes much to the site's location. Like other fourth-millennium alluvial centers, Warka was located at the bottom of the huge transportation funnel created by the Tigris-Euphrates watershed. However, as Jennifer Pournelle (2003a, figs. 7a, 8) has recently noted, the site was also situated precisely at the point where the main channel of the Euphrates, as it existed in the fourth millennium, broke (and/or was channeled) into a corona of smaller distributaries as the river reached the then receding mid-Holocene Persian Gulf coastline. The resulting radial patterning of water channels partially encircling Warka (figs. 5, 21) allowed its inhabitants an ease of access, via water transport, to resources, labor, and information drawn from both the site's immediate hinterland and the vast Tigris-Euphrates watershed that was unmatched by neighboring polities in the alluvium and entirely unachievable by contemporary polities outside of the alluvium.

In fact, as predicted by the core premises of the new economic geography (chap. 3), differential transport costs alone might well account for the seemingly monocentric urban structure of the Warka area in the Middle–Late Uruk period versus the more multicentric character of the Nippur-Adab area, a divergence recently highlighted in Pollock's (2001, 218) reexamination of Adams's survey data.[9] The fact is that however privileged they may have been in terms of their access to waterborne transport in comparison with nonalluvial polities, cities in the northern reaches of the Mesopotamian alluvium did not possess the natural radial channels that surrounded Warka at the time early Sumerian civilization crystallized in the second half of the fourth millennium. Nor, because of the slowly receding mid-Holocene coastline, did they have as extensive an area of navigable marshes in their immediate environs. Speaking in the abstract about the relationship between location, transportation, and development, sociologist Amos Hawley (1986, 90) has observed that "[l]ocation proves critical in the initiation of an expansion process. The strategic site is possessed by the center with the easiest access to both regional and interregional influences. It is there that the requisite information for improvements in transportation and communication technologies has the greatest probability of accumulating."[10]

Hawley's insights apply not only to the specific case of Warka but also more broadly to the Mesopotamian alluvium as a whole. How farsighted those insights really are in terms of the explanation of the Sumerian takeoff will become clear in the chapter that follows. Before proceeding to that assessment, however, we must take a few moments to contrast the

developmental sequence just outlined for southern Mesopotamia with
contemporary developments elsewhere in the Near East.

Aborted Urbanism in Upper Mesopotamia

The long sequence of urban growth in the southern Mesopotamian alluvium that is evident throughout all phases of the Uruk period and the
whole of the fourth millennium contrasts starkly with the developmental trajectory of contemporary northern Mesopotamian societies. To be
sure, as Henry Wright (2001, 145) presciently noted, both sequences similarly start the fourth millennium with an burst of settlement growth and
expansion of social complexity, but in the north this initial spurt came to
an end approximately 3500–3400 BC or so (i.e., the end of the so-called
"Northern Middle Uruk period"). Development differences between the
two areas through the fourth millennium have come into sharper focus
only recently as a result of new excavations and surveys centered at Tell
Brak (Emberling et al. 1999; Emberling and McDonald 2001; Matthews
2003; Oates 2002; Oates and Oates 1997; Oates et al. 2007) along the
Jagh Jagh branch of the Upper Khabur River in Syria, new excavations
at Nineveh, near Mosul, which dominated a natural ford on the Upper
Tigris River in Iraq (Stronach 1994), new surveys at Tell el-Hawa and
its environs (Wilkinson and Tucker 1995), in the Jebel Sinjar Plains of
northern Iraq, and older surveys in the vicinity of Samsat (summarized
in Algaze 1999), which controlled a natural ford on the Upper Euphrates
area of southeastern Turkey.

This new body of work shows that the scale of individual sites situated in disparate areas of the northern Mesopotamian plains during the
first half of the fourth millennium was roughly comparable to that of
contemporary sites in the southern Mesopotamian alluvium. Nowhere
is this clearer than at Tell Brak (fig. 20), a site situated at the juncture
of a historical east-west overland route across Upper Mesopotamia and
the north-to-south waterborne route formed by the Jagh Jagh River, a
tributary of the Khabur River. At this position, Brak functioned in effect
as a natural gravity-fed collection and bulk-breaking point for metals and
other commodities procured from the Anatolian highlands and brought
into the Upper Mesopotamian plains, first through overland routes cutting across the Karaca Dağ and the Mazi Dağ mountains of southeastern
Turkey and then shipped downstream the Jagh Jagh using boats or rafts.

From Brak, in turn, resources could be shipped to markets in southern Iraq via the Khabur and Euphrates rivers or, alternately, be transferred onto porters or donkeys and distributed laterally across northern Mesopotamia.

Almost certainly on account of its privileged position, Brak grew to a minimum of 65 hectares (Emberling et al. 1999) in the Northern Middle Uruk period (ca. 3800–3400 BC), and a new detailed surface survey of the immediate environs of the mound suggests that the site may have been as large as 130 hectares at this time, if one takes into account contemporary but not contiguous occupations in suburbs surrounding the main mound (Oates et al. 2007). In terms of total occupied area, though not necessarily in density or compactness (Ur, Karsgaard, and Oates 2007), Brak was thus broadly similar in scale to Warka during Adams's (1981) "Early/Middle Uruk" phase and was at least twice as large as the second-largest center in the southern alluvium at this time, site 1306. Moreover, the recent excavations in the main mound of Brak (area TW) show that substantial buildings existed at the site at this time and that elite inhabitants of the settlement had access to a variety of exotic imported resources (Oates et al. 2007).

Brak may have been exceptional but was not unique. Though less well documented, Nineveh is also likely to have been a sizeable settlement in the first half of the fourth millennium. Its most recent excavator, David Stronach (1994), gives a preliminary estimate in the 40-hectare range for the Late Chalcolithic period. Hawa is reported to have been at this time in the range of 30-plus hectares (Wilkinson and Tucker 1995), and Samsat (Algaze 1999) and Hamoukar (Ur 2002b) were about half that size.

Similarities in the scale of individual sites in northern and southern Mesopotamia, however, mask important differences in the overall complexity of the settlement systems of both areas as a whole throughout the fourth millennium. Outside of the areas and sites noted, large portions of the extensive northern Mesopotamian plains were characterized by largely undeveloped rural landscapes and lacked any evidence for indigenous hierarchies approaching urban scope at the time. Such was the case, for instance, for all of the Tigris Basin in southeastern Turkey (Algaze et al. 1991; Algaze 1999; Wilkinson 1990a, 1994), and much of Upper Euphrates both in Turkey and Syria (Algaze et al. 1994; Algaze 1999) away from selected Uruk enclaves near natural fords. A similar situation obtained in the Aleppo plains of Syria west of the Euphrates (Matthers 1981; Schwartz et al. 2000), and even in branches of the Upper

FIGURE 20. The High Mound at Tell Brak, as seen from the surrounding plain.

Khabur in Syria other than the Jagh Jagh (Wilkinson 2000b; Stein and Wattenmaker 1990).

Even where substantial Late Chalcolithic polities did exist in northern Mesopotamia, those polities hardly equaled their southern counterparts in complexity (but see Frangipane 1997 and Lamberg-Karlovsky 1999 for a contrary view). This conclusion can be inferred from comparisons of available survey data bearing on the density and hierarchical structure of settlement grids surrounding large settlements in both areas throughout the fourth millennium. Pending the full publication of the results of the Brak regional survey, the best data we have for the north are derived from systematically conducted and published surveys conducted by Tony Wilkinson in the environs of Tell al-Hawa in the Jezirah of Iraq, Tell Beydar in the Balikh Basin of northern Syria, and Samsat on the Upper Euphrates in southeastern Turkey. His results show that during the first half of the fourth millennium each of those sites was surrounded by a corona of uniformly small village or hamlet-sized sites (Algaze 1999; Wilkinson 1990a, 2000a; Wilkinson and Tucker 1995, fig. 35, *top*). This compares unfavorably with the more complex settlement grids of variously sized dependent settlements that surrounded contemporary (Early/Middle Uruk) urban centers in the south (Adams 1981; Johnson 1980; Pollock

2001). Further, surveys of the Hawa and Samsat environs show that while a more complex three-tiered settlement pattern structure did eventually appear in the vicinity of both mounds in the second half of the fourth millennium, in both cases it did so only *after* the onset of contacts with the Uruk world and not before (Algaze 1999; Wilkinson and Tucker 1995, fig. 35, *bottom*).

More important still is a further difference between northern and southern Mesopotamia. Substantial Late Chalcolithic settlements in the Upper Mesopotamian plains such as Nineveh, Hawa, Hamoukar, Brak, and Samsat had no peers within their own immediate regions, were situated in different drainages, and were separated from each other by hundreds of kilometers that could only be traversed overland. Thus, they were largely isolated from one another in terms of day-to-day contacts. This was not the case in the south, where multiple competing peer cities connected by waterways existed within relatively short distances and easy communication (via water) of each other.

In light of the above, it should not be surprising to find sharp differences in the overall developmental trajectories of both areas through the fourth millennium. Most salient among these is that in the north, unlike the south, the initial burst of growth and development was not sustained for long. Because of chronological problems and inadequate exposures, data from Nineveh, Hawa, and Samsat are unreliable on this point, but new research at Brak and Hamoukar shows that both settlements contracted substantially in the second half of the fourth millennium (Emberling et al. 1999, 25–26; Emberling 2002; Oates et al. 2007, 597; and Gibson et al. 2002; Ur 2002a, 2002b, respectively), just as the expansion of southern sites such as Warka reached their Late Uruk peak. This was likely not an isolated phenomenon limited to these two sites, as a similar demographic retrenchment is reflected at a regional scale in the recalibrated north Jazirah survey data noted above (fig. 19).

Available data are not precise enough to discern whether the reversal of long-standing demographic trends in Upper Mesopotamia and the contraction of the remarkable protourban settlement at Brak were caused by the intrusion of Late Uruk elements into the area and the site, as Emberling (2002) suggests, or whether the intrusion took advantage of a broader and unrelated endogenous process of decline. Either way, the contraction of the previously quite substantial settlement at Brak in the second half of the fourth millennium meant that urban centers in the alluvium of Late Uruk date were now significantly larger than all contemporary Late Chalcolithic polities in the Mesopotamian periphery. In fact, at 250 hectares, Late Uruk Warka was many times larger than any contemporary peripheral competitor. The fact that this huge differential developed at precisely the time of the maximum expansion of the Uruk colonial network is unlikely to be a mere coincidence.

Developments at Brak, Hamoukar, and the north Jazirah region during the second half of the fourth millennium appear representative of Upper Mesopotamia as a whole and clearly indicate the start of a centrifugal process that would culminate in the widespread ruralization of the northern plains by the end of the fourth and the transition to the third millennium. Surveys of portions of the Upper Mesopotamian plains within modern-day Iraq, Syria, and southeastern Turkey consistently show that sites across the area dating to the end of the fourth and beginning of the third millennia ("Kurban V" and "EBI" along the Euphrates and "Painted Ninevite V" along the Khabur and Tigris basins) were uniformly small villages or hamlets (data summarized in Algaze 1999, table 3). By this time, the few indigenous protourban centers that had existed in the preceding period had shriveled in size, and they would not recover their importance until the final phases of the Ninevite V period, sometime in the second quarter of the third millennium (Matthews 2003; G. Schwartz 1994; Weiss 1990; Wilkinson 1994).

In sharp contrast to the aborted protourban experiment of the north, urbanism in the south continued to flourish and expand not only though the Uruk period but throughout the fourth- and third-millennium transition (Jemdet Nasr/Early Dynastic I) as well (Adams 1981; Postgate 1986). In fact, by the first quarter of the third millennium, at a time when no urban centers are positively documented in the north, the urban spiral of the south continued unabated (Early Dynastic I): older sites such as Ur, Kish Nippur, Abu Salabikh, Warka, and possibly, Umma grew further, and new cities were founded across the alluvium, including most notably Lagash (al-Hiba) and Shuruppak (Fara; Adams 1981; H. Wright 1981b; Gibson 1972). Warka reached 600 hectares in extent at this point (Finkbeiner 1991) but this was no longer exceptional; al-Hiba situated at the edge of the easternmost marshes in the alluvium was almost as large (Carter 1985).

These differences matter considerably. As Hawley (1986, 18) has noted, the greater the number of individuals that comprise a coherent unit of social interaction, the greater the capacity of that society for collective action, and the greater the size discrepancy between two societies, the greater the difference in their overall capabilities. Larger societies are not mere aggregates of preexisting social units, unchanged except for scale, but rather are qualitatively different because increasing social size is multiplicative rather than additive in its consequences. The reasons for this will be outlined in the chapter that follows, which examines the contributions of increasing social scale and propinquity to the Sumerian takeoff as well as the new technologies of labor control and communication that ultimately made the takeoff possible.

CHAPTER EIGHT

The Synergies of Civilization

Propinquity and Its Consequences

Multiple repercussions would have arisen from the just-discussed differences in population density and distance between polities typical of southern Mesopotamia and areas on its periphery throughout the second half of the fourth millennium. These repercussions represent in effect socioevolutionary synergies that help explain why the earliest urban and state-level societies of southwestern Asia appeared in southern Mesopotamia and not elsewhere.

The first synergy arises from the greater concentration of polities that existed in the Mesopotamian alluvium throughout the seven-hundred-year or so duration of the Uruk period, as compared to neighboring areas. As Colin Renfrew and his colleagues (Renfrew and Cherry 1986) have repeatedly argued, the long-term presence of multiple polities within relatively short distances of each other invariably engenders important processes of competition, exchange, emulation, and technological innovation—processes that are archaeologically visible in changes in how commodities were produced in Mesopotamia of the Middle and Late Uruk periods. The impact of these mutually reinforcing processes has been explained by Robert Wright (2000, 165–68), who notes that in situations where antagonistic but mutually communicative polities exist, social and economic innovations that prove maladaptive in any one

society are likely to be weeded out more quickly than in less competitive settings. Conversely, innovations that prove advantageous are more
likely to spread quickly across the various polities in competition, thus
accelerating the pace of change of the system as a whole.

The second synergy arises from the greater proportion of the population of southern Mesopotamia that lived in towns and cities and their
immediate dependent hinterlands through the Uruk period, as compared to the more dispersed settlement typical for surrounding areas at
the time. This had several important consequences. The first is one that
logically follows from the models of urban growth discussed above and
was originally noted by Adam Smith ([1776] 1976 [I.i.1–3]): the assemblage of a critical mass of both producers and consumers is a necessary
precondition for the division of labor and resulting economies of scale.
Second, proximity between workers and employers lowers training costs
and increases labor flexibility (Malecki 1997, 49), thus providing southern institutions quicker access than their competitors to skilled workers/
builders/soldiers when needed.

Finally, increasing population density in towns and cities would have
compounded the natural advantages of the alluvial environment by further efficiencies in transportation and communication arising from the increasingly compact arrangement of the inhabitants of the area throughout
the fourth millennium. One such compounding efficiency falls squarely
in the realm of Cronon's created landscape and was provided by the start
of construction of minor irrigation canals across portions of the southern
alluvium through the Uruk period. Some of these manmade canals are
situated between the principal natural river channels that existed in the
fourth-millennium alluvium and can be inferred from the presence of
small, linearly arranged, villages dating to the Early, and, particularly,
the Middle and Late Uruk periods. Examples have been detected both
in the Warka (e.g., fig. 21) and Eridu-Ur areas (Pournelle 2003a, 11, figs.
2, 8, 2003b, 197, fig. 80; see also Wilkinson 2003b, 89; H. Wright 1981b,
326, fig. 18).

No doubt, the primary role of these small canals was enhancing agricultural production but, in addition, some of the canals served other productive uses as well. This is clear in the case of two groups of three small
mounds each, which were recorded by Wright in the plain between Ur
and Eridu. Arranged at right angles to each other, the mounds consisted
largely of heaps of ceramic and kiln slag. Wright suggests, plausibly, that

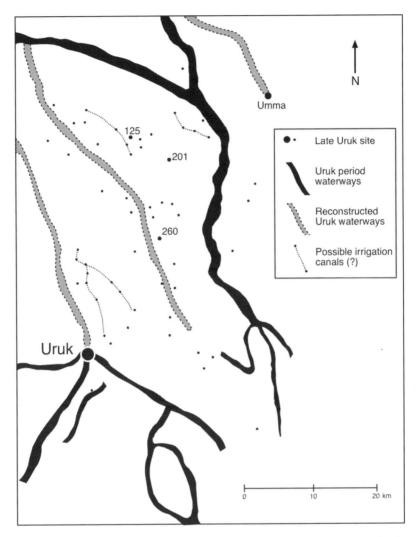

FIGURE 21. Location of Late Uruk period sites and principal waterways of the time in Warka survey area. Note the presence of linearly arranged villages, possibly indicating the existence of intervening man-made irrigation channels, in the alluvial plain between the main waterways of the time.

they represent the remains of specialized facilities for pottery manufacture lining the banks of two small intersecting manmade canals, no longer
visible, which facilitated the transport of potting clay, wood, and other
kindling for the kilns as well as the finished pots to and from nearby urban
towns (H. Wright 1981b, 326, fig. 26).

Whether agricultural or industrial in purpose, the small manmade
canals that started to dissect the alluvial plains of southern Iraq in the
Uruk period served to extend the natural transportation advantages of
the Mesopotamian landscape to areas beyond the natural flow of the
rivers. In so doing, they reinforced ongoing urbanization processes in
the alluvium. This effect, no doubt inadvertent, may be inferred from
studies that clearly link reductions in transport costs of agricultural commodities in traditional societies to the expansion of existing agricultural
boundaries and the movement of population into cities (Fujita and Krugman 1995, 520).

The third synergy is related to the preceding and arises from the conjuncture of two linked processes: the increasing density of the urban
landscape of Uruk Mesopotamia during the second half of the fourth
millennium and the expansion of Uruk colonies and colonists across the
Mesopotamian periphery at that time. In an earlier chapter I noted that
these processes are related in that both are partly explainable in terms
of evolving patterns of trade between southern Mesopotamian societies
and polities at their periphery. A further correlation between the two
processes may now be added: both involved a multiplication of the number of interpersonal interactions possible at every level of the Uruk world
system (Algaze 1993, 2005a). This included contacts between people in
ever closer physical proximity to each other within the growing cities
themselves, between city dwellers and peasants in surrounding dependent rural settlements, between the various independent but, no doubt,
mutually communicative urban polities that dotted the southern Mesopotamian lowlands through all phases of the Uruk period, between those
polities and associated colonial settlements abroad, and, lastly, between
Uruk colonists and the preexisting indigenous peoples in the areas into
which they intruded. As interpersonal interactions multiplied, information flow would have been enhanced. In turn, this radically improved the
possibility that unforeseen technological improvements and inventions
would emerge in Uruk cities and the Uruk cultural sphere as opposed to
elsewhere in southwest Asia.[1]

Why this should be so is explained by Gerhard Lenski (1979, 16), a sociologist, and Joel Mokyr (1996, 71), an economist. Employing arguments that elaborate on Myrdal's observation about the relationship between knowledge and innovation and that mirror, but in a narrower context, Spencer's and Jacobs's ideas about the inherently open-ended and self-amplifying nature of social evolution (chap. 3), Lenski and Mokyr note that technological innovation is essentially a process of recombining existing elements of information so that the rate of innovation is bound to rise as the store, diversity, and flow of information increase. At a minimum, this means that the potential for innovation in the Uruk world system must have increased at an exponential rate many times greater than the actual increase in the number of people in Uruk cities, dependencies, and colonies, or in the stock of information within early Sumerian culture itself. It is not simply that in a larger population there will be proportionally more people lucky enough or smart enough to come up with new ideas (Korotayev 2005, 80), but rather it is that with each doubling of the number of people in contact, the number of possible vectors of interaction is actually squared (Krugman n.d.).[2] In reality, however, the increase in possible new ideas would have been dramatically greater than the mere square of the number of people connected by the Uruk urban and colonial network because each person would have actually possessed multiple elements of information capable of recombination at different times, and because interaction may take place between multiple individuals or groups at any one time. Since these imponderables are beyond the reach of archaeological data, it is simply not possible to quantify with any degree of precision the actual increase in the probability of innovation within the Uruk world of the second half of the fourth millennium. However, it stands to reason that that increase would have more closely conformed to the parameters of a quadratic growth curve rather than to those of an exponential one (i.e., the number of individual *pairs* of elements of information potentially free to interact at any one time would rise foursquare with the squaring of their basic number).[3]

Technologies of the Intellect

As the web of interpersonal communications became increasingly dense in southern cities that, by the second half of the fourth millennium, were growing many times larger than peripheral population centers, and that were embedded in ever wider networks of relationships with foreign cultures as a result of the Uruk colonial network, the likelihood that unforeseen innovations would arise in southern cities and that advantageous inventions would be quickly diffused among them was greatly enhanced. In the Mesopotamian case, this does not appear to have taken the form of any significant new material technologies, although a plausible argument can be made for the invention of the wheel in southern cities at this time (see Bakker et al. 1999 for references and a discussion of available evidence). Rather, as noted earlier, when it came to material technologies, Uruk centers were better at adopting innovations made by others than they were in creating their own. Minimally, this applies to wool weaving, metal smelting, and the use of domestic donkeys as pack animals.

Where the Uruk world excelled, however, was in the realm of what the eminent social anthropologist Jack Goody (2000) has termed "technologies of the intellect" and what the equally notable sociologist, Michael Mann (1986), has termed "technologies of power." In the early Sumerian case, these "technologies" primarily consisted of new modes of social control, most notably new and more efficient ways to organize labor, increase economic production, and process and disseminate socially useful information. These interrelated "technologies of the mind," so to say, were as much a part of the emerging "created landscape" of early Mesopotamia as the new Uruk period irrigation canals and, once developed, arguably became the single most important source of developmental asymmetries between southern Mesopotamia and neighboring areas.

Without doubt, one of the most salient among the ideational innovations of the Uruk period was the *systematic* use of various types of dependent laborers receiving rations for the production of subsistence and sumptuary commodities and for building and agricultural activities. Borrowing a page from V. Gordon Childe, we may use the term "labor revolution" to describe this new way to reliably convert the muscle power of the many into socially useful commodities benefiting the few. Underlying this transformation was a conceptual shift in the way some categories of human labor were looked at in southern Mesopotamian societies. Southern elites came to view and use fully encumbered laborers in the same exploitive way that human societies, over the immediately preceding millennia, had viewed and used the labor of domesticated animals. This represents a new paradigm of the nature of social relations in human societies. I suspect that a comparable shift in the way in which human labor is perceived (and exploited) is integral to all cases of early state formation, but in reality we do not know exactly when this perceptual change occurred in the Mesopotamian case. All we can say for certain is that it had already taken place by the end of the Uruk period, as can be observed in the Archaic Texts. Scribal summaries detailing the composition of groups of foreign and nativeborn captives used as laborers describe them with age and sex categories identical to those used to describe state-owned herded animals, including various types of cattle and pigs (Englund 1995a, 1998, 176–81). Because these parallels are repeated in numerous texts, they cannot be explained away as either accidents or scribal idiosyncrasies. Rather, it would appear that the two classes of labor (captive "others" and domestic animals) were considered equivalent in the minds of Uruk scribes and in the eyes of the institutions that employed them. Early Near Eastern villagers domesticated plants and animals. Uruk urban institutions, in turn, domesticated humans.

While available documentation is not sufficient to quantify the contribution of encumbered workers to the economy of Uruk city-states with any degree of precision, it would appear that their number was significant (contra Weiss 1989). One recently published Archaic Text fragment (Uruk IV script), for instance, is a summary of several smaller individual accounts and refers to a total of 211 male and female captive laborers (Englund 1998, 178–79, fig. 66). Admittedly, there is no way to know how representative this tablet is. However, a crude but perhaps useful measure of the relative importance of slaves and encumbered workers to the portion of the Uruk economy that was being recorded by state scribes may be obtained by looking at the frequency of attestations of the pertinent signs for the various types of captive laborers in the Archaic Texts (5,820 complete and fragmentary tablets to date, including Uruk IV and III scripts). This can be done because the sumerologist Robert Englund (1998, 70–71, 176–78) has compiled a comprehensive list of every known use of each non-numerical sign in the Archaic Texts. His compilation shows that the second most frequently mentioned commodity in these texts was female slaves (SAL), with 388 attestations (for comparative purposes, barley, the most frequently noted commodity, had 496 attestations). To this must be added 113 attestations of laborers described as male slaves (KUR_a) who are often qualified further as being of foreign origin (i.e., from the mountains), and at least 159 attestations of laborers in temporary or permanent captivity described by

FIGURE 22. Uruk seal impressions depicting labor scenes. Agricultural labor (A, B, D, H); weaving (C); porters (E); filling of granaries (G, H). Not to scale.

means of the pictograms ERIM or SAG+MA, visually indicating that they represented some sort of yoked or shackled class of people (Nissen, Damerow, and Englund 1993, 74).

A less direct measure of the importance of encumbered labor to the Uruk economy may also be available. Many of the Archaic Texts record disbursements of textiles and grain to individuals and presumably represent rations given to some sort of fully or partly dependent workers (Englund 1998, 178–79, fig. 67). Again, the contribution of such workers to the Uruk economy cannot be gauged with any precision. However, if we presume that Nissen (1976) is correct in assuming that the ubiquitous beveled rim bowls (fig. 23) were used as ration bowls, their incidence in Uruk cities in amounts so large that they frequently defy quantification suggests that the number of workers receiving state rations in return for their labor in southern Mesopotamia during the second half of the fourth millennium must have been quite substantial indeed.

In practical terms, the perceptual shift in how human labor was conceptualized meant that Uruk elites probably had a greater variety of encumbered laborers at their disposal than did their northern counterparts, that they could extract more energy from those laborers, and that they were better able to move them around as needed at little cost—an ability often identified as a key factor in economic development (Krugman 1995, 19). More important, it also means that Uruk elites could organize laborers in nontraditional ways so as to take advantage of increases in productivity and other economies of scale arising from (1) the specialized production of commodities and (2) the integration of procurement, production, and distribution activities in related industries (forward and backward linkages) under a single organizational structure.

The available archaeological record does provide evidence for these organizational quantum leaps. The start of specialized production of commodities, for instance, can be directly inferred from the well-documented shift to standardized ceramics that is observable throughout the Uruk period (Nissen 1976). The moldmade beveled rim bowls already noted are only one of the many mass-produced pottery types that become typical at this time. The overwhelming portion of the Uruk ceramic repertoire, in fact, consists of vessels made on the fast wheel by specialized producers. Comparable changes based on task specialization and standardization can also be seen in the way other commodities were produced at the time. As noted earlier, minimally this includes how wool was processed (Englund 1998; Green 1980; Nissen 1986) and metals cast (Nissen 2000).

Attempts to integrate economically related activities under a single organizational structure, in turn, are also inferable from available data. Just over twenty years ago, the archaeologist Rene Dittmann (1986) published an innovative study of the iconography of Uruk glyptic from Susa in which he sought to gain insights into how labor was organized and controlled at the time by plotting the associations and superimpositions of images within the corpus of sealings and sealed devices from the site.

FIGURE 23. Uruk beveled rim bowl from Chogha Mish, Iran.

His basic premises were (1) that the glyptic represented the bureaucratic records of state administration in Susa, (2) that scenes depicting laborers performing specific productive activities stood for discrete organizational groupings recognized by the city's administrators, (3) that images depicting specific individuals and distinctive buildings associated with those activities stood for the institutions managing their labor and reaping its rewards, and (4) that the hierarchical relationship between the labor groupings and institutions alluded to in the seal narratives can be inferred when different seals are impressed on single devices, with later superimposed impressions reflecting the actions of higher level authorities.

Preliminarily, two broad sets of correlations are immediately apparent from Dittmann's work. At Susa, scenes depicting ideologically charged activities, such as combat and the performance of religious rituals, most commonly associate with a larger-than-life male figure typically thought to represent a "priest-king" or "city ruler," while scenes depicting various types of economic activities, such as agricultural labor and the storage of agricultural products, the transport of commodities, the herding of caprids and bovines, and the processing of wool and dairy products are most commonly associated, in turn, with buildings with niched façades, generally thought to represent temples and/or palaces on the basis of parallels with excavated architecture. It is this latter linkage that is immediately pertinent to the present discussion. More specifically, the visual association in the sealed devices of particular institutional symbols and specific commodity production sequences, for instance, those depicting herding and the various stages of textile production (fig. 14), can plausibly be interpreted to mean that the benefits accruing from the vertical integration of sequential economic activities were well understood by whatever controlling institution or institutions were represented in the seals by the niched structures.

The second ideational technology appearing in Uruk cities by the second half of the fourth millennium is less ambiguous. Closely related to the changes in commodity production and labor organization just discussed, it consisted of new forms of record keeping that were exponentially more expressive than the simpler systems used by contemporary societies elsewhere and that were capable of conveying knowledge across space and time with much greater efficiency than any and all rival systems in existence at the time. This contention is borne out by a comparison of the very different glyptic, reckoning, and writing practices that were in use contemporaneously in southern Mesopotamian cities and peripheral polities during the second half of the fourth millennium.

Starting with the glyptic. Seal impressions on clay have traditionally accompanied the movement of goods across the Near East starting already in prehistoric times and were also used from the very beginning as an oversight mechanism for stored goods in the area. They served as a crude means of accounting identifying the senders of the commodities to which they were attached, the individuals or groups responsible for the storerooms that they sealed, or the individuals or functionaries disbursing stored commodities (Fiandra 1979; von Wickede 1990). Glyptic continued to be used in similar fashion well into the historic periods, and a substantial corpus of evidence exists for both early Sumerian and peripheral societies of the second half of the fourth millennium. For southern Mesopotamia, pertinent evidence is provided by thousands of cylinder seal impressions, and a much smaller number of actual seals, recovered in Uruk sites in southern Iraq and Khuzeztan and in Uruk colonial settlements in northern Iraq, northern Syria, and southeastern Anatolia (Amiet 1961, 1972; Boehmer 1999; Delougaz and Kantor 1996; Pittman 2001; Strommenger 1980). A glyptic corpus of comparable size but consisting mostly of stamp seal impressions and seals is available from a handful of Late Chalcolithic sites across the north and northwest periphery of Mesopotamia, most notably Arslan Tepe in the Anatolian

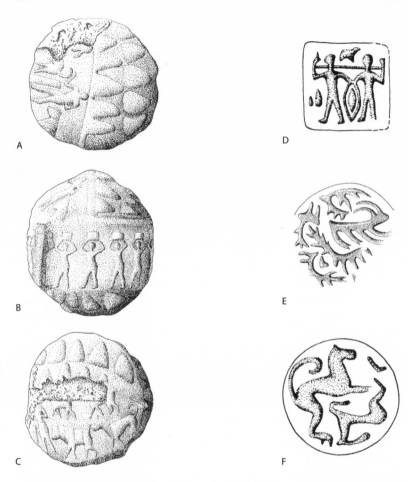

FIGURE 24. Middle/Late Uruk period impressed ball from Chogha Mish, Iran, showing the impressions of three different cylinder seals on its surface (A–C). Various Late Chalcolithic stamp seal impressions from Arslan Tepe VIA (D–F). Not to scale.

highlands (Ferioli and Fiandra 1983 [1988]), and Tepe Gawra in the Zagros piedmont of northern Iraq (Rothman 1994, 2002).

Comparing these two bodies of contemporary glyptic data is instructive. Immediately striking is the fact that owing to their larger size and lateral orientation, the cylinder seals used by southern polities in the second half of the fourth millennium lent themselves better to the expression of complex linear visual narratives than the smaller stamp seals of various sizes and shapes used by contemporary polities in the north.

Uruk glyptic was thus engineered to convey much more—and better organized—information than the glyptic used by their northern counterparts, a point made by Nissen (1977) many years ago and recently reargued in greater detail by Schmandt-Besserat (2007). Equally important, the numerous mid- and late-fourth-millennium sealings found discarded at various locations within Late Chalcolithic levels at Arslan Tepe (periods VII and VIA) commonly bear the impression or impressions of but a single seal (e.g., fig. 24d–24f). A similar case obtains in the contemporary Late Chalcolithic levels of Tepe Gawra (Levels IX–VIII). At both sites, impressions of more than one seal on a single sealing surface are exceptional (Fiandra 1994, 168; M. Frangipane, personal communication, 1999; M. Rothman, personal communication 1999). In contrast, as noted earlier in reference to Susa, contemporary glyptic procedures in Middle and Late Uruk cities and their colonial outposts regularly exhibit the imprints of multiple seals, particularly in the case of balls and bullae (Delougaz and Kantor 1996; e.g., fig. 24a–24c). This difference in sealing practice decisively reversed earlier trends toward increasing complexity in glyptic use that had in fact favored the north until the first half of the fourth millennium (Oates et al. 2007, 593) and is relevant because the number of impressions of different seals in a single sealing gives us a glimpse of the number of agents and, possibly, witnesses involved in whatever transaction is being recorded. In addition, if Nissen (1977) and Dittmann (1986) are correct in seeing the seals as encoding information about the hierarchical ranking of specific authorizing individuals and the institutions they worked for, then the much greater frequency of complex devices with multiple impressions of different superimposed seals in Middle and Late Uruk centers can be taken as a proxy for the greater number of levels of bureaucratic control and accountability that existed within those centers, compared with the then much smaller northern sites (Pittman 1993).

An examination of ways of recording and disseminating information that transcend mere iconography reveals even more glaring disparities. Particularly telling is the fact that no Late Chalcolithic site has yet provided evidence for the existence of indigenous systematic reckoning and writing systems comparable in their complexity to those that evolved in southern Mesopotamian Uruk sites during the second half of the fourth millennium. This process started in earnest in the later part of the Middle Uruk period and the earlier part of the Late Uruk period (ca. 3400/3300 BC) with the introduction, in seemingly quick succession, of

hollow seal-impressed balls filled with tokens and seal-impressed numerical notation tablets (figs. 24a–24c and 22b and 25, respectively).
The Late Chalcolithic counterpart to these southern devices are but a
single unimpressed numerical notation tablet from "northern Middle
Uruk" contexts at Tell Brak (fig. 26b) and a few rounded tallying slabs
found in an indigenous administrative complex at Arslan Tepe (period
VIA). The slabs (fig. 26a) have evenly sized indentations on their otherwise blank surfaces, presumably representing numbers, and apparently
served as mnemonic devices (Liverani 1983 [1988], figs. 1–4).

Because the Tell Brak or Arslan Tepe devices were not impressed
with seals, they carried only a fraction of the information that could be
transmitted by the more elaborate token-filled balls and numerical notation tablets of southern societies at this time, which overwhelmingly
relied on complex combinations of numbers and superimposed layers of
iconic images (seal impressions). Moreover, unlike the more complex
southern systems, the mnemonic devices of Late Chalcolithic societies
were incapable of communicating any information beyond their immediate institutional and temporal context.

The divergence in the efficiency and complexity of the accounting
and information processing systems possessed by groups in each of the

FIGURE 25. Seal impressed Late Uruk period numerical notation tablet from Chogha Mish.
Scale indicated.

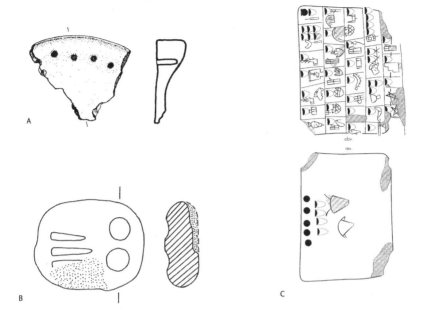

FIGURE 26. Late Chalcolithic numerical mnemonic device from Arslan Tepe VIA (A); un-impressed Late Chalcolithic numerical notation tablet from Tell Brak (B); and Late Uruk pictographic tablet from Uruk/Warka [cattle account: Uruk IV script] (C). Not to scale.

two areas (and, by inference, the differences in the scale and complexity of their economies) becomes particularly marked by the very end of the Uruk period (ca. 3200/3100 BC) with the appearance in the south of the earliest tablets with pictographic writing (i.e., the Archaic Texts in Uruk IV script: approximately 1,900 out of approximately 5,820 Archaic tablets and fragments [Englund 1998, 86]; e.g., fig. 26c). This took place contemporaneously with the Arslan Tepe VIA remains, as shown by available radiocarbon dates (Wright and Rupley 2001). Almost all of these pictographic tablets were simple accounts recording flows of commodities. They thus served the same basic function as the seal-impressed lumps of clay available to Late Chalcolithic societies and as the more elaborate impressed balls and numerical tablets of earlier phases of the Uruk period in the south. Even though these tablets are not fully comprehensible to us (Damerow 2006), they are profoundly revolutionary in terms of what came before. By using pictograms to represent objects amenable to illustration and as rebuses (singly or in combination) to denote abstract concepts and verbs not amenable to concrete depiction, these tablets were now capable of recording commodity flows of significance to controlling institutions in a manner that allowed for the expression of nuances of time, location, persons involved, administrative action effected, and that was fully transmissible through space and time within the confines of early Sumerian culture. As Robert Englund (1998, 2004) has noted, even the earliest pictographic tablets show that by the end of the Uruk period southern scribes had developed the ability to abstract and summarize detailed data about collections and disbursements of goods and labor in a form usable by themselves at a later time, by higher-level supervisory officials at any time, and by later generations of similarly trained bureaucrats. The significance of this development was succinctly summarized by Michael Hudson (2004), who notes that "[b]y quantifying ... resource flows, accounting became a management tool for forward planning" (see also Steinkeller 2004). Planning, in turn, allowed Late Uruk urban administrators to deploy available labor and resources so as to maximize their future revenues and power. In this sense, writing was a key component of the "labor revolution" of Uruk Mesopotamia alluded to above. To the extent that it was so, the renowned anthropologist Claude Lévi-Strauss (1964, 292) was disturbingly correct when he noted that "[t]he primary function of writing, as a means of communication, is to facilitate the enslavement of other human beings."[4]

But the importance of writing in early Mesopotamian civilization went much further than accounting for resources at hand and planning for future gain. A small but critically important proportion of the earliest Archaic Texts consists of thematically and conceptually arranged word lists ("Lexical Texts") that, no doubt, served as scribal training exercises. These compilations provide unique insights about many aspects of the material, social, and ideological world of early Sumerian urban dwellers that are not generally referenced elsewhere (Englund 1998, 2004). More to the point, they presuppose the existence of a formally constituted and self-perpetuating scribal profession (and class?) dedicated to the transmission of knowledge across generations. Aided by scribes, early Sumerian elites and institutions would have had better and more detailed access to the accumulated knowledge of earlier generations than their rivals in neighboring areas, where the lack of comparably accurate and efficient forms of communication systems meant that the past would only be known through fallible human memories and ever mutable oral traditions (Goody 2000).

Bluntly put, this meant that by the final phase of the Uruk period, the web of interpersonal communications across the Uruk world was being thickened by interaction not only between the living but also, and for the first time in human history, between the living and the dead. Equally important, because writing is a form of "cognitive scaffolding" or "external memory" that permits individuals to perform cognitive tasks above and beyond those normally possible by the unassisted brain (Mouck 2004; Lévi-Strauss 1964, 291), the presence of a scribal class in Uruk cities guaranteed that, as a group, Sumerian elites would have been more likely than their peers elsewhere to possess the problem-solving tools and institutional memory that are needed to efficiently integrate larger populations and more diverse territorial realms, to successfully react to recurring environmental perturbations and social threats, and to profitably recognize and take advantage of opportunities for gain arising in a more unpredictable manner.[5]

There is no mystery to understanding why a scribal tradition first appeared in the context of early Mesopotamian cities that were fast-growing in demographic density and socioeconomic diversity. Studies of modern cities show that expanding population density commonly leads to a disproportionately large expansion in the size of communicative sectors of the managerial institutions in those cities. The reasons for this are explained by John Kasarda (1974), a sociologist, who notes that in human societies, as in biological organisms, increasing size exacerbates particular system problems and often results in disproportionate growth in sectors serving to solve those problems. According to Kasarda, the most critical problem faced by large-scale social systems is articulating communications between their parts. For this reason, as they grow increasingly large and diverse, complex societies divert an ever larger proportion of their human resources to collecting, processing, and transmitting information. Though Kasarda never considered the possibility that his insight could be applicable to premodern urbanism, the emergence of a scribal profession in the Uruk period is itself evidence that the managerial multiplier Kasarda identified for modern cities was at work in fourth-millennium southern Mesopotamia as well, where cumulative innovations in the way knowledge was manipulated provided the nascent city-states of the time with what, arguably, became one of the most important competitive advantages they possessed over contemporary polities elsewhere, in which comparable breakthroughs in accounting, accountability, classification, and access to information (current and past) appear to have been absent.

The Urban Revolution Revisited

Just as there is a connection between increasing population size and the likelihood that a culture will develop formal mechanisms and institutions to ensure efficient communications, increases in the efficiency of communication, once effected, themselves feed the evolving urban process. Economic geographers have implicitly understood this since the time of Adam Smith ([1776] 1976, 13–15 [I.i.1–3]), who observed that gains in the efficiency of communication always act as a spur for economic specialization and growth in human societies. At the same time, Smith also noted that equally important gains in economic specialization and differentiation could be obtained from reductions in mobility costs arising from advances in transportation efficiency. It follows logically from Smith's insights that human settlements will naturally tend to grow to the maximum size afforded by the technologies for communication and transportation possessed by their population at any one time and, further, that the introduction or development of new technologies to convey commodities and information will result in additional settlement expansion (Hawley 1986, 7). The reasons for this are explained by Amos Hawley (1986, 65–66), noted above, who observed that social units engaged in specialized functions are necessarily spread over space, which naturally decreases the efficiency of information flow and increases the cost of value-added production and services. Thus, increases in communication efficiency and reductions in mobility costs always result in gains in economic specialization and differentiation—processes that, as noted earlier, are central to the origins and growth of urban societies. It is not difficult to see how the Sumerian takeoff relates to the processes described by Smith and Hawley: it involved both enhanced communication efficiency in the form of new reckoning and writing systems and reductions in mobility costs as population across southern Mesopotamia became increasingly concentrated, production facilities consolidated, and production itself standardized.

A further source of savings in mobility costs must also be considered in any attempt to evaluate why the takeoff happened when it did: improvements in the facility for overland movement in and out of the alluvium in the Middle–Late Uruk periods as a result of the introduction of domesticated donkeys and, possibly, wheeled carts (Bakker et al. 1999). While these new transportational technologies were shared by a wide cross section of contemporary ancient Near Eastern societies (Kohl 2001) in the mid- and late fourth millennium, they must have affected southern Uruk polities with disproportionate intensity. This is explained by the process of circular and cumulative causation, which implies that the adoption of a new technology, for instance, a new mode of transport, will affect societies with varying developmental trajectories very differently, depending on when exactly the technology is introduced in the cycle of mutual determinations that always exists between population growth, market size, innovation, and increasing returns from new economies of scale.

Against this background, it is easy to understand why the domestication of donkeys, which, when used in caravans, are capable of carrying substantially more cargo overland over much greater distances than unassisted humans, must have had a greater impact on Uruk societies than on neighboring Late Chalcolithic polities. Only in the south did advances in overland travel complement both the natural advantages in ease of transport of the area and the compounding of those advantages by the start of construction of modest manmade canals (fig. 21). Moreover, and more importantly, only in the south were both of these processes reinforced and compounded further by advances in commodity production using task-specialized labor and in the ability to transmit information accurately across time and space. Thus, southern societies would have been better situated than their competitors to profitably exploit the new opportunities for export provided by donkey caravans in the fourth millennium.

Some circumstantial evidence for the role of donkeys in Uruk trade actually exists. In a recent synthesis of available faunal evidence for equid remains in Upper Mesopotamia from the fourth and third millennia BC, Emmanuelle Vila (2006), a paleozoologist, notes that Uruk sites in northern Syria (e.g., El Kowm-2, Sheikh Hassan, Mashnaqa) generally exhibit higher relative frequencies of equid bones in their faunal assemblages than later Early Bronze Age sites in the same area, and this applies not only to immediately post-Uruk levels in small Upper Mesopotamian sites but late third-millennium levels in fully urban centers in the area as well, such as Tell Chuera, for example. She notes further that the majority of those bones can be identified as domestic donkeys (*Equus asinus*). A similar pattern appears to exist in Uruk sites on the Turkish side of the border, for instance, at Zeytinlibahçe Höyük, some 5 kilometers downstream from Hacınebi. Preliminary analysis of the faunal remains from the earliest Uruk level yet found at Zeytinlibahçe (two rooms forming part of a storehouse of Middle Uruk date built using riemchen bricks) shows that asses appear to have been unusually common at the time.[6] The site's excavator, Marcela Frangipane, interprets this as reflecting "an emphasis on trading or movements of people and/ or goods" (Frangipane et al. 2004, 40, figs. 11–12). In my opinion, this explanation is likely correct and is applicable not only to the Zeytinlibahçe data but also to the otherwise difficult-to-explain equid data found by Vila in Uruk outposts in Syria.

Be that as it may, by making it possible for southern traders and colonists to travel northward in large numbers while carrying loads of trade items for the first time, donkey caravans added fuel to a cybernetic process of economic development that had already been underway for centuries in southern Mesopotamia but that had until then been based largely on intraregional trade.

CHAPTER NINE

Conclusions:
The Mesopotamian Conjuncture

As by means of water-carriage a more extensive market is opened to every sort of industry than what land-carriage alone can afford it, so it is upon the sea coast, and along the banks of navigable rivers, that industry of every kind naturally begins to subdivide and improve itself, and it is frequently not till a long time after that those improvements extend themselves to the inland parts of the country. —Adam Smith, *The Wealth of Nations*

If anything is clear from the foregoing chapters it is that we must acknowledge that processes of social evolution are always the result of both regional and transregional patterns of interaction (Kohl 1987b). A case in point is provided by the roughly parallel development of early state and urban polities in Upper and Southern Mesopotamia during the first half of the fourth millennium BC. Because complex social systems can neither exist nor evolve in isolation, and because there is in fact substantial evidence for contacts between these two areas going as far back as the Neolithic period (H. Wright 1969; Connan 1999), this lockstep development is best explained as the result of processes of competitive emulation fueled by interaction between otherwise independent polities in the two regions. In this, the formative phases of Mesopotamian civilization now appear similar to those of Mesoamerica with its multiple but distinct regional traditions of social complexity (the Maya, Monte Alban, Teotihuacan) developing independently but roughly in tandem as a result of comparable socioevolutionary processes made widespread by extensive long-distance contacts (Marcus 1998).[1]

When seen against this background, the Sumerian takeoff and the intrusion of Middle and Late Uruk settlers into parts of Upper Mesopotamia represent, in fact, a sharp reversal of the preexisting historical trajectory of northern societies. If we are to understand why the balance of urbanization, social complexity, and power in the ancient Near East shifted so decisively to the southern alluvial lowlands of Mesopotamia in the second half of the fourth millennium BC, we must delineate the sequence of mutually reinforcing necessary and sufficient conditions that came together in the south at that time but were absent (in the aggregate) from neighboring contemporary social groups. Only then can we begin to elucidate why the Sumerian takeoff took place at all, why it occurred when it did, and why comparable developments failed to materialize in Upper Mesopotamia, an area that only a few centuries before had appeared as poised for an urban takeoff as the south or elsewhere in southwest Asia.

Early on the stage was set by advantages in productivity, reliability, and ease of transport inherent to the "natural landscape" of southern Mesopotamia. Absent in the aggregate from neighboring regions, these advantages can be considered as the initial set of necessary conditions in the conjuncture. No doubt, the most important of these advantages was ease of transport. As the economist Pierre Desrochers (2001b, 31) insightfully notes, "[T]he overwhelming fact about past trends is that a general reduction in the transportation costs of both goods and information has always tended to encourage geographical concentration rather than discourage it."

The divergent developmental sequences of southern and northern Mesopotamia through the fourth millennium are very much a case in point. The centrality of transport in structuring this divergence becomes clear when we contrast the two areas at the time and the locational circumstances of the main settlements in each area. Those of the south, as already noted, invariably lined the banks of waterways. So, for that matter, did many of the known large Late Chalcolithic settlements across the north. Nineveh, Brak, and Samsat, for instance, are all situated along the principal navigable waterways crisscrossing the area. Each controls a historical fording place where the principal east-west overland routes across Upper Mesopotamia intersect the rivers (Algaze 1993 [2005a]). Paradoxically, however, water transport, the same factor that fostered interaction between early centers in the closely intertwined fourth-millennium fluvial system of the south, limited interaction in the north, where the major waterways were both quite distant from each other and too deeply incised for multiple channels to exist or to allow for the construction of artificial canals linking the cities to their hinterlands.

The vast intervening plains across the north also impeded both interaction and agglomeration, at least in comparison to the south. The historian Edward Whiting Fox (1971, 25) reminds us quite clearly that geography matters in history, because the units of economic organization cannot be larger than the radius of practical transport prevailing at any one time, and because that economic radius will, more often than not, limit the extent of regular social contact. Thus, even after the introduction of donkeys and carts in the mid-fourth millennium, limitations inherent to overland travel across the Upper Mesopotamian plains imposed enduring natural limits to population agglomeration away from the rivers (Wilkinson 1995). Whereas geography in the south both permitted and encouraged linearly arranged agglomerations based on boat and barge transport, and whereas irrigation agriculture provided the practical means to support such enlarged populations, the geography and rainfall patterns of the northern plains encouraged population dispersal instead so as to maximize the amount of territory under cultivation. Thus, without a way to defeat the friction of overland travel by means of more efficient communication, *in the aggregate,* the geography of the northern plains naturally tended to foster smaller agglomerations than were possible in the south, and significantly more dispersed ones as well.

Under these circumstances, a critical mass of compact and closely interacting peer polities such as existed throughout the Uruk period in alluvial Mesopotamia failed to form across the hinterlands of northern Mesopotamia as a whole in the fourth millennium. Absent this critical mass, processes of intraregional exchange, competition, and emulation would have been less likely to occur in northern Mesopotamia than was the case in contemporary southern Mesopotamian societies. At the same time, however, northern societies would also have had both less need and less ability than their southern counterparts to engage in bulk external trade with its many social ramifications. Less need because Upper Mesopotamian societies were generally situated in areas closer to the principal bulk resources they needed, such as timber for instance, which could therefore be obtained locally without substantial organization. And less ability, because the means of transportation available to northern societies away from the rivers simply did not lend themselves to the cost-effective movement of anything other than low-bulk, high-value exotics. In contrast, for southern societies, the rivers provided a particularly efficient mode of channeling and distributing both episodic trade in exotics and recurring transfers of bulk commodities.

Accordingly, the initial protourban social systems of the north were not likely to expand significantly in size beyond a certain threshold, because of the "tyranny of friction" or, when they did, as in the thus far unique case of Brak, they were not likely to endure. Nor were the early northern centers likely to significantly enhance their productivity relative to that possible in the south because they lacked the critical mass of closely packed populations to permit much specialization of labor or to encourage the development of new, more complex technologies of communication, such as proved fundamental for the Sumerian takeoff. This left an indelible mark on the historical development of the north because those types of social synergies were in fact precisely what was required in order for northern social systems to successfully circumvent the inherent constraints of their geographical framework.

Indigenous city-states comparable (in complexity, if not always in scale) to those that had thrived in the south since the fourth millennium did emerge across the Upper Mesopotamian plains sometime just before the middle of the third millennium (Weiss 1990; Wilkinson 1994), eight hundred years or so after the Sumerian takeoff. This time lag reflects the operation of processes outlined by Adam Smith in the epigram that introduces this chapter, whereby economic activity and its multipliers first arise in coastal/riverine areas as a result of advantages provided by cheap transport and only at a later time diffuse into inland areas where higher transportation costs prevail. Indeed, it was only by adopting forms of economic production and social organization derived from southern models and, eventually, by embracing full-fledged southern-style writing systems (Postgate 1988), that Upper Mesopotamian polities of the Early Bronze Age were able to marshal the organizational efficiencies needed to overcome the natural friction of overland travel across their hinterlands that had prevented their Late Chalcolithic predecessors from forming enduring regionally organized societies such as emerged in the south.

Stated simply, the initial—and precocious—experiment with urbanism in Upper Mesopotamia represented by sites such as Brak in the first half of the fourth millennium ultimately failed because urbanism in the north was only possible as a created landscape: it became viable only as a result of innovations in communication and labor control created elsewhere. In southern Mesopotamia, on the contrary, urbanism was a logical outgrowth of natural and socially created synergies that compounded and reinforced each other from the very beginning.

In the end it turns out that the sociologist Karl Wittfogel (1957), who initially noted the close correlation that exists between early Old World civilizations and major river systems, was right but for the wrong reasons. Rivers were indeed central to the development of early Mesopotamian civilization, but not so much as a source of irrigation water, as he argued, but rather because of their role as conduits of transportation for subsistence commodities, building materials, necessary resources, and sumptuary goods. After all, in Mesopotamia as along other old world river basins where pristine civilizations formed, cities emerged not at random along the courses of the rivers but rather in fertile areas downstream, where a minimal threshold of access to local agricultural resources was ensured and where, more importantly, transport costs were lowest and access to diverse resources within the river's watershed and information about them was highest (Bairoch 1988, 12). This is not a particularly new conclusion in the context of ancient Mesopotamia. Forty years ago, in his study of canals and irrigation in Umma at the time of the Ur III Empire, the assyriologist H. Sauren (1966, 36) concluded that the role of canals in allowing for efficient transportation within the empire was as important as their role as conduits of irrigation water. Sauren's conclusion is as valid to discussions of the origins of ancient Mesopotamian cities as it is to the analysis of early Mesopotamian imperial administration. Though there are exceptions (mostly so-called disembedded capitals established de novo by political fiat), the importance of rivers and waterborne transport to the emergence and growth of many urban societies is elegantly explained by Felipe Fernández-Armesto (2001, 182), a historian, who notes "civilizations of scale can only be built with concentrated resources. Resources can be concentrated only by means of good communications. And for almost the whole of history, humankind has depended for long-range communications on waterways."

And yet, natural advantages derived from geography and environment do not explain in and of themselves the crystallization of early Mesopotamian civilization—or that of any other pristine civilization for that matter. In the final analysis, environmental and geographical factors are only permissive, not prescriptive. Whether individuals and groups react to environmental changes and take advantage of geographical possibilities, and how they do so, are always constrained by culturally determined perceptions of opportunities and threats at any one time. These, in turn, are partly shaped by available technologies and capital (both human and material). Moreover, the present is also shaped from the past by inherently unpredictable accidents and innovations that add an element of indeterminacy to any attempt at historical prognostication (or explanation). For these reasons, history displays a wide range of results of the interaction of societies and their environment, and this range can only become greater and more unpredictable as the density and intensity of social interactions grows in increasingly complex societies. Nonetheless, environment and geography do constitute important selective pressures that often impose an important measure of directionality on human affairs, as Edward Fox (1971, 1989) has repeatedly and persuasively warned us. The reason for this is explained by Joel Mokyr (1990), who notes that environmental factors commonly act as "focusing devices" that limit the range of options that are perceived as viable by individual societies at any one time and that powerfully influence the direction that those societies take in their search for technological innovations.

Against this interplay between indeterminacy and directionality, the natural advantages of the southern Mesopotamian landscape merely provided a backdrop wherein some social responses became more likely than others. In light of the diversified but dispersed resources prevalent in southern Mesopotamia throughout the late fifth and fourth millennia BC, and given the naturally reduced cost of mobility in the area, one of the most probable such responses was for pre- and protohistoric elite individuals and groups to specialize in the production of a limited number of commodities for which they had comparative advantage owning to their location within the alluvial environmental mosaic of the late fifth and fourth millennia and to engage in trade with differently specialized local rivals from relatively early on. By the same token, the absence of important necessary resources from the Mesopotamian environment, most notably roofing-grade timber and metals, also made it likely that early southern elites would seek to engage in trade with foreign counterparts in areas where such resources occurred naturally. This, however, had to await, first, the accumulation of surpluses, human capital, and productive capacity accruing from the earlier stage of largely internal exchange, and second, the domestication of the donkey, which both enlarged the geographical horizon of southern elites and physically enabled them to engage in bulk export trade for the first time in their history and to establish colonies in far away strategic locations of the Mesopotamian periphery.

We can only speculate about the historical consequences of these early patterns of trade, but I would suggest that their self-amplifying social ramifications would have created a situation in which the parallel development of multiple competing independent centers was a likely outcome, which may well help explain why competing city-states continued to be the most characteristic political formation of alluvial Mesopotamia long after the end of the Uruk period. However, while trade may have been a powerful force underlying the emergence of such centers, it was by no means the only form of interaction between them, as is shown by the fact that martial themes, the taking of prisoners, and even scenes depicting sieges of fortified cities are repeatedly depicted in Uruk iconography (e.g., Amiet 1961, pls. 46–47, nos. 659–61; Boehmer 1999, fig. XXVI, pls. 11–27; Brandes 1979, 117–73, pls. 1–13; Delougaz and Kantor 1996, 146–47, pls. 150–51). Indeed, it stands to reason that as external trade grew in importance through the Uruk period, competition over access to trade routes would have increased. In an earlier chapter I argued that competition between the emerging city-states of Uruk Mesopotamia for access to external resources may well explain many aspects of the "Uruk expansion" into southwestern Iran and various parts of Upper Mesopotamia. Here, it may be added that such competition was likely also a prime source of conflict within the alluvium itself, as probably depicted in the glyptic. This matters because, as already noted, political fragmentation, economic competition, and warfare often promote accelerated social change. A case in point in suggested by Patricia Crone (1989, 161), who argues that political fragmentation and interpolity competition were crucial for what she perceives as the unique vitality of developmental rates in European polities of the late medieval and early modern eras as compared with those characteristic of other areas of the world at that time: "Far from being stultified by imperial government, Europe was to be propelled forward by constant competition between its component parts." Such is likely to have been the case in ancient Mesopotamia as well.

In any event, in turning to trade and colonization earlier and more intensively than neighboring societies, elite individuals and institutions in alluvial Mesopotamia surely had no understanding of the long-term developmental consequences of the actions they were undertaking. Rather, trade simply became an efficient way to accomplish in the southern context what elites naturally want to do in all human societies, namely, sanction existing social inequalities, extend the amounts and varieties of commodities and labor at their disposal, and increase their political power.

In this light, the Sumerian takeoff became, in effect, an unanticipated consequence of long-term trade patterns that differentially favored the development of societies in the alluvial lowlands of Mesopotamia over polities in neighboring regions. This trade was inherently asymmetrical in its impact because, with some exceptions, it involved the import of raw or only partially modified resources from highland areas of the ancient Near East that required further processing before they could be incorporated into the economies of southern cities and the export of multistage value-added manufactured commodities from those cities. At first, the trade was spurred by differences in productivity that favored the south and that were largely the result of geographical and environmental factors—what Cronon refers to as the "natural landscape." Once a significant measure of exchange was in place, however, further conditions expanding and compounding the competitive advantages of Sumerian societies now arose mostly from the "created landscape" ensuing from the social ramifications of the trade. One such condition was provided by synergies derived from the greater density of population in rapidly urbanizing Uruk polities possessing ever larger markets and ever larger and more diverse pools of skilled and unskilled labor, usable, as needed, for commodity production, or building or agricultural activities, as soldiers engaged in warfare against local rivals, or as colonists and emissaries sent to faraway lands.

In turn, synergies derived from greater density and larger labor pools were compounded and expanded by the only sufficient conditions in the conjuncture: socially created organizational efficiencies delivering ever increasing returns to scale from an ever more specialized labor force and allowing for exponentially more efficient and more accurate ways of conveying information across space and time. More than anything else, these social innovations, which took place, no doubt, within the context of palace and temple "households" controlling substantial resources and labor, explain why complex, regionally organized city-states emerged earlier in southern Iraq than elsewhere in the Near East, or the world.

Early Sumerian Societies:
A Research Agenda

There is both challenge and opportunity in misfortune. Between the Iranian Revolution, the Iran-Iraq War, and the two Gulf Wars and their aftermath, the extensive regional survey programs in southern Iraq and southwestern Iran came to a premature end, and ongoing archaeological work by both local and foreign teams in Iraq and southwestern Iran has, for all practical purposes, also stopped. This is thus an ideal time to take stock of what already has been done in the core of the Uruk world and, where possible, to rethink the data through new interpretative models. This push has already begun. Central to this effort is the publication of the final reports of early German excavations at Warka, which is proceeding with admirable speed as part of the series Ausgrabungen in Uruk-Warka Endberichte. At the same time, a number of Belgian (Gasche and Tanret 1998) and American (Hritz and Wilkinson 2006; Pournelle 2003a, 2003b, 2006; Wilkinson 2000b) researchers are using old but recently available satellite imagery and an array of new remote sensing technologies to squeeze more and different information from southern Mesopotamian survey data that only a few years ago appeared spent.

But if world systemic perspectives have any validity—and I believe they do—we must look beyond the confines of the southern Mesopotamian alluvium and the closely associated southwestern Iranian plains in our quest to understand the fourth-millennium origins of early Mesopotamian civilization. Accordingly, this is also the time to start correlating the corpus of existing, newly published, and reinterpreted materials from the Uruk core with the growing body of recent and ongoing work in northeastern Syria and southeastern Turkey relevant to what has often been termed the Uruk expansion (summarized in Algaze 2005a, chap. 8). Stemming from opposite extremes of the Uruk world system, each of these bodies of materials provides a different but complementary perspective on the "great leap forward" of fourth-millennium early Sumerian societies.

Lastly, this is a time for reflection as a prelude to further action. Sooner or later archaeological research will again be possible in Iraq and southwestern Iran, and, when that happens, a new generation of researchers will need a clear understanding of the gaps remaining to be filled if our comprehension of the emergence of early Sumerian civilization is to improve substantially over present levels. The need for carefully targeted research will be particularly acute in the case of Iraq, because existing evidentiary gaps there are being compounded on a daily basis, and made less amenable to remediation, by the systematic looting of the country's rich archaeological heritage, which continues appallingly unabated at present.

In what follows, by way of getting a discussion started, I list some of those evidentiary shortcomings and briefly provide some preliminary, and necessarily naïve, suggestions for possible ways to address some of them.

Agency

The first research agenda for the future is without a doubt one of the most difficult to successfully bring to fruition, but is also one that can be started immediately with data at hand. In a cogent criticism of one of my earlier papers, Claudio Cioffi-Revilla (2001), a sociologist, argued that the sorts of environmental and economic variables that are the focus of this book fail to address the *proximate* causes of the formation of early cities and states, which he sees as entirely political and historically contingent. Taken to its ultimate logical conclusion, Cioffi-Revilla's argument means that to truly understand how cities and states form we must also be able to reconstruct in detail the various strategies used by early elites to convince dependent commoners in their grasp that their interests were in fact coterminous—what he terms the "collective action problem."

Cioffi-Revilla is certainly correct, and his comment raises a serious issue that was noted earlier and that must now be addressed: how are we to achieve a thorough understanding of historically contingent strategies of social manipulation in the case of early pristine civilizations—societies that commonly are documented only through chronologically imprecise archaeological work, and that typically lack detailed historical and literary documentation? Or, to rephrase the question in terms specific to the early Mesopotamian case: how did the first rulers of newly formed Uruk city-states manage to persuade and/or coerce people in surrounding villages, marshes, and pasture lands to relinquish autonomy, resources, and, most importantly, labor to urban institutions they had never known before; and how did the new urban elites get the laborers to work in ways that must have been quite different—in terms of organization—from those that they were accustomed to in traditional tribal societies?

To be frank, given the nature of the evidence that exists for fourth-millennium Mesopotamia (chaps. 2 and 7, above), I doubt that we will ever be able to answer such questions with any degree of precision. However, I suspect that important insights can still be obtained from further iconographic analysis of the available corpus of Uruk period images. One example will suffice to illustrate what I mean. As noted earlier, much of Uruk art deals with the activities of a larger-than-life bearded male figure, who wears his hair in a chignon and sports a net skirt. Typically depicted as a hunter of wild animals, as a leader in battle, as a fountain of agricultural wealth, and as the main officiator in various religious rituals (Schmandt-Besserat 1993, 2007; Bahrani 2002; Winter 2007), this individual is generally thought to represent a "priest-king" (Amiet 2005) or "city ruler" (Delougaz and Kantor 1996). This attribution is largely based on parallels between the manner in which he is depicted in Uruk art and the way historic Mesopotamian kings were later portrayed.[1]

While this interpretation is almost certainly correct in its broad claims, it begs the question of whether the institution of kingship as it existed in the earliest Mesopotamian cities differed in any substantive way from its better-documented later counterparts. It may be possible to begin to approach this question by modeling the activities of the iconic male figure at issue not only in terms of what later Mesopotamian kings and provincial governors are known to have done but also in terms of the strategies that rulers of ethnohistorically documented premodern states elsewhere are known to have used in their respective quests to solve their own collective action problem(s). In my opinion, the fastest—and possibly greatest—

payoff along these lines would come from extending the methodology of glyptic analysis that Dittmann pioneered in his analysis of the Susa sealings, noted in an earlier chapter, to other pertinent corpora of Uruk glyptic published since Dittmann's study first appeared, most notably the materials from Chogha Mish (Delougaz and Kantor 1996), Tell Brak and other Uruk colonial sites in northern Syria (Pittman 2001) and, most importantly, from Warka itself (Boehmer 1999).

Paleoenvironment

Building on the prescient work of Frank Hole (1994), a central claim in this book has been that the environmental framework of fourth-millennium alluvial Mesopotamia was quite different from that which prevailed in the area in the historic periods and that this environment presented particularly propitious opportunities for human settlement that were recognized and exploited by early populations in the area. With some exceptions, however, this picture of conditions at the time early Sumerian societies became urban is based on extrapolations of large-scale climatological models and sedimentological research derived from areas outside the Mesopotamian alluvium itself (chap. 4). Helpful as these models are, they generally have neither the geographical nor chronological resolution that we would require to tackle issues of causality in human-environmental relations during the formative stages of Mesopotamian civilization.

From the point of view of palaeoclimatology, what is needed is a coordinated effort to incorporate available data into mesoscale computer simulation programs reconstructing climatic trends at specific crucial stages in the formation of Mesopotamian civilization. Particularly informative would be simulations focusing on conditions prevalent in the Tigris-Euphrates watershed (1) during the first quarter of the fourth millennium (Early Uruk), when available settlement pattern data (Adams 1981) show that southern Mesopotamia became a cauldron of competing statelets that, in the aggregate, was unparalleled elsewhere in the ancient Near East, and (2) during the third quarter of the millennium (Middle Uruk), when Warka starts growing exponentially and, perhaps not coincidentally, southern Mesopotamian polities first start to expand into the Upper Euphrates and Upper Tigris.

More difficult to obtain given present political conditions, but even more necessary, would a systematic geomorphologic coring program up and down the Mesopotamian alluvium that would build upon the earlier effort by the Iraqi Geological Service (chap. 4) but be much broader in scale. Subsets of this coring program could focus on areas immediately surrounding known early urban centers in both the northern and southern portions of the alluvium as well as yet-to-be identified centers in the still unsurveyed southeastern portion of the alluvial plains (below).[2] This would allow us to identify, directly and precisely, the local impact of the northward intrusion of the Persian Gulf on emerging Mesopotamian societies, both in the aggregate and on individual Uruk cities in particular. Provided good chronological resolution can be obtained, such a program could well also provide insights as to the relationship, if any, between the changes in the demographic profile of particular portions of the Mesopotamian alluvium through the various phases of the Uruk period, as documented by Adams's surveys, and the slow but certain retreat of the gulf littoral taking place at that time.

More specifically, could the demographic shift from the Nippur-Adab area to the Warka area that Adams (1981) observed as taking place between what he termed the Early/Middle and Late Uruk periods be related not only, as he argued, to shifts in the watercourses of the time, but also to the drying up of highly productive marsh resources in the northern portions of the alluvium, as the Persian Gulf coastline shifted southward? Phrased differently, if we could obtain a detailed record of the rate of the maritime recession within the alluvial plain of southern Mesopotamia through the fourth millennium it might be possible to model with some precision the impact of that recession on the dynamics of the evolving Tigris-Euphrates fluvial system of the time and in so doing, to better understand the connections between the coevolving natural and created environments of early Sumerian civilization as it first crystallized.

Trade

Perhaps one the most basic gaps from the point of view of this book is that of the current lack of evidence for changes in the nature and scale of trade in and out of southern Mesopotamia throughout the fifth and fourth millennia. In the preceding chapters, I repeatedly argued that trade was a key transformative agent in the crystallization of early Sumerian urban societies. To be candid, however, at this stage of our knowledge, this assertion is more a proclamation of faith than a conclusion made necessary by evidence at hand, for claims presented here for the primacy of trade are not based on actual data showing increases in the movement of imports and exports between southern Mesopotamian societies and neighboring regions from the Ubaid through to the Uruk period, but are based instead on my explicit theoretical orientation concerning the root forces that generally underlie endogenous urban processes. To be sure, to judge from excavations at central sites such as Warka, there appears to be a substantial increase in the variety, and presumably frequency, of imports being brought into southern Mesopotamia from resource-rich highland areas during the Middle and Late Uruk periods compared to the preceding Ubaid period, but the data we have were mostly obtained from early excavations and are neither fully representative (below) nor fully published.[3] Accordingly, existing data are not quantifiable in any reliable way.

The fact is that we will not know with certainty whether trade and its many social multiplier effects were a cause or a consequence of urban and state formation in Mesopotamia (chap. 6) until we start excavating some of the large urban sites through which such trade would have been funneled using the sorts of pioneering excavation methodologies and recording protocols used by Henry Wright at sites such as Farukhabad, in the Deh Luran plain of southwestern Iran, which were designed specifically to address whether (1) "Increased participation in exchange networks begins with . . . an increase in export rather than an initial increase in imports," whether (2) "Increased participation in systems of export leads to increased administrative specialization and state formation," and whether (3) "Increased participation in systems of export and import leads to the growth of central towns" (Wright 1981a, 3). Wright addressed these interrelated questions by careful sieving of all in situ deposits and by recording the relative densities of specific materials imported and exported into and from the site in terms of finds per cubic meter of excavated deposit per phase.[4] This methodology points the way forward to assessing the importance of interregional trade to processes of urbanization and state formation at other Uruk period centers, possibly even at Warka itself. More specifically, even if used as a complementary strategy deployed side by side with more traditional excavation programs, the wider application of sieving coupled with relative (density) counts should permit us to compare in a quantifiable way changes in the relative frequencies of nonperishable imports brought into alluvial cities throughout the various phases of Uruk and Ubaid periods and to contrast the pertinent results across different sites, provided the comparison is restricted to materials from similar functional areas within the sites.

Getting archaeological evidence bearing on the scale of exports from the Mesopotamian alluvium in the fourth millennium will be much more difficult, however, because as noted earlier those exports consisted primarily of perishable products that naturally leave few traces in the material record. Particularly vexing is the issue of the identification of textiles and wool, which in spite of their key importance to early Mesopotamian development remain "specially difficult to trace and their study tends to fall between disciplinary cracks" (Kriger 2006, 7). More feasible with technologies at hand, and more likely to provide results in the short term, would be a coherent program geared to identify exports of dairy products via chemical characterization analyses (e.g., Rottlander 1990; Heron and Evershed 1993) focusing on lipid remains embedded in Uruk jars found in peripheral sites, of which there are many (for a partial listing organized by region, see Algaze 1993 [2005a], 63–74).

Households and Property

The issue of exchange brings us to a related evidentiary problem: while we have a relatively good idea of what public ritual/administrative spaces looked like in fourth-millennium Mesopotamian cities, and of the sorts of materials commonly found within those spaces, after 150 years or so of excavations we still know almost nothing about the nature and extent of intramural or extramural industrial areas in those cities, about the nature and variability of households in them (Nissen 2002), or about the patterning of activities within individual households through the various phases of the Uruk period. In short, intrasite spatial analyses as practiced by the current generation of archaelogists has never had an impact on research in southern Mesopotamia, possibly because the heydey of this approach took place in the last two or so decades and largely coincided with periods when Iraq was closed to fieldwork.

There is, to be sure, much evidence for Uruk households at Uruk colonial sites in northern Syria, particularly at Jebel Aruda and Habuba
Kabira-süd, but the final publication of these finds has not yet appeared.
This prevents systematic analyses of the types and scale of economic activities that took place within the colonial outposts and of the spatial
patterning of such activities. That such patterning existed is clear from
preliminary reports, which allude to various specialized industries within
Habuba Kabira, including lapidary production and, of course, metallurgical activity. Tantalizing as these data may be, at best they serve as testable hypotheses about the types of economic activities that took place
within fourth-millennium households in southern Mesopotamia itself.
At present we have no way to address questions about the production of
trade goods for export at the household level in the Uruk heartland or
the ways in which households at different levels of the Uruk settlement
hierarchy in the south had access to, and consumed, long-distance trade
imports acquired through colonial outposts. These evidentiary gaps must
be closed as soon as practicable once Iraq reopens to systematic archaeological work.

The lack of archaeological evidence on fourth-millennium households
in the Mesopotamian alluvium is problematic for other reasons as well.
One is that it effectively prevents any archaeological consideration of
issues of ethnicity in the formation of early Mesopotamian civilization
(i.e., the so-called Sumerian problem). The right archaeological research
design (e.g., Goldstein 2005) applied to sites in different portions of the
Mesopotamian alluvium and to different quarters within Uruk town and
cities could significantly add much to what we presently know about this
potentially key subject, which in Mesopotamia has thus far only been addressed through textual or linguistic evidence (e.g., van Soldt 2005).

Another drawback of the lack of information on households in the
Uruk period is that it prevents us from addressing the equally thorny issue of property. As noted earlier, complex social transformations such as
those implied by the emergence of early Sumerian cities and states cannot be fully explained without reference to concurrent ideological transformations, which may include new understandings about property and
property rights (North and Thomas 1973). However, because sites such
as Warka have never been properly sampled away from central public
areas, we cannot ascertain the ways in which, if any, the Sumerian takeoff correlates with changes in how property was conceptualized in early

Mesopotamian societies. Again, the Uruk colonial outposts in Syria offer tantalizing clues. For instance, separate analyses by Rene Vallet (1996, 1998) and Jean Daniel Forest (1997) of the principles of urban planning inferable from published plans of the architecture in the Jebel Aruda/Habuba Kabira-süd urban complex agree in that newly founded Late Uruk colonial cities were systematically divided into parcels and that, at a minimum, some extended families did enjoy restrictive access to scarce urban plots within those sites. This raises important questions regarding (1) the degree to which the restricted property rights inferable from the urban layout of Uruk colonies is matched by comparable situation in the Mesopotamian core itself at the time, and (2) whether comparable restrictions in access to property existed in southern Mesopotamia in phases of the Uruk period predating the Uruk expansion.

Excavation and Survey

Survey

In an earlier chapter I argued that there is a missing tier in the Uruk urban hierarchy as presently known from existing surveys of Mesopotamian alluvium and suggested that ancient Umma probably anchored the missing tier. I also suggested that further Uruk centers and their dependencies might be found in the Lagash area. These hypotheses are testable as part of a larger program to document what is left of the heavily looted site of Umma (Tell Jokha) itself and to survey portions of the alluvium along the Tigris where Adams was unable to work because of security concerns in the late 1970s, particularly in the general area of the ancient city-states of Umma and Lagash (i.e., areas surrounding Tell Jokha and Tell al-Hiba, and areas of the Shatt al Gharraf immediately to the south and east, up to the Iranian border. For the location of the area in question, see now Wilkinson 2003b, fig. 5.3, "7b").

Excavation

Our lack of understanding of the physical layout of Uruk cities in the south beyond their relatively well-understood central ritual/administrative quarters can be remedied, of course, by concentrating future excavation efforts in the periphery of such sites so as to document a fuller range of the activities that took place within them. This is most easily done at Warka itself because detailed surface surveys led by Uwe Finkbeiner (1991) have identified the location and extent of Uruk period remains within the walls of the later city (fig. 18).

Equally unrepresentative is our understanding of urban-rural hierarchies in the Uruk period, which for all practical purposes are known only from survey. What did towns and villages look like at the time the initial urban-rural continuum was created in Mesopotamia? We simply do not know because contemporary villages and hamlets have not been excavated in the environs of large Uruk sites in the alluvium, and what exposures we do have in mid- and small-sized Uruk towns are either unrepresentative, for instance, at Tell Uqair, where only the central ceremonial district was sampled (Lloyd and Safar 1943), or too limited in scope, as, for example, at the Uruk mound of Abu Salabikh, where the outbreak of the first Gulf War terminated a promising research design (Pollock 1990; Pollock, Steele, and Pope 1991). This state of affairs is regrettable both in and of itself and because it prevents us from understanding the ways in which lower-order Uruk sites may have differed from comparable sites in the historical periods, which are generally better documented both archaeologically and, above all, textually.

In short, what was the nature of interactions between early Mesopotamian cities and their dependencies, and what was the intensity of such interactions? To rephrase the question in archaeologically testable terms: can we identify the outflow of patronage-affirming (imported) sumptuary goods from Mesopotamian cities to surrounding towns and villages and the inflow of subsistence and exportable resources that those cities received from their hinterlands in return? In addition, what was the spatial extent of such interactions: how large on average were the territories administered by Uruk city-states and how variable where they—as compared to the better-understood city-states of the third millennium? To be sure, some of these questions have been addressed already via survey data (Adams 1981; Pollock 2001) but they can be tackled differently, and more directly, when systematic archaeological work restarts in Iraq by means of coherent excavation programs targeting smaller dependent Uruk sites in the immediate orbit of the better-known cities—preferably single-period sites that are likely to survive the present wave of destruction because they are smaller and less attractive to looters. The program I have in mind is one modeled in part on work that

Henry Wright and Gregory Johnson conducted at various lower-order Uruk sites in the Susiana Plain during the 1970s (Johnson 1976; Wright, Miller, and Redding 1980), which came to a premature end because of the Iranian revolution.

Paleozoology

Faunal data are conspicuous for their absence from excavated Uruk levels in the Mesopotamian alluvium itself. Most of the systematic data available comes from marginal sites, such as Tell Rubeidheh (Payne 1988) in the Hamrin region of Iraq or from Uruk outposts outside the alluvium proper, either in Turkey (Bigelow 1999; Syracusano 2004) or Syria (Vila 2006). This situation must be remedied if we are to ascertain when exactly wooly sheep were first brought into the Mesopotamian alluvium and how much time elapsed between that event and the start of the late fourth-millennium "fiber revolution"—to borrow a well-turned phrase from Joy McCorriston—that had so central a role in the historical development of early Mesopotamian civilization.

Another issue of central importance for which we need representative faunal samples is that of the contribution of resources from marshes, lagoons, and estuaries to the growth of Uruk centers, principally in the form of fodder for cattle and sheep and protein-rich fish. Following on insights by Pournelle (2003a, 2003b), throughout this book I have emphasized the contribution of littoral resources to Uruk societies, maintaining that those resources were potentially more significant in relative terms than was the case later on in the historic periods. More specifically, dried and salted fish used as rations were certainly an important component of the economy of Mesopotamian city-states in the historical periods (Englund 1990), and it stands to reason that fish should have been even more central to the economy of emerging Uruk city-states because of their greater abundance and greater accessibility at the time (above, chap. 4). This is to some degree testable. The caloric contribution of littoral resources to early Mesopotamian civilization could easily be gauged by systematic sieving for faunal and marine resources in future excavations in any of the southernmost Uruk period centers. Potentially, the issue could also be investigated through analyses of bone stable isotope ratios of carbon and nitrogen (Schoeninger and Moore 1992) in pertinent human osteological material, but this avenue of research remains blocked by our puzzling lack of success in identifying the location of Uruk burials, an issue to which we now turn.

Mortuary Evidence

The almost total lack of mortuary evidence that presently exists for the Uruk period prevents us from properly evaluating the degree to which the McNeill hypothesis about demographic processes in early cities, noted in an earlier chapter, fits the situation in early Mesopotamia. Equally important, this lack also keeps us, in my opinion, from fully realizing the scale and breadth of imports flowing into southern Mesopotamia through the various phases of the Uruk period, many of which would have been taken out of circulation as burial offerings. This absence of evidence is a situation so vexing that at least one author has been reduced to suggesting that bodies were floated down the river en route to the Persian Gulf (Pollock 1992, 298). There is no need, however, for deus ex machina explanations. Extramural cemeteries are known for the Ubaid period, most notably at Eridu (Safar, Mustafa, and Lloyd 1981), whereas intramural burials in houses are common for infants in the Ubaid period (Jasim 1989) and for all segments of the demographic spectrum of early Mesopotamian cities throughout the third millennium, starting with the ED I period (Algaze 1984). It is likely, therefore, that the puzzling lack of burials in the intervening Uruk period just means we have not been looking in the right places.

I suspect that the mystery of Uruk burial practice will be solved once Uruk households in southern Mesopotamia are properly sampled, although, to be fair, it is worrisome that no associated burials have thus far been reported from Uruk houses in the Late Uruk colonial sites in Syria. In addition, however, we also need a systematic program to sample the outskirts of Uruk sites to test for the presence of dedicated extramural cemeteries of fourth-millennium date. On this issue Warka is unlikely to produce meaningful results—or at least not produce them easily—as the expansion of the city in the early third millennium may have obscured earlier external cemeteries, if any. Indeed, it may very well be that millennia of canal building, plowing, and other types of agricultural activity have erased much of the relevant evidence for extramural cemeteries of the Uruk period around long-lived sites, if they existed. However, it

is possible—and well worth checking—that some cemeteries might still
be preserved in the environs of smaller single-period sites in areas that
quickly became agriculturally marginal after the Uruk period because of
river course changes.

Chronology

Few things are more important in terms of our understanding of the
emergence of Mesopotamian civilization than correlating the processes
of internal and external expansion of Uruk societies throughout the
fourth millennium. Yet, a synthesis of Uruk-related work in core and peripheral areas is not easily accomplished at this time. As more and more
work takes place in Uruk and Uruk-related sites in Syria and southeastern Turkey, archaeologists are beginning to amass a small but coherent
corpus of absolute dates pertaining to the Middle and Late Uruk periods
(assembled and recalibrated under a single standard by Henry Wright
and Eric Rupley 2001; Rupley 2003). Sadly, however, this corpus finds
no parallels in contemporary Uruk sites in southern Mesopotamia and
Susiana, where the number of available fourth-millennium dates remains
negligible. The situation is compounded by the fact that our understanding of the internal relative chronology of the Uruk period is equally defi-
cient, as Hans Nissen (2002) has recently noted.

Lacking a secure chronological foundation, our ability to delineate
causality across space is hampered. A few examples of key questions that
at present we are unable to answer will suffice to illustrate the point.
For instance, what was the relationship between the Uruk expansion and
the growth of Warka as the paramount center in the southern alluvium?
It is quite unlikely that the two phenomena are entirely unrelated, as I
have argued earlier, but clear correlations still elude us. Other no less important questions that remain unanswerable at present include (1) What
was the relationship, if any, between the Uruk intrusion into the Susiana
Plain of southwestern Iran and the timing of north-to-south population
movements in the Mesopotamian alluvium, which Adams believes took
place sometime toward the very end of the Early Uruk period? (2) What
was the relationship, if any, between the colonization of the Susiana plain
and the start of expansion northward along the Euphrates and, possibly,
the Tigris? To rephrase this last question: was the intrusion into Susiana
the first step in a broader expansionary scramble by competing alluvial

polities that expanded in different directions at different times, in part reacting to the actions of their rivals and in part motivated by the desire to acquire needed resources?

Questions such as these will not be fully addressable until new excavations at the core of the Uruk world and southwestern Iran produce clusters of pertinent radiocarbon dates that can be contrasted against the existing dates from Uruk colonies across the north. A cost-effective way to start that process might be by cleaning existing sections at previously excavated Uruk centers both in the alluvium and in Susiana and, where possible, mine still-standing architecture (e.g., the Anu Ziggurat and White Temple at Warka) for datable samples.

The Early Uruk Problem

A final research agenda for the future is one that Hans Nissen (1993) laid out in an important article written more than a decade ago. If we are to elucidate the processes that gave rise to Mesopotamian civilization, as exemplified by the Middle–Late Uruk expansion and cultural explosion, we must invest some time on clarifying the nature of the immediately preceding Early Uruk period societies, which for all practical purposes are documented only through settlement pattern data. What makes the Early Uruk period so important is that, as noted earlier (chap. 7), what settlement data we do have for the period can readily be interpreted to show that a system of (competing?) city-states was already in place at that time—even if in embryonic form.

Yet, it has been almost seventy-five years since von Haller (1932) published the results of soundings into early levels at Warka, and improbably, his results have not yet been superseded. We need more excavations into Early Uruk levels, and much wider exposures, both at Warka and at contemporary urban sites in the Nippur-Adab area. In addition, we need excavations at smaller Early Uruk sites in their vicinity. Only then will we be able to fully assess whether the tempo and scale of the internal growth and external expansion of Middle and Late Uruk polities were as abrupt as they seem to be at present, or whether developments in those later phases were prefigured in significant ways in the Early Uruk period. Moreover, only then will we be able to compare the nature of the very earliest urban experiments of northern and southern Mesopotamia, and thereby better understand why the two experiments, so similar in their beginnings, eventually led to such diverging outcomes. The important Early Uruk site of Tell al-Hayyad, site 1306 in Adams's survey, possibly the fabled antediluvian city of Larak (Adams 1981, 348, n. 3), is still out there in the desert steppe waiting for a better political climate and for the next generation of researchers investigating the origins of early Mesopotamian civilization.

Appendix 1

Surveyed Early/Middle Uruk Sites in the
Mesopotamian Alluvium Organized by Size
and Presumed Functional Category

Site Number	Area (in hectares)
"Hamlets" (ca. 0.1–2.5 ha):[1]	
WS 22	2.5
WS 23	1
WS 24	1
WS 42	0.1 ("present")
WS 103	1
WS 110	0.1 ("present")
WS 129	1
WS 156	0.1
WS 169	2
WS 178	0.7
WS 209	1
WS 215	0.1
WS 229	0.1
WS 237	0.9
WS 258	0.5
WS 267	1.9
WS 317	0.1
WS 318	1.1
WS 330	1.2
WS 386	0.1 ("present")
WS 402	0.5
WS 409	0.9
WS 410	0.2
WS 460	1

[1] Total category number of sites: 123; total category occupied hectares: 67.3; average hectare per site in category: 0.55.

Continued

Site Number	Area (in hectares)
"Hamlets" (ca. 0.1–2.5 ha):[1]	
NS 573	1
NS 574	1
NS 639	0.1
NS 655	0.1
NS 667	0.1
NS 671	0.5
NS 677	0.3
NS 680	0.1
NS 706	0.1
NS 711	0.1
NS 722	0.2
NS 743	2
NS 749	0.1
NS 782	0.1
NS 783	0.1
NS 793	0.4
NS 802	0.2
NS 804	1.7
NS 818	0.5
NS 821	0.1
NS 824	1.4
NS 826	0.5
NS 829	0.3
NS 837	1.4
NS 838	0.1
NS 854	0.2
NS 935	0.8
NS 936	0.2
NS 939	2.4
NS 940	1.7
NS 952	0.2
NS 964	0.7
NS 976	0.2
NS 977	0.6
NS 980	0.8
NS 981	1.5
NS 982	0.1
NS 1019	1.4
NS 1021	1
NS 1024	1.3
NS 1027	0.1
NS 1044	1
NS 1054	0.1
NS 1067	0.1
NS 1069	0.5
NS 1070	0.1
NS 1071	0.1

[1] Total category number of sites: 123; total category occupied hectares: 67.3; average hectare per site in category: 0.55.

Continued

Site Number	Area (in hectares)
"Hamlets" (ca. 0.1–2.5 ha):[1]	
NS 1096	2
NS 1109	0.5
NS 1112	0.1
NS 1115	0.5
NS 1118	0.6
NS 1129	2.4
NS 1135	0.1
NS 1152	0.1
NS 1164	1
NS 1169	0.5
NS 1170	0.5
NS 1174	0.1
NS 1178	0.1
NS 1180	0.1
NS 1195	0.1
NS 1196	0.5
NS 1199	1
NS 1208	0.1
NS 1210	0.1
NS 1216	0.1
NS 1217	0.1
NS 1230	0.5
NS 1247	0.1
NS 1271	0.5
NS 1278	0.1
NS 1284	0.5
NS 1294	0.8
NS 1304	0.1
NS 1312	0.2
NS 1316	0.1
NS 1318	0.1
NS 1337	0.1
NS 1375	0.2
NS 1383	1
NS 1386	0.1
NS 1416	0.6
NS 1428	0.5
NS 1432	1.7
NS 1434	0.1
NS 1437	0.1
NS 1440	1
NS 1443	0.1
NS 1448	0.9
NS 1451	1.4
NS 1460	0.1
NS 1465	0.1
NS 1471	0.1

[1] Total category number of sites: 123; total category occupied hectares: 67.3; average hectare per site in category: 0.55.

Continued

Site Number	Area (in hectares)
"Hamlets" (ca. 0.1–2.5 ha):[1]	
NS 1615	0.6
AS 221	1
AS 259	0.2
AS 261	0.1
"Villages" (2.6–5 ha):[2]	
WS 34	4.2
WS 107	2.6
WS 163	4
WS 168	5
NS 744	3.6
NS 781	5
NS 831	5
NS 832	3
NS 835	2.9
NS 853	4
NS 912	3
NS 1032	3
NS 1034	2.6
NS 1072	3.4
NS 1103	5
NS 1113	4
NS 1114	4
NS 1137	3.8
NS 1159	4.5
NS 1198	3.4
NS 1353	4.2
NS 1355	3
"Small towns" (5.2–9 ha):[3]	
WS 71	6.7
WS 113	5.3
WS 181	5.8
WS 218	6.5
WS 245	6
NS 755	5.3
NS 790	5.5
NS 792	6.8
NS 845	8
NS 975	5.8
NS 1020	8.2
NS 1046	8.6
NS 1124	6.8
NS 1165	5.3
NS 1205	7.9

[2] Total category number of sites: 22; total category occupied hectare: 83.2; average hectare per site in category: 3.8.

[3] Total category number of sites: 15; total category occupied hectares: 98.6; average hectares per site in category: 6.57.

[4] Total category number of sites: 7; total category occupied hectares: 76; average hectares per site in category: 10.85.

Continued

Site Number	Area (in hectares)
"Large towns" (10–14 ha):[4]	
WS 4	10
WS 171	10
WS 201	11
NS 678	13.5
NS 1166	10.6
NS 1194	11.5
Abu Salabikh	10
"Small towns" (24–25 ha):[5]	
NS 1172	25.5
Nippur	25
"Cities" (40–50 ha):[6]	
NS 1237	42
NS 1306	50
Eridu	40
"Primate cities" (100 ha):[7]	
Warka	70–100

Note: data abstracted from Adams (1981), table 7 and H. Wright (1981).

Key: WS = Warka Survey, NS = Nippur-Adab Survey, AS = Akkad Survey; ES = Eridu Survey. Named sites indicated.

[5] Total category number of sites: 2; total category occupied hectares: 50.5; average hectares per site in category: 25.25.

[6] Total category number of sites: 3; total category occupied hectares: 132; average hectares per site in category: 44.

[7] Total category number of sites: 1; total category occupied hectares: 70–100; average hectares per site in category: 70–100.

Appendix 2

Surveyed Late Uruk Sites in the Mesopotamian Alluvium Organized by Size and Presumed Functional Category

Site Number	Area (in hectares)
"Hamlets" (ca. 0.1–2.5 ha):[1]	
WS 6	0.3
WS 44	0.8
WS 48	0.5
WS 60	1.8
WS 76	2
WS 82	0.5
WS 95	0.1
WS 105	0.6
WS 106	1.7
WS 108	1
WS 112	1
WS 115	1.7
WS 128	1.8
WS 133	0.2
WS 137	1.5
WS 144	2
WS 153	2
WS 160	0.4
WS 164	1
WS 190	0.6
WS 203	0.6
WS 219	1.4
WS 237	0.9
WS 264	1.9

[1] Total category number of sites: 74; total category occupied hectares: 69.31; average hectare per site in category: 0.93.

Continued

Site Number	Area (in hectares)
"Hamlets" (ca. 0.1–2.5 ha):[1]	
WS 267	0.3
WS 272	0.5
WS 274	1.1
WS 276	0.5
WS 285	0.9
WS 286	0.5
WS 292	1.9
WS 293	1.7
WS 309	0.6
WS 310	0.9
WS 314	0.6
WS 325	0.1
WS 331	0.9
WS 334	0.4
WS 350	0.8
WS 367	2
WS 373	0.5
WS 386	1.5
WS 387	1
WS 406	0.8
WS 417	0.3
WS 418	0.4
WS 460	1
NS 539	2
NS 573	0.2
NS 574	1
NS 786	0.6
NS 805	0.5
NS 940	1.7
NS 975	0.6
NS 977	0.2
NS 1031	0.01
NS 1096	2
NS 1124	1
NS 1129	2.4
NS 1163	0.9
NS 1164	0.2
NS 1196	0.5
NS 1197	1.1
NS 1261	0.8
NS 1357	1.2
NS 1375	0.2
NS 1432	1.7
NS 1448	0.9
NS 1615	0.6
ES 5	0.1 "traces"
ES 7	0.7

[1] Total category number of sites: 74; total category occupied hectares: 69.31; average hectare per site in category: 0.93.

Continued

Site Number	Area (in hectares)
"Hamlets" (ca. 0.1–2.5 ha):[1]	
Tell 'Ubaid (ES 8)	0.1 "traces"
ES 29	1.6
ES 141	1
"Villages" (2.6–5 ha):[2]	
WS 9	4.7
WS 20	6
WS 28	2.9
WS 42	3
WS 51	3.6
WS 86	4.2
WS 114	2.9
WS 126	4
WS 127	4
WS 163	4
WS 166	4
WS 168	5
WS 174	2.6
WS 187	4.4
WS 191	3
WS 193	4
WS 199	3
WS 236	4.8
WS 282	2.6
WS 338	2.6
WS 376	4.8
WS 453	4.9
NS 1072	3.4
NS 1131	3
NS 1137	3.8
NS 1154	2.6
NS 1216	4.8
NS 1293	5
NS 1315	2.8
NS 1353	4.2
NS 1355	3
ES 171	3.5
"Small towns" (5.2–9 ha):[3]	
WS 12	7.8
WS 18	5.8
WS 71	6.7
WS 87	7.8
WS 109	5.2
WS 110	9
WS 152	6.6

[2] Total category number of sites: 32; total category occupied hectares: 118.1; average hectare per site in category: 3.7.

[3] Total category number of sites: 16; total category occupied hectares: 103.3; average hectares per site in category: 6.6.

Continued

Site Number	Area (in hectares)
"Small towns" (5.2–9 ha):[3]	
WS 162	6
WS 185	5.8
WS 218	6.5
WS 245	6
WS 407	6
NS 790	5.5
NS 1165	5.3
NS 1394	7.7
Abu Salabikh	5.5
"Large towns" (10–14 ha):[4]	
WS 4	10
WS 201	11
WS 242	10
WS 262	14
NS 678	13.5
NS 1194	11.5
Ur	10
"Small cities" (24–25 ha):[5]	
WS 125	24
NS 1172	25.5
Nippur	25
"Cities" (50 ha):[6]	
NS 1306	50
"Primate cities" (250 ha):[7]	
Warka	250

Note: Data abstracted from Adams (1981), table 7 and H. Wright (1981).

Key: WS = Warka Survey, NS = Nippur-Adab Survey, AS = Akkad Survey; ES = Eridu Survey. Named sites indicated.

[4] Total category number of sites: 7; total category occupied hectares: 80; average hectares per site in category: 11.4.

[5] Total category number of sites: 3 total category occupied hectares: 74.5; average hectares per site in category: 25.

[6] Total category number of sites: 1; total category occupied hectares: 50; average hectares per site in category: 50.

[7] Total category number of sites: 1; total category occupied hectares: 250; average hectares per site in category: 250.

Notes

Prologue

1. A better but more cumbersome term would be "Sumero-Akkadian" civilization, as this would acknowledge the long debates in the field about the undoubted contribution of Semitic speakers and cultural traditions to the making of early Mesopotamian civilization as a whole (see now, for example, van Soldt 2005). In the interest of brevity, I use the term "Sumerian" instead. This convenient label is being used in a cultural rather than a linguistic sense. It presupposes an unbroken line of continuity between the creators of the early cities that arose in the Mesopotamian alluvium during the fourth millennium and the people that inhabited those cities later on in the third millennium, who wrote in the Sumerian language—irrespective of what their ethnic affiliation may have been. Thus, the designation "Sumerian" in this book does not in any way deny the possible presence of non-Sumerian speakers in early Mesopotamian cities or their potential contributions to early Sumerian civilization.

I am fully aware, of course, of the sumerologist Robert Englund's (1998, 73–81) contention that it is not possible to demonstrate that the early proto-cuneiform tablets of fourth-millennium date (i.e., the Uruk IV–III script-type "Archaic Texts") were written in Sumerian. This is not in itself particularly unusual, as the earliest written records in many areas of the world, e.g., Egyptian and Zapotec, also cannot be shown to have been written in the language of the civilizations that later inhabited those areas (Houston 2004). While I have no doubt that Englund is technically correct, there is no need to interpret, as he does, the lack of explicit Sumerian linguistic traits in the Archaic Texts as meaning that Sumerian speakers immigrated into the Mesopotamian alluvium *after* the Uruk period. Rather, in my opinion, a more parsimonious explanation for the linguistic ambiguity of those early texts is that proposed by Roger Matthews (1999):

[T]he polyglot nature of life in the city of Uruk around the last quarter of the fourth millennium B.C., with slaves and traders being brought in from the furthest reaches of a far-flung world system, may in fact have stimulated the invention and development of a system of administrative communication which was specifically designed to transcend the idiosyncrasies of any single language, and thus be comprehensible and user-friendly to all participants within specific social and economic contexts of a multi-ethnic society.

2. In addition to the authors included in Rothman (2001), see also Amiet (1994); Cuyler Young (1995); Joffe (1994); Keith (1995); Lamberg-Karlovsky (1995); Matthews (1994); Pollock (1994); Postgate (1996); Rothman (2004); Stein (1999a); and H. Wright (1995).

3. Unless otherwise further qualified, throughout this book the terms "trade," "exchange," and "commerce" are used interchangeably, and in their most basic and generic sense, to simply denote reciprocal transactions where goods are exchanged for other goods of perceived equal value.

Chapter One

1. In the words of DeWitt Clinton, who successfully lobbied for the construction of the canal while serving as New York City major between 1803 and 1815 and who initiated the construction of the canal as the then newly elected governor of New York State in 1817: "As an organ of communication between the Hudson, the Mississippi, the St. Lawrence, the Great Lakes of the north and west and their tributary rivers, it will create the greatest inland trade ever witnessed. The most fertile and extensive regions of America will avail themselves of its facilities for a market. All their surplus productions, whether of the soil, the forest, the mines, or the water, their fabrics of art and their supplies of foreign commodities, will concentrate in the city of New York, for transportation abroad or consumption at home. Agriculture, manufactures, commerce, trade, navigation, and the arts will receive a correspondent encouragement. The city will, in the course of time, become the granary of the world, the emporium of commerce, the seat of manufactures, the focus of great moneyed operations and the concentrating point of vast disposable, and accumulating capital, which will stimulate, enliven, extend and reward the exertions of human labor and ingenuity, in all their processes and exhibitions. And before the revolution of a century, the whole island of Manhattan, covered with inhabitants and replenished with a dense population, will constitute one vast city" (Finch 1925, 4).

Chapter Two

1. This has led the assyriologist Claus Wilcke (2007, 114) to suggest that the differentiation between "public" or "official" versus "private" economic realms is a modern abstraction of little applicability to ancient Mesopotamian economic behavior. While Wilcke may be correct in terms of the cognitive processes of ancient Mesopotamian traders in, say, the third millennium BC, this differentiation is still quite useful to us as an analytical tool for their activities.

2. According to Snell (1977, 48), domestic products included alkalis, honey, wax, bitumen, gypsum, fish, grains, leather hides, livestock, oils, reeds, tanning agents, vegetables, and some types of wood; imported products include fruits, metals, and various types of resins, spices, and woods.

3. To be fair, unlike many who have used central place models outside of the historical context of early twentieth-century Bavaria, Christaller himself never claimed that his analysis was applicable to other areas and historical periods—or that his work was pertinent to issues of origin, even in the southern German case itself. On the contrary, he was quite explicit in that his study was solely descriptive and entirely particularistic in nature. His aim, in his own words, was to "determine geographic reality *at present,* that is, to explain the number, sizes, and distribution of central places in southern Germany" (Christaller ([1933] 1966, 133, emphasis added).

Chapter Three

1. This is based, of course, on the pioneering insights of the great economist Alfred Marshall, who famously contended that "economics is a branch of biology, broadly interpreted." Although often cited, his views on this subject were never achieved wide currency among modern economists (Hogson 1993).

2. This is an example of the process that modern economists, following the ideas of Alfred Marshall, often term "knowledge or technological spillovers" (Desrochers 2001a, 2001b; Fujita and Krugman 2004, 153–54).

3. Although Krugman and his coworkers have never claimed that their approach is applicable beyond the modern capitalistic world system, for reasons outlined in the preceding chapter I believe that their analyses of urban process today are of substantial heuristic value in understanding how early Mesopotamian cities came to be.

4. While this premise may sound both obvious and even trite, it represents, in fact, a significant departure from the underlying assumption of a homogeneous landscape allowing equal mobility for all that many archaeologists implicitly

accept when applying models derived from central place theory to the interpretation of their data (see chap. 2). The same is the case for many economists that study the relationship between trade, urban process, and economic development in the modern world, who seldom take into account in their analyses the impact of differential ease of transport (Martin and Sunley 1996, 260; Meardon 2001, 26) or varying geographic landscapes (Gallup, Sachs, and Mellinger 1999, 212).

5. The geographer Frederick Ratzel, writing in the late nineteenth century, was the first to note that cities tend to aggregate at end points of transport routes. Their tendency to form at junctures of different types of transport, in turn, was noted at about the same time by the sociologist C. H. Cooley (Bairoch 1990, 148, n. 26). For more modern treatments of Ratzel's and Cooley's pioneering insights about the relationship between transport and urban location, see also Burghardt (1971, 1979) and Hirth (1978).

6. To be sure, the concept of cumulative causation itself is hardly unique to Myrdal. See Meardon (2001, 43–44), for a discussion of Myrdal's intellectual debt to earlier economic thinkers on this particular issue.

Chapter Four

1. Available evidence on regional subsidence versus local uplift in the Shatt el-Arab area during the last six thousand or so years is somewhat contradictory and not amenable to precise dating. For a review of the pertinent literature, see Uchipi, Swift, and Ross (1999).

2. While there is little pertinent faunal data of fourth-millennium date from sites in the immediate environs of the mid-Holocene marshes, available faunal data from Ubaid III levels at Ras al-Amiya near the northern edge of the alluvium and Ubaid IV levels at the Hut Sounding in Eridu and Tell el-'Ouelli, both near the southern edge of the alluvial delta, suggest that cattle was the main domestic species exploited by alluvial societies through the end of the Ubaid period (Flannery and Wright 1966; Desse 1983). In contrast, available faunal evidence of ED I date from Sagheri Sughir, a small village near Ur, and of ED III date from Tell al-Hiba (Lagash), shows that sheep and goat were predominant in the area during the third millennium, and cattle, while present, were by then much less common (Mudar 1982). However, given the paucity of pertinent data and how unrepresentative is what data we do have, there is simply no way to ascertain the extent to which the changing proportions in the ratio of sheep/goat versus cows in the southern alluvium from the fifth to the third millennia represent an adaptation to environmental changes, reflect conscious choices made by early Sumerian populations to maximize textile production by the historic periods, or both.

3. Reed boat impressions on bitumen dating to the late sixth and fifth millennia BC have been recovered at As-Sabiyah site H3, an Arabian Neolithic

coastal Persian Gulf settlement in Kuwait, and Kosak Shamali, a small Ubaid site along the Euphrates in northern Syria (Connan et al. 2005). Late Chalcolithic levels from Hacınebi Tepe, also along the Euphrates but in southeastern Turkey, provide further examples dated to the late fifth or early fourth millennium (M. Schwartz 2002).

4. For the fourth millennium, for instance, see Amiet (1961, pl. 13 bis, e, g; 46, no. 655, all from Warka, and Delougaz and Kantor (1996a, pl. 151b) from Chogha Mish.

5. Existing analyses focus mostly on tablets published thus far, which largely consist of archives plundered from the site from Kültepe in the late nineteenth and early twentieth centuries. The Assyrian Quarter at Kanesh/Kültepe has been under systematic excavation since 1948 by Turkish expeditions led by Tashin Özgüç and his successors. About 20,000 more tablets have been recovered in those excavations, and these are now starting to be published. The principal existing syntheses of the Old Assyrian trading phenomenon, however, still mostly reflect the earlier unprovenanced but more fully published materials.

6. In addition to substantial amounts of grain and reeds, shipments of the following products are frequently attested: various types of flour, beer, agricultural oils, (preserved) fish, vegetables, fruits, animal fodder, bundles of wood, timber, and various types of wood implements, bitumen, pottery, leather sacks and leather products, as well as a small number of unidentified commodities. In addition, but more rarely, shipments by boat included various types of livestock, wool, dairy products, silver, copper implements, and encumbered workers, both male (GURUŠ) and female (GEME) (Sharlach 2004, 289–311, chart 2.14).

7. Robert Englund (personal communication, 2005), tells me a liter of threshed barley weighs on average between 0.6 and 0.67 kg. Lionel Casson (1971, 26, n. 5) estimates a liter of grain at 0.85 kg. Mindful of these two calculations, I use here 0.7 kg as a convenient average.

8. The texts considered in these calculations include:

A. Cargoes sent from Lagash to Nippur (Sharlach 2004, chart 3.6): ITT 4.7497: 173 gur; MVN 7.514: 148 gur; MVN 2.8: 433 gur; MVN 7.257: 60 gur; MVN 6.148: 244 gur; ASJ 3.103: 1 gur; BM 21680: 300 gur; ASJ 3.145: 480 gur; MVN 11.11: 3020 gur; ASJ 3.157: 3581 gur; MVN 12.16: 196 gur; MVN 12.18: 480 gur; MVN 12.21: 180 gur; MVN 12.20: 498 gur; MVN 12.161: 180 gur; MVN 12.22: 663 gur; BM 21876a: 300 gur; MVN 12.19: 938 gur; BM 21848a: 150 gur; BM 21229a: 485 gur; MVN 12.40: 670 gur; MVN 12.63: 293 gur; BM 21610: 669 gur; MVN 9.26: 57 gur; ASJ 9.11: 58 gur.

B. Cargoes sent from Lagash to unknown destinations (Sharlach 2004, chart 3.7): MVN 2.11: 211 gur; MVN 2.10: 181 gur; MVN 6.73: 378 gur; MVN 6.190: 180 gur; MVN 6.211: 360 gur; MVN 6.22: 78 gur; MVN 6.87: 199 gur; MVN 12.62: 752 gur; MVN 12.68: 730 gur; MVN 12.178: 240 gur; MVN 12.194: 1078 gur; MVN 12.195: 904 gur; MVN 12.207: 242 gur; MVN 12.215: 117 gur; MVN

2.9: 170 gur; HSS 4.23: 100 gur; MVN 12.288: 561 gur; HLC 1.244: 709 gur; MVN 9:52: 1740 gur; UDT 62: 314 gur; HLC 1.47: 300 gur; MVN 17.44: 122 gur; MVN 12.389: 122 gur; MVN 12.398: 100 gur; TCTI 2.2545: 565 gur; CTMMA 1.38: 5 gur; MVN 15.257: 10 gur.

9. The texts considered in these calculations include:

A. Cargoes sent from Umma to Nippur (Sharlach 2004, chart 2.5): MVN 21.296: 610 gur; MVN 16.891: 48 gur; SAT 2/3.335: 58 gur; Limet, TS 48: 10 gur; NYPL 288: 244 + gur; MVN 4.36: 106 gur; MVN 15.87: 68 gur; AAICAB2.1937–71: 522 gur; Syracuse 160: 216 gur; BCT 2.253: 318 gur; BIN 5.132: 400 gur; MVN 4.55: 2 gur; Contenau, Cont. 5: 532 gur.

B. Cargoes sent from Umma to Uruk and Ur (Sharlach 2004, chart 2.7): MVN 21.272: 360 gur; Touz. 314: 64 gur; MVN 20.162: 66 gur; AAICAB2.1935–557: 160 gur; NYPL 291: 3 gur; SAT 2/3.647: 820 gur; SAT 2/3.965: 373 gur; SAT 2/3.1022: 81 gur; BIN 5.119: 724 gur.

10. Distances noted here between southern Mesopotamian sites are abstracted from Adams's (1981, figs. 27–28) maps of ancient settlements in the alluvium.

Chapter Five

1. This suggestion follows from Charles Spencer's (1997, 232) insightful examination of the applicability of the biological concept of exaptation to social evolutionary processes. As defined by the noted paleontologist S. J. Gould (1988, 331–32), exaptation refers to biological features that evolved to solve problems at one evolutionary level but that end up playing a different functional adaptive role in evolutionary processes of a higher order than those in which the feature initially arose. Gould even suggested that exaptive possibilities rather than direct adaptation form the principal basis of (biological) complexity. A case could be made that Gould's insight about the role of exaptation in creating complexity is equally—if not more—applicable to human societies. Following the insights of Jacobs (chap. 3 above), it stands to reason that the greater the degree of internal diversity of a social system, the greater the exaptive possibilities of that system, and the greater the likelihood of emergent social complexity.

2. Traces of wine have been chemically identified as the contents of one of the common types of Uruk spouted jars often found in Late Chalcolithic sites (Badler, McGovern, and Glusker 1996). As southern Mesopotamia was not suitable for grape cultivation, the wine contained within such jars must have been a bulk import into Uruk colonial sites in Upper Mesopotamia that was then processed further (?), before being repackaged into smaller containers and exported to both peripheral and alluvial consumers (Algaze 1995).

3. Human porterage: at the low end of the spectrum, J. E. Holstrom (1934, 33) uses ethnographic reports to suggest that African porters can carry an average of

27 kg over 9.4 km/day. At the high end of the spectrum, Robert Drennan (1984, 105) uses ethnohistoric data to suggest that Aztec porters carried ca. 30 kg for about 36 km/day, while Paul Bairoch (1990) arrives at similar results using economic texts from eighteenth- and nineteenth-century Europe and Britain, which indicate averages of 37.5 kg over 32.5 km/day.

Donkey porterage: at the low end of the spectrum, nineteenth- and twentieth-century British Army data show that donkeys carried an average of 50 kg over a distance of 24 km/day (cited in Dercksen 2004, 265, n. 703). At the high end of the spectrum, donkeys in early twentieth-century Iran are reported as able to carry between 54 and 68 kg over distances of 24–40 km/day (Holstrom 1934, 34).

4. See Derksen (2004, 257–58) for a compilation of available osteological data for donkey size in northern Mesopotamian sites of third- and second-millennium date.

5. It should be noted, however, that the Godin outpost, unlike the Hacınebi one, lacks evidence for Uruk-type cooking pots (i.e., strap-handled jars). Virginia Badler (2002, 87) plausibly suggests that this difference is indicative of gender differences in the Uruk settlers present at the two outposts, with southern females present at Hacınebi but presumably absent in the more difficult-to-reach Iranian outpost.

6. Made of an unusual copper-silver alloy, this weapon was almost certainly imported from the Taurus highlands, where implements cast using the same alloy were relatively common in the late fourth millennium (Palmieri, Hauptmann, and Hess 1997).

7. While in situ evidence of metal-processing installations in Uruk cities is still rare, at least when compared to the more ubiquitous evidence for such installations in Uruk colonies in Syria and southeastern Turkey, the paucity of such installations in the south is easily explained. One possible explanation is that noted by the late Roger Moorey (1994, 243), who pointed out that early metal industries would have used simple but effective technologies, such as crucible smelting, that have largely escaped the attention of archaeologists looking only for more substantial installations such as furnaces. An alternative—and complementary—explanation is that evidence at our disposal concerning the frequency and location of metallurgical activities within southern centers may simply be unrepresentative. Early excavations at sites such as Warka, Eridu, Uqair, etc., overwhelmingly concentrated their efforts on exposing the central administrative quarters of those sites. Accordingly, they would have missed evidence of metal-processing activities situated away from central quarters. In fact, this is precisely where such activities are likely to have been located, possibly as a way for elites to avoid foul-smelling smelting fumes. At the Uruk colonial enclave of Habuba Kabira-süd in Syria, which by any account has the largest and most representative exposures of any Uruk settlement thus far explored, for instance, metal

processing took place only at a cluster of installations in the northeastern quarter of the site, the portion of the city farthest away from its ritual/administrative area (Kohlmeyer 1997, 447).

8. It is possible that these axes/ingots already served as a standardized unit of value. The assyriologist Marvin Powell (1996, 238) notes that the Sumerian sign for shekel (*gin*) is actually a stylized picture of an axe and that gin is used interchangeably to mean both shekel and axe.

9. There is little direct evidence for when exactly wooly sheep were introduced into southern Mesopotamia. *A terminus post quem* in the last quarter of the fifth millennium is suggested by faunal data, noted in chapter 4, suggesting that cattle was the main domestic species exploited by alluvial societies through the end of the Ubaid period and that sheep and goats were still rare in the south at that time.

10. This may be inferred from the fact that between 457 and 549 workdays (the work of three herders) would be necessary to maintain a flock of 100 animals throughout the year (Russell 1988, 83). After rounding, this boils down to about 5 workdays per sheep per year. Since an average of 3.5 sheep are necessary, including processing wastage, to produce 2 kilograms of wool (McCorriston 1997, 524), about 9 workdays would be required per year for each unprocessed kilogram of fiber produced.

11. Other relevant images in this category include Amiet (1961, pl. 16, no. 273, 19, no. 320, and 1972, nos. 673–74).

12. Other relevant images in this category include Amiet (1961, pl. 14, 238) and Delougaz and Kantor (1996, pl. 153 a, c–e).

13. This proportion was arrived at dividing Waetzoldt's total employment estimate (15,000) by the number of actual weavers (6,800 and 4,754) receiving rations at different times (Waetzoldt 1972, 94).

14. This weight is extrapolated from a summary tablet from Ur, recording 5,800 individual pieces of cloth sent to fullers, which weighed 155 talents (4,650 kg; Waetzoldt 1972, 106). From this, an average weight per piece of 0.80 kg can be inferred.

15. Note, however, that because the ceramic assemblages are so similar, Adams was forced to lump together the Ur III and Isin-Larsa periods in his survey results. See Adams (1981, fig. 16 and table 12) for a summary of pertinent Uruk and Ur III/Isin-Larsa data, respectively. Nonetheless, in spite of this lack of chronological precision, trends are clear. If arbitrarily, but conservatively, we designate an extent of 40 or more hectares as the minimum size required to warrant the use of the term "urban" in southern Mesopotamia during both the late fourth and late third millennia, then Adams's data show that, depending on the region, between 33 and 50 percent of the population in the alluvium was urbanized in the Late Uruk period versus 55 for the Ur III/Isin-Larsa period. These proportions are actually closer than they seem. Adams's numbers for the degree

of urbanization of the alluvium in the Uruk period need to be revised upwards, as his calculations are based on an estimate of 100 hectares for Warka in the Late Uruk phase, but new research has shown that a much higher estimate of roughly 250 hectares is in order (chap. 7).

16. This is the *gún ma-da* tax payable in sheep and oxen by Ur III military personnel holding land allotments in areas outside of Babylonia itself. As of 1987, this tax is attested in only about 100 or so of the Puzrish-Dagan texts. This number, of course, represents only a minute portion of the known texts from the site, which number in the thousands (Steinkeller 1987). However, because the relevant archives were not systematically excavated, there is no reliable way to ascertain what proportion of the total collections of animals at Puzrish-Dagan came from areas external to the Ur III empire as opposed from the internal (Babylonian) provinces.

17. This is worked out presuming a total (average) of 5,500 textile workers in the Uruk period, that weavers would have been between 32 and 45 percent of that total (Waetzoldt 1972, 99), and that the ratio of fullers to weavers was between 1:45 and 1:18 (Waetzoldt 1972, 92).

18. The contracts studied by Postgate stem from a variety of sites in northern Babylonia. Marc Van De Mieroop has studied a second group of contemporary herding contracts, all stemming from Ur in the southern portion of the alluvium. He concludes that a single shepherd could handle between 106 and 1,002 animals at that city (Van De Mieroop 1993, 165). In my opinion, however, it is highly unlikely that a single shepherd could have handled the many tasks associated with pasturing and ensuring the safety and reproduction of so many animals. Rather, it seems more plausible that the Ur herding contracts simply record the principal (adult) shepherd responsible for the flock and make no mention of the many minor workers (adolescents and children) that necessarily would have also been involved in pasturing such large flocks.

19. In fact, Englund (1998, 146) identifies the sign combination $SE_a + NAM_2$ in the herding contracts in the Archaic Texts as designating a professional name, which he believes may have acted as a "feeder."

20. Ryder (1993, 14–16) suggests that the introduction of wool shearing based on the availability of sharp iron scissors sometime during the first millennium BC prompted ancient Near Eastern herdsmen to start selecting for continuous wool growth throughout the year. After millennia of such selection, modern sheep populations in the area no longer molt their wool, and plucking is no longer practiced.

21. As discussed in detail in chapter 7, it is almost certainly not accidental that the growth of the city of Uruk and its immediate area in the Late Uruk period correlates with declines in population not only in the northern (i.e., Nippur-Adab area) and southern (i.e., Eridu-Ur basin) reaches of the Mesopotamian alluvium but with population in southwestern Iran and northern Mesopotamia as well.

Chapter Six

1. For a more detailed discussion and specific references to archaeologically attested imports in Uruk period levels of southern Mesopotamian sites, see Algaze (1993 [2005a], 74–84); and Moorey (1994). The following references should be added to the aforementioned discussions by Algaze and Moorey: bitumen, see Connan (1999) and Schwartz, Hollander, and Stein (1999); wood, see Moorey and Postgate (1992); and Engel and Kürschner (1993); wine, see Algaze (1995); Badler, McGovern, and Glusker (1996); and McGovern (2003, 43–63, 160–64).

2. While the Sammelfund was found in the Jemdet Nasr–period level at Warka (Eanna III), the hundreds of objects comprising this hoard appear to consist principally of heirlooms that can be dated to the Uruk period on stylistic grounds (Heinrich 1936).

3. Woven textiles, being entirely organic, leave no trace in the archaeological record, save for occasional impressions of cloth preserved on metal corrosion (e.g., Barber 1991, 132–33) or sealing clay (Ochsenschlager 1993, 55). However, those impressions are likely to be representative only for the coarser grades of cloth, grades that would not have featured significantly in exports.

4. Note, however, that some tools associated with weaving have been noted in the context of Uruk sites, although we still lack a comprehensive study of the data that would allow us to differentiate which of these objects were used in the context of domestic versus industrial weaving. Cases in point for the tools are a variety of elongated spatula-like implements made of bone (e.g., Delougaz and Kantor 1996, 110; pl. 128x, y, aa), which may have served as loom shuttles. Archaeology also provides evidence, however fragmentary and nonquantifiable, for other aspects of the textile production process at the time, including spinning, storing of thread, and sewing. These can be inferred, respectively, from stone or terracotta spindle whorls (e.g., Delougaz and Kantor 1996, 104–9, n. 26, pls. 29q–z, 30j–o, 126a–m), terracotta thread spools (e.g., Delougaz and Kantor 1996, 107, n. 31, pls. 30a–g, 126y–bb), and bone needles (e.g., Delougaz and Kantor 1996, 110, pl. 128v–y).

5. In later periods, Mesopotamian societies imported substantial amounts of wine from the Upper Euphrates region, which was shipped downstream via the river from either Carchemish and/or Mari (Finet 1969), and it would stand to reason that similarly situated Uruk outposts along the Euphrates (Habuba-süd, etc.) may have served as collection, bottling, and transshipment points for wine produced in the high plains of Upper Mesopotamia, where both wild and domestic grapes thrived in antiquity.

6. See chapter 6, note 1.

7. The Limestone Temple in Eanna V was approximately 27 × 80 m in size (2,160 m^2). The principal Eanna IVb-a structures in the same area include (all measurements are approximate and derived from fig. 3): Temple D: 80 × 50 m

(4,000 m^2); Temple C: 20 × 55 m (1,100 m^2); Palace E ("Square Building") 55 × 55 m; (3,025 m^2); Pillared Hall: 40 × 17 m (680 m^2); Stone Cone Mosaic Temple: 20 × 30 m (600 m^2); Riemchengebaüde: 20 × 20 m (400 m^2); Building F: 20 × 33 m (660 m^2); and Mosaic Court Building: 20 × 33 (660 m^2). To this must be added the roughly contemporary White Temple (18 × 22 m = 396 m^2) and Steingebaüde (25 × 30 m = 600 m^2) in the Anu Ziggurat area (fig. 2). Thus, the known (i.e., excavated) area of public structures at the core of Warka in the final phase of the Uruk period minimally occupied an area of approximately 12,121 square meters, requiring anywhere between 16,800 and 33,600 linear meters of roofing timber at rates comparable to those calculated by Margueron for the Limestone Temple. To be sure, while all of this timber had to have been imported into the alluvium over the long term, not all of it needed to have been procured at any one time since, no doubt, a significant portion of the timber used in any one building phase would have been salvaged from earlier architecture.

8. Adams (1981, 122) notes, however, that stone bowls in complex shapes and exhibiting particularly skilled craftsmanship were much more common in Uruk period sites in the Warka region than in the Nippur-Adab area.

Chapter Seven

1. Note, however, that the two data sets are not entirely comparable insofar as Pollock's cutoff for town-sized settlements is 8 hectares as opposed to Adams's 10 hectares.

2. In arriving at this number, Nissen follows Adams's (1981, 69, 349–50) equally conservative estimate of 100 persons per hectare of occupied area as determined by surface survey. The difficulties of making precise correlations between area and population in the Mesopotamian case have been the subject of a review by Nicholas Postgate (1994), who uses the actual layout of neighborhoods in third- and second-millennium Mesopotamian cities to estimate their population, and concludes that actual densities in those cities could have been as high as 900 plus persons per hectare.

3. According to Adams (1981, 69, 75, tables 3 and 5, respectively), sites 10 hectares in extent and larger amounted to 39 percent of a total occupied area of the Uruk survey area in the Late Uruk period (382 ha). This comes out to about 149 ha worth of "urban-sized" occupations. To this must be added a further 150 hectares to account for the increased estimate of the urban extent of Uruk itself at this time. Urban-sized occupations in the Uruk area in the Late Uruk phase thus amounted to about 299 hectares out of a total of 532 hectares, or just under 60 percent.

4. See chapter 7, note 1.

5. It should be noted that Wilkinson (2000b, fig. 5) had originally suggested

that regional population densities in the north Jazirah region were higher than those in the south throughout the fourth millennium, but after comparing both data sets using Dewar's algorithm he no longer believes that this was the case (Kouchoukos and Wilkinson 2007, 16–18, fig. 10).

6. Both Umma (WS 197) and Aqarib (WS 198) were at the edge of Adams's 1968 survey area, but could not be properly surveyed at that time because of extensive sand dunes covering the area (Adams and Nissen 1972, 227–28). The dunes obscuring these sites have now cleared the Umma-Aqarib region.

7. I am grateful to Douglas White for helping me understand the principles underlying power-law growth patterns and their applicability to the study of urban settlement systems.

8. Jennifer Pournelle (2003b, 155) proposes a further possibility, which, again, does not preclude any of the preceding explanations. She suggests that the absence of sites in the Abu Salabikh/Tell al-Hayyad arc may be due in part to decreased wind erosion in this area (hampering site recognition), as opposed to areas directly north and south of the arc.

9. Although this statement may have to be revised once systematic surveys are extended to the Umma and Lagash areas of the Tigris.

10. In this light, the fact that the overwhelming amount of evidence we possess for the development of early Mesopotamian writing during the Uruk period (a communication technology par excellence) happens to come from Warka may well not be accidental. See chapter 8, below, for a fuller discussion of the role of writing and related technologies on the evolution of early Sumerian civilization.

Chapter Eight

1. See Desrochers (2001a, 2001b) for a discussion of the role of geographical proximity as a spur for innovation.

2. This principle represents a transposition to the dynamics of human communication of an idea of Robert Metcalfe (one of the inventors of the Ethernet) about the nature of computer-based communication networks. He argued that the aggregate value of a network (i.e., usefulness in creating and disseminating information) is proportional to the square of the number of its users (Krugman n.d.).

For illustrative purposes, if we presume that something like Metcalfe's Law can be used to model what would happen in human societies as physical propinquity increased the likelihood of communication, a doubling of a population from, say, 5,000 to 10,000 people would increase the number of *possible* interactions within that population from 25 to 100 million and a further doubling of the population to 20,000 people would yield 400 million possible interactions.

3. For illustrative purposes, quadratic growth means that a squaring of an initial population of, say, 10 people would result in a total of 10,000,000,000,000,000,000 *possible* interactions—although, to be sure, the number of *actual* interactions at any one time is likely to be many, many times smaller than the theoretical quadratic maximum. I am grateful to Douglas White for explaining to me the principles underlying power-law growth patterns.

4. I am grateful to Joyce Marcus (personal communication, 2006) for bringing this citation to my attention. See also Marcus (1996).

5. The advantages of societies possessing fully developed writing systems over those lacking them are summarized by Lévi-Strauss (1964, 291) in a passage so eloquent that it deserves to be cited in full:

> Writing is a strange thing. It would seem as if its appearance could not have failed to wreak profound changes in the living conditions of our race, and that these transformations must have been above all intellectual in character. Once men know how to write, they are enormously more able to keep in being a large body of knowledge. Writing might, that is to say, be regarded as a form of artificial memory, whose development should be accompanied by a deeper knowledge of the past and therefore by a greater ability to organize the present and the future. Of all the criteria by which people habitually distinguish civilization from barbarism, this should be the one most worth retaining: certain peoples write and others do not. The first group can accumulate a body of knowledge that helps it move ever faster towards the goal that it has assigned to itself; the second group is confined within limits that the memory of individuals can never hope to extend, and it must remain a prisoner of a history worked out from day to day, with neither a clear knowledge of its own origins nor a consecutive idea of what its future should be.

6. The faunal remains from Hacınebi are uninformative on this point, as there were so few equid bones overall that no attempt was made to differentiate between wild (*E. hemionus*) and domestic (*E. asinus*) animals (Bigelow 1999, table 1).

Chapter Nine

1. The development of the Harappan civilization, centered on several large and roughly equidistant urban sites along the Indus and Hakra rivers of modern Pakistan, may well follow an evolutionary pathway similar to that described here. However, the nature of the political structures that characterized these cities, and the territorial boundaries between them, are widely debated among Indus specialists.

Epilogue

1. But note, however, that the existence of a kingly figure with religious over-tones in Uruk Mesopotamia is disputed by some specialists (e.g., Glassner 2003, 204–12), who argue that there is little supporting textual evidence for the title "king" in the Archaic Texts. While this is largely true, there is one exception, and it happens to be a significant one. One of the earliest and most important lexical lists in the corpus of Archaic Texts is a document conventionally referred to as the "Titles and Professions List." Fragmentary scribal copies of this standard-ized list are known at Warka already in the earliest Uruk IV–type script (Nissen, Damerow, and Englund 1993, 110–15). In its complete version, the document lists over 120 categories of specialized administrative and priestly personnel in some sort of hierarchical order. Entries include the titles of administrators in charge of various state offices and in many cases also detail the ranks of lesser officials within individual offices. What makes this list pertinent to the discussion of kingship in the Uruk period is that it starts with a functionary designated by an enigmatic sign combination, $NAM_2+\acute{E}SDA$. This official is attested already in Uruk III script-type versions of the list, which date to the very end of the fourth millennium (Jemdet Nasr period). Because of its position at the head of a list of officials presented in declining order of importance, it is highly likely that the $NAM_2+\acute{E}SDA$ functionary stands at the very top of the administrative pyramid in early Sumerian cities.

Who is this man and what does he do? In answer to these questions, Hans Nissen notes that since the sign combination at issue is equated in a much later Sumerian-Akkadian dictionary with the Akkadian word *Šarrum*, which incon-testably means *king* (Nissen, Damerow, and Englund 1993, 111), it stands to rea-son that a comparable meaning can be ascribed to the earlier fourth-millennium attestation of $NAM_2+\acute{E}SDA$.

In addition, views that deny the existence of kings in fourth-millennium Mes-opotamia are undermined, in my opinion, by the striking iconographic continu-ity that exists between the "priest-king/city ruler" images of the Uruk period and the way Sumerian kings of third-millennium date were represented, whose identity is established without a doubt by associated inscriptions.

2. What I envision is a project similar in research goals, scale, and level of ana-lytical precision to the exhaustive coring program recently undertaken by Dutch, U.S., and Egyptian scholars on the Egyptian Delta (Butzer 2001) and Belgian and Iranian researchers in southwestern Iran (Baeteman, Dupin, and Heyvaert 2004, 2005).

3. The materials published in the series Ausgrabungen in Uruk-Warka End-berichte may not include many artifacts left in Baghdad as part of the Iraqi share of the finds. In addition, the materials in question were not excavated, collected, or recorded using modern problem-oriented procedures (Nissen 2002).

4. After assessing changes in the relative density of imported and exported materials (chert and, more rarely, copper and lapis lazuli, and bitumen, respectively) at Farukhabad throughout the fourth millennium, Wright concluded that increases in the participation of the site's inhabitants in long distance trade networks did not take place until after the Uruk period. Elsewhere, I have argued that while this conclusion is warranted by the Farukhabad data it is unlikely that results from the site, a small center 4–5 hectares in extent in a somewhat marginal location, are representative of conditions in the much larger centers at the core of the Uruk world (Algaze 1993 [2005a], 119).

Reference List

Adams, R. McC. 1965. *Land Behind Baghdad*. Chicago: University of Chicago Press.

———. 1966. *The Evolution of Urban Society: Early Mesopotamia and Prehispanic Mexico*. Chicago: Aldine.

———. 1974. "Anthropological Perspectives on Ancient Trade." *Current Anthropology* 15: 239–58.

———. 1978. "Strategies of Maximization, Stability, and Resilience in Mesopotamian Society, Settlement, and Agriculture." *Proceedings of the American Philosophical Society* 122: 329–35.

———. 1981. *Heartland of Cities*. Chicago: University of Chicago Press.

———. 2005. "Critique of Guillermo Algaze's "The Sumerian Takeoff." *Structure and Dynamics: eJournal of Anthropological and Related Sciences:* Vol. 1, article 9. Http://repositories.cdlib.org/imbs/socdyn/sdeas/vol1/iss1/art.

Adams, R. McC., and H.-J. Nissen. 1972. *The Uruk Countryside*. Chicago: University of Chicago Press.

Algaze, G. 1984. "Private Houses and Graves at Ingharra: A Reconsideration." *Mesopotamia* 18–19: 135–94.

———. 1989. "The Uruk Expansion: Cross-cultural Exchange in Early Mesopotamian Civilization." *Current Anthropology* 30: 571–608.

———. 1993. *The Uruk World System: The Dynamics of Expansion of Early Mesopotamian Civilization*. Chicago: University of Chicago Press.

———. 1995. "Fourth Millennium Trade in Greater Mesopotamia and the Question of Wine." In *The Origins and Ancient History of Wine*, ed. by S. Fleming, P. McGovern, and S. Katz, 89–96. New York: Gordon and Breach.

———. 1999. "Trends in the Archaeological Development of the Upper Euphrates Basin of Southeastern Anatolia during the Late Chalcolithic and Early Bronze Ages." In *Archaeology of the Upper Syrian Euphrates: The Tishrin Dam Area*, ed. by G. del Olmo Lete and J.-L. Montero Fenollós, 535–72. Barcelona: Editorial Ausa.

———. 2001a. "Initial Social Complexity in Southwestern Asia: The Mesopotamian Advantage." *Current Anthropology* 43: 199–233.

————. 2001b. "The Prehistory of Imperialism: The Case of Uruk Period Mesopotamia." In *Uruk Mesopotamia and Its Neighbors*, ed. by M. Rothman, 27–83. Santa Fe: SAR Press.

————. 2005a. *The Uruk World System: The Dynamics of Expansion of Early Mesopotamian Civilization*. Second revised edition. Chicago: University of Chicago Press.

————. 2005b. "The Sumerian Takeoff." *Structure and Dynamics* 1: Http://repositories.cdlib.org/imbs/socdyn/sdeas/vol1/iss1/art2/.

Algaze, G., R. Breuninger, C. Lightfoot, and M. Rosenberg. 1991. "The Tigris-Euphrates Archaeological Reconnaissance Project, 1989–90." *Anatolica* 17: 175–240.

Algaze, G., A. Mısır, and T. Wilkinson. 1992. "Sanlıurfa Museum/University of California Excavations and Surveys at Titris, Höyük, 1991: A Preliminary Report." *Anatolica* 18: 33–60.

Algaze, G., R. Breuninger, and J. Knudstad. 1994. "The Tigris-Euphrates Archaeological Reconnaissance Project: Final Report of the Birecik and Carchemish Dam Survey Areas." *Anatolica* 20: 1–96.

Amiet, P. 1961. *La glyptique mésopotamienne archaïque*. Paris: Centre National de la Recherche Scientifique.

————. 1972. *Glyptique susienne*. Mémoires de la Délégation Archéologique Française en Iran, 43. Paris: Geuthner.

————. 1994. "Review of G. Algaze's The Uruk World System—The Dynamics of Expansion of Early Mesopotamian Civilization." *Revue d'Assyriologie* 88: 92–93.

————. 2005. "L'effigie royale aux origins de la civilisation mésopotamienne." *Revue Biblique* 112: 5–19.

Aqrawi, A. A. M. 2001. "Stratigraphic Signatures of Climatic Change during the Holocene Evolution of the Tigris-Euphrates Delta, Lower Mesopotamia." *Global and Planetary Change* 28: 267–83.

Badler, V. R., P. E. McGovern, and D. L. Glusker. 1996. "Chemical Evidence for a Wine Residue from Warka (Uruk) inside a Late Uruk Period Spouted Jar." *Baghdader Mitteilungen* 27: 39–43.

Badler, V. R. 2002. "A Chronology of Uruk Artifacts from Godin Tepe." In *Artefacts of Complexity: Tracking the Uruk in the Near East*, ed. by N. Postgate, 79–109. Warminster: Aris and Phillips.

Baeteman, C., L. Dupin, and V. Heyvaert. 2004. "Geo Environmental Investigation." In H. Gasche, ed., "The Persian Gulf Shorelines and the Karkheh, Karun, and Jarrahi Rivers: A Geo-Archaeological Approach. First Progress Report." *Akkadica* 125: 155–215.

————. 2005. "Geo Environmental Investigation." In H. Gasche, ed., "The Persian Gulf Shorelines and the Karkheh, Karun, and Jarrahi Rivers: A Geo-Archaeological Approach. First Progress Report–Part 2." *Akkadica* 126: 5–12.

Bakker, J. A., J. Kruk, A. E. Lanting, and S. Milisauskas. 1999. "The Earliest Evidence of Wheeled Vehicles in Europe and the Near East." *Antiquity* 73: 778–90.

Bairoch, P. 1988. *Cities and Economic Development.* Chicago: University of Chicago Press.

———. 1990. "The Impact of Crop Yields, Agricultural Productivity, and Transport Costs on Urban Growth between 1800 and 1910." In *Urbanization in History: A Process of Dynamic Interactions,* ed. by A. D. van der Woude, A. Hayimi, and J. de Vries, 134–151. Oxford: Clarendon Press.

———. 1993. *Economics and World History: Myths and Paradoxes.* Chicago: University of Chicago Press.

Ballinger, C. J. 2001 "City, Society, and State: The Role of Transport Costs in European State Development." Master's thesis, University of North Carolina at Chapel Hill.

Bahrani, Z. 2002. "Performativity and the Image: Narrative, Representation, and the Uruk Vase." In *Leaving No Stones Unturned: Essays on the Ancient Near East and Egypt in Honor of Donald P. Hansen,* ed. by E. Ehrenberg, 15–22. Eisenbrauns: Winona Lake.

Barber, E. W. 1991. *Prehistoric Textiles.* Princeton: Princeton University Press.

———. 1994 *Women's Work: The First 2000 Years.* New York: W. W. Norton.

Beinhocker, E. D. 2006. *The Origin of Wealth.* Cambridge: Harvard Business School Press.

Benco, N. 1992. "Manufacture and Use of Clay Sickles from the Uruk Mound, Abu Salabikh." *Paléorient* 18: 119–34.

Berger, J.-F., S. Cleuziou, G. Davtian, M. Cattani, F. Cavulli, V. Chapentier, M. Cremaschi, J. Giraud, P. Marquis, C. Martin, S. Méry, J.-C. Plaziat, and J.-F. Saliege. 2005. "Evolution paléogéographique du Ja'alan (Oman) a l'Holocene Moyen: Impact sur l'evolution des paléomilieux littoraux et des strategies d'adaptation des communautés humaines." *Paléorient* 31: 46–63.

Bigelow, L. 1999. "Zooarchaeological Investigations of Economic Organization and Ethnicity at Late Chalcolithic Hacınebi: A Preliminary Report." *Paléorient* 25: 83–89.

Boese, J. 1995. *Ausgrabungen in Tell Sheikh Hassan. Vol. 1. Vorläufige Berichte über die Grabungskampagnen 1984–1990 und 1992–1994.* Saarbrucken: Saarbrucker Druckerei und Verlag.

Boessneck, J. 1992. "Besprechung der Tiernochen und Molluskresten von Hassek Höyük." *Hassek Höyük: Naturwissenschaftliche Untursuchungen und lithische Industrie,* ed. by M. R. Behm-Blancke, 58–74. Tübingen: Ernst Wasmuth Verlag.

Boehmer, R. M. 1999. *Uruk, Früheste Siegelabrollungen.* Ausgrabungen in Uruk-Warka Endberichte, 25. Mainz am Rhein: Philipp von Zabern.

Bourke, S. 2001. "The Chalcolithic Period." In *The Archaeology of Jordan,* ed.

by B. MacDonald, R. Adams, and P. Bienkowski, 107–61. Sheffield: Sheffield Academic Press.

Brandes, M. A. 1979. *Siegelabrollungen aus den archaischen Bauschichten in Uruk-Warka*. Weisbaden: Franz Steiner Verlag.

Burghardt, A. F. 1971. "A Hypothesis about Gateway Cities." *Annals of the Association of American Geographers* 61: 269–87.

———. 1979. "The Origin of the Road and City Network of Roman Pannonia." *Journal of Historical Geography* 5: 1–20.

Butler, A. 2006. *Sheep*. New York: O Books.

Butzer, K. W. 2001. "Geoarchaeological Implications of Recent Research in the Nile Delta." *In Egyptian-Canaanite Interaction—The 4th Millennium Background,* ed. by E. van den Brink and T. E. Levy, 83–97. London: Leicester University Press.

Carter, E. 1985. "Lagash (Tell Al-Hiba)." *Iraq* 47: 222.

Casson, L. 1971. *Ships and Seamanship in the Ancient World*. Princeton: Princeton University Press.

Christaller, W. 1966 [1933]. *Central Places in Southern Germany*. Translated by C. W. Baskin. Englewood Cliffs, NJ: Prentice Hall.

Cioffi-Revilla, C. 2001. "Comment." *Current Anthropology* 42: 216–17.

Clark, C., and M. Haswell. 1970. *The Economics of Subsistence Agriculture*. London: Macmillan.

Clark, G. 2007. *A Farewell to Alms*. Princeton: Princeton University Press.

Collins, P. 2000. *The Uruk Phenomenon: The Role of Social Ideology in the Expansion of Uruk Culture during the Fourth Millennium BC*. BAR International Series, 900. Oxford: Archeopress.

Connan, J. 1999. "Use and Trade of Bitumen in Antiquity and Prehistory: Molecular Archaeology Reveals Secrets of Past Civilizations." *Philosophical Transactions of the Royal Society, London: Biological Sciences* 354: 33–50.

Connan, J., R. Carter, H. Crawford, M. Tobey, A. Charrié-Duhault, D. Jarvie, P. Albrecht, and K. Norman. 2005. "A Comparative Geochemical Study of Bituminous Boat Remains From H3, As Sabiyah (Kuwait), and RJ-2, Ra's al-Jinz (Oman)." *Arabian Archaeology and Epigraphy* 16: 21–66.

Cornog, E. 2000. *The Birth of Empire: Dewitt Clinton and the American Experience, 1769–1828*. New York: Oxford University Press.

Crawford, H. E. W. 1973. "Mesopotamia's Invisible Exports in the Third Millennium B.C." *World Archaeology* 5: 232–41.

Crone, P. 1989. *Pre-industrial Societies*. Oxford: Basil Blackwell.

Cowgill, G. 2000. "Intentionality and Meaning in the Layout of Teotihuacan, Mexico." *Cambridge Archaeological Journal* 10: 358–65.

Cronon, W. 1991. *Nature's Metropolis Chicago and Great West*. New York: W. W. Norton.

Davis, S. J. M. 1984. "The Advent of Milk and Wool Production in Western Iran:

Some Speculations." In *Animals in Archaeology: 3. Early Herders and Their Flocks*, ed. by J. Clutton-Brock and C. Grigson, 265–78. Oxford: BAR.

———. 1993. "The Zooarchaeology of Sheep and Goat in Mesopotamia." *Bulletin on Sumerian Agriculture* 7: 1–7.

Damerow, P. 2006. "The Origins of Writing as a Problem of Historical Epistemology." *Cuneiform Digital Library Journal*. Http://cdli.ucla.edu/pubs/cdlj/2006/cdlj2006_001.pdf.

Delougaz, P., and H. J. Kantor. 1996. *Chogha Mish I: The First Five Seasons of Excavations, 1961–1971*, ed. by A. Alizadeh. Oriental Institute Publications, 101. Chicago: Oriental Institute.

De Noblet, N., P. Braconnot, S. Joussaume, and V. Masson. 1996. "Sensitivity of Simulated Asian and African Summer Monsoons to Orbitally Induced Variations in Insolation 126, 115, and 6 kBP." *Climate Dynamics* 12: 589–603.

Dercksen, J. G. 1996. *The Old Assyrian Copper Trade in Anatolia*. Leiden: Nederlands Instituut Voor Het Nabije Oosten.

———. 2004. *Old Assyrian Institutions*. Leiden: Nederlands Instituut Voor Het Nabije Oosten.

Desrochers, P. 2001a. "Local Diversity, Human Creativity, and Technological Innovation." *Growth and Change* 32: 369–94.

———. 2001b. "Geographical Proximity and the Transmission of Tacit Knowledge." *Review of Austrian Economics* 14: 25–46.

Desse, J. 1983. "Les faunes du gisement obeidien final de Tell el'Ouelli." In *Larsa et 'Ouelli: Travaux de 1978–1981*, ed. by J.-L. Huot, 193–99. Paris: Éditions Recherches sur les Civilizations.

Dewar, R. 1991. "Incorporating Variation in Occupation Span into Settlement Pattern Analysis." *American Antiquity* 56: 604–20.

Drennan, R. 1984. "Long-Distance Transport Costs in Pre-Hispanic Mesoamerica." *American Anthropologist* 86: 105–12.

Dymski, G. 1996. "On Krugman's Model of Economic Geography." *Geoforum* 27: 439–52.

Dittmann, R. 1986. "Seals, Sealings, and Tablets: Thoughts on the Changing Pattern of Administrative Control from the Late Uruk to the Proto-Elamite Period at Susa." In *Gemdet Nasr: Period or Regional Style?* ed. by U. Finkbeiner and W. Röllig, 332–66. Wiesbaden: Ludwig Reichert.

Eckholm, K. 1977. "External Exchange and the Transformation of Central African Social Systems." In *The Evolution of Social Systems*, ed. by J. Friedman and M. J. Rowlands, 115–36. London: Duckworth.

Edens, C. 1999. "The Chipped Stone Industry at Hacınebi: Technological Styles and Social Identity." *Paléorient* 25: 23–34.

Eichmann, R. 1989. *Uruk, Die Stratigraphie*. Mainz am Rhein: Philipp von Zabern.

el-Moslimany, A. 1990. "Ecological Significance of Common Nonarboreal Pollen: Examples from the Drylands of the Middle East." *Review of Paleobotany and Palynology* 64: 343–50.

———. 1994. "Evidence of Early Holocene Summer Precipitation in the Middle East." *Radiocarbon* 36: 121–30.

Ellerman, D. 2005. "How Do We Grow?" *Challenge* 48: 50–83.

Emberling, G. 2002. "Political Control in an Early State: The Eye Temple and the Uruk Expansion in Northern Mesopotamia." In *Of Pots and Plans: Papers on the Archaeology and History of Mesopotamia and Syria Presented to David Oates in Honor of His 75th Birthday*, ed. by L. Al-Ghailani Werr, J. Curtis, H. Martin, A. McMahon, J. Reade, and J. Oates, 82–90. London: Nabu Publications.

Emberling, G., and H. McDonald. 2001. "Excavations at Tell Brak 2000: Preliminary Report." *Iraq* 63: 21–54.

Emberling, G., J. Cheng. T. Larsen, H. Pittman, T. Skuldboel, J. Weber, and H. T. Wright. 1999. "Excavations at Tell Brak 1998: Preliminary Report." *Iraq* 61: 1–41.

Engel, T., and H. Kürshner. 1993. "Weitere Holzkohlen und Holzreste aus Uruk." *Baghdader Mitteilungen* 24: 127–35.

Englund, R. K. 1990. *Organization und Verwaltung der Ur III-Fischerei*. Berlin: D. Reimer.

———. 1995a. "Late Uruk Pigs and Other Herded Animals." In *Beiträge zur Kulturgeschichte Vorderasiens*, ed. by U. Finkbeiner, R. Dittmann, and H. Hauptmann, 121–33. Mainz: Philipp von Zabern.

———. 1995b. "Late Uruk Period Cattle and Dairy Products. The Evidence from Protocuneiform Sources." *Bulletin on Sumerian Agriculture* 8: 32–48.

———. 1998. "Texts from the Late Uruk Period," In *Mesopotamien: Späturuk-Zeit und Frühdynastische Zeit*, ed. by P. Attinger and M. Wafler, 15–236. Freiburg Schweiz: Universitätsverlag, and Gottingen: Vandenhoeck and Ruprecht.

———. 2004. "Proto-Cuneiform Account-Books and Journals." In *Creating Economic Order: Record-Keeping, Standarization, and the Development of Accounting in the Ancient Near East*, ed. by M. Hudson and C. Wunsch, 23–46. Bethesda, MD: CDL Press.

Farber, Howard. 1978. "A Price and Wage Study for Northern Babylonia during the Old Babylonian Period." *Journal of the Economic and Social History of the Orient* 21: 1–51.

Feinman, G. 1998. "Scale and Social Organization: Perspectives on the Archaic State." In *Archaic States,* ed. by G. Feinman and J. Marcus, 95–134. Santa Fe: School of American Research Press.

Ferioli, P., and E. Fiandra. 1983. "Clay Sealings from Arslantepe VIA: Administration and Bureaucracy." *Origine* 12: 455–509.

Fernández-Armesto, F. 2001. *Civilizations*. New York: Free Press.

Fiandra, E. 1979. "The Connection between Clay Sealings and Tablets in Administration." In *South Asian Archaeology, 1979*, ed. by H. Hartel, 29–43. Berlin: Dietrich Reimer.

———. 1994. "Discussion." In *Archives before Writing*, ed. by P. Ferioli, E. Fiandra, G. G. Fissore, and M. Frangipane, 168. Rome: Centro Internazionale di Recerche Archaeologiche Anthropologiche e Storiche.

Finch, R. G. 1925. *The Story of the New York State Canals: Historical and Commercial Information*. New York: New York State Canal Corporation. Reprinted in http://www.canals.state.ny.us/cculture/history/index.html

Finet, A. 1969. "L'Euphrate, route commerciale de la Mésopotamie." *Annales Archéologiques Arabes Syriennes* 19: 37–48.

Finkbeiner, U. 1991. *Uruk Kampagne 35–37, 1982–1984. Die archäologische Oberflächenuntersuchung (Survey)*. Ausgrabungen in Uruk-Warka Endberichte, 4. Mainz: Philipp von Zabern.

Finley, M. I. 1985. *The Ancient Economy*. Second edition. Berkeley: University of California Press.

Flannery, K. V. 1995. "Prehistoric Social Evolution." *Research Frontiers in Anthropology*, ed. by C. R. Ember and M. Ember, 1–26. Englewood Cliffs, NJ: Prentice-Hall.

———. 1999. "Process and Agency in Early State Formation." *Cambridge Archaeological Journal* 9: 3–21.

Flannery, K. V., and H. T. Wright. 1966. "Faunal Remains from 'Hut Sounding' at Eridu." *Sumer* 22: 61–64.

Forest, J.-D. 1997. "L'habitat urukien du Djebel Aruda: Approche fonctionnelle et arrière-plans symboliques." In *Les maisons dans la Syrie Antique du III'e millénaire aux débuts de L'Islam*, ed. by C. Castel, M. al-Maqdissi, and F. Villeneuve, 217–43. Beirut: Institut Français D'Archaéologie du Proche Orient.

———. 1999. *Les premieres temples de Mésopotamie*. British Archaeological Reports, 765. Oxford: Archeopress.

Foster, B. 1977. "Commercial Activity in Sargonic Mesopotamia." *Iraq* 29: 31–43.

———. 1993. "'International' Trade at Sargonic Susa." *Altorientalische Forschungen* 20: 59–68.

Fox, E. W. 1971. *History in Geographic Perspective: The Other France*. New York: W. W. Norton.

———. 1980. "The Range of Communications and the Shape of Social Organization." *Communication* 5: 275–87.

———. 1989. "The Argument: Some Reinforcements and Projections." In *Geographic Perspectives in History*, ed. by E. D. Genovese and L. Hochberg, 331–42. Oxford: Basil Blackwell.

———. 1991. *The Emergence of the Modern European World*. Cambridge: Blackwell.

Frangipane, M. 1997. "A Fourth Millennium Temple/Palace Complex at Arslan-tepe-Malatya: North-south Relations and the Formation of Early State Societ-ies in the Northern Regions of Southern Mesopotamia." *Paléorient* 23: 45–73.

———. 2001a. "Centralization Processes in Greater Mesopotamia: Uruk Ex-pansion as the Climax of Systemic Interactions among Areas of the Greater Mesopotamian Region." In *Uruk Mesopotamia and Its Neighbors*, ed. by M. Rothman, 307–48. Santa Fe: SAR Press.

———. 2001b. "On Models and Data in Mesopotamia." *Current Anthropology* 42: 415–16.

———. 2002. "Non-Uruk" Developments and Uruk-Linked Features on the Northern Borders of Greater Mesopotamia." In *Artefacts of Complexity: Tracking the Uruk in the Near East*, ed. by J. N. Postgate, 123–48. Warminster: Aris and Phillips, Ltd.

Frangipane, M., F. Balossi, G.-M. Di Nocera, A. Palmieri, and G. Syracusano. 2004. "The 2001 Excavation Campaign at Zeytinbahce Höyük: Preliminary Report." In *Salvage Project of the Archaeological Heritage of the Ilisu and Carchemish Dam Reservoirs. Activities in 2001*, ed. by N. Tuna, J. Greenhalgh, and J. Velibeyoğlu, 19–56. Ankara: Middle eastern Technical University.

Frankfort, H. 1951. *The Birth of Civilization in the Near East*. Bloomington: In-diana University Press.

Fujita, M., P. Krugman, and A. J. Venables. 1999. *The Spatial Economy: Cities, Regions, and International Trade*. Cambridge: MIT Press.

Fujita, M., and P. Krugman. 1995. "When Is the Economy Monocentric—Von Thünen and Chamberlin Unified." *Regional Science and Urban Economics* 25: 505–28.

———.2004. "The New Economic Geography: Past, Present, and Future." *Papers in Regional Science* 83: 139–64.

Gallup, J. L., J. D. Sachs, and A. Mellinger. 1999. "Geography and Economic Development." *International Regional Science Review* 22: 179–232.

Garfinkle, S. J. 2005. "Public versus Private in the Ancient Near East." In *A Companion to the Ancient Near East*, ed. by D. C. Snell, 384–96. Malden, MA: Blackwell.

Gasche H., and M. Tanret, eds. 1998. *Changing Water Courses in Babylonia. Towards a Reconstruction of the Ancient Environment in Lower Mesopotamia*. Chicago: Oriental Institute.

Gibson, McG. 1972. *The City and Area of Kish*. Miami: Field Research Proj-ects.

Gibson, McG., A. al-Azm, C. Reichel, S. Quntar, J. A. Franke, L. Khalidi, C. Fritz, M. Altaweel, C. Coyle, C. Colantoni, J. Tenney, G. Abdul Aziz, and T. Hartnell. 2002. "Hamoukar: A Summary of Three Seasons of Excava-tions." *Akkadica* 123: 11–34.

Glassner, J.-J. 2000. "Les petits états mésopotamiens a la fin du 4e et au cours du

3e millénaire." In *A Comparative Study of Thirty City-State Cultures*, ed. by Mogens Herman Hansen, 35–54. Copenhagen: C.A. Reitzels Forlag.

———. 2003. *The Invention of Cuneiform*. Baltimore: John Hopkins University Press.

Goldstein, P. S 2005. *Andean Diaspora: The Tiwanaku Colonies and the Origins of South American Empire*. Gainesville: University Press of Florida.

Goody, J. 2000. *The Power of the Written Tradition*. Washington, DC: Smithsonian Institution Press.

———. 2006. *The Theft of History*. Cambridge: Cambridge University Press.

Gould, S. J. 1988. "On Replacing the Idea of Progress with an Operational Notion of Directionality." In *Evolutionary Progress,* ed. by M. Nitecki, 319–38. Chicago: University of Chicago Press.

Green, M. V. 1980. "Animal Husbandry at Uruk in the Archaic Period." *Journal of Near Eastern Studies* 39: 1–35.

Gunder Frank, A. 1993. "Bronze Age World System Cycles." *Current Anthropology* 34: 383–429.

Harrison, S. P., D. Jolly, F. Laarif, A. Abe-Ouchi, B. Dong, K. Herterich, C. Hewitt, S. Joussaume, J. E. Kutzbach, J. Mitchell, N. de Noblet, and P. Valdes. 1998. "Intercomparison of Simulated Global Vegetation Distributions in Response to 6 kyr BP Orbital Forcing." *Journal of Climate* 11: 2721–41.

Hawley, A. 1986. *Human Ecology: A Theoretical Essay*. Chicago: University of Chicago Press.

Heinrich, E. 1936. *Kleinfunde aus den archaischen Tempelschichten in Uruk*. Leipzig: Otto Harrassowits.

Helms, M. W. 1988. *Ulysses' Sail: An Ethnographic Odyssey of Power, Knowledge, and Geographical Distance*. Princeton: Princeton University Press.

———.1993. *Craft and the Kingly Ideal*. Austin: University of Texas Press.

Heron, C., and R. P. Evershed. 1993. "The Analysis of Organic Residues and the Study of Pottery Use." In *Archaeological Method and Theory,* ed. by M. B. Schiffer, 5: 247–84. Tucson: University of Arizona Press.

Hicks, J. 1969. *A Theory of Economic History*. Oxford: Clarendon.

Hirth, K. 1978. "Interregional Trade and the Formation of Prehistoric Gateway Communities." *American Antiquity* 43: 35–45.

Hoelzmann, P., D. Jolly, S. P. Harrison, F. Laarif, R. Bonnefille, and H. J. Pachur. 1998. "Mid-Holocene Land-surface Conditions in Northern Africa and the Arabian Peninsula: A Data Set for the Analysis of Biophysical Feedback in the Climate System." *Global Biochemical Cycles* 12: 35–51.

Hodgson, G. M. 1993. "The Mecca of Alfred Marshall." *Economic Journal* 103: 406–15.

Hole, F. 1994. "Environmental Instabilities and Urban Origins." In *Chiefdoms and Early States in the Near East,* ed. by G. Stein and M. S. Rothman, 121–52. Madison, WI: Prehistory Press.

Holmstrom, J. E. 1934. *Railways and Roads in Pioneer Development Overseas: A Study of Their Comparative Economics*. London: P. S. King & Son.

Houston, S. D., ed. 2004. *The First Writing: Script Invention as History and Process*. Cambridge: Cambridge University Press.

Hritz, C., and T. J. Wilkinson. 2006. "Using Shuttle Radar Topography to Map Ancient Water Channels in Mesopotamia." *Antiquity* 80: 415–24.

Hudson, M. 2004. "Introduction: The Role of Accounting in Civilization's Economic Takeoff." In *Creating Economic Order: Record-Keeping, Standarization, and the Development of Accounting in the Ancient Near East*, ed. by M. Hudson and C. Wunsch, 1–22. Bethesda, MD: CDL Press.

———. 2005. Review of David A. Warburton, *Macroeconomics from the Beginning: The General Theory, Ancient Markets, and the Rate of Interest*. "A Free Market Critique of Ancient Economies." *Journal of the Economic and Social History of the Orient* 48: 118–22.

Jacobs, J. 1969. *The Economy of Cities*. New York: Vintage.

———. 2000. *The Nature of Economies*. New York: Modern Library.

Jacobsen, T. [1953] 1970. "On the Textile Industry at Ur Under Ibbi-Sin." In *Towards the Image of Tammuz*, ed. by W. L. Moran, 216–30. Cambridge: Harvard University Press.

———. 1982. *Salinity and Irrigation Agriculture in Antiquity: Diyala Basin Archaeological Projects; Report on Essential Results, 1957–58*. Malibu: Undena.

Jasim, S. A. 1989. "Structure and Function in an Ubaid Village." In *Upon this Foundation: The Ubaid Reconsidered*, ed. by E. F. Henrickson and I. Thuesen, 79–90. Copenhagen: Carsten Niebuhr Institute of Ancient Near East Studies.

Joffe, A. 1994. Review of G. Algaze's *The Uruk World System—The Dynamics of Expansion of Early Mesopotamian Civilization*. *Journal of Field Archaeology* 21: 512–15.

———. 1998. "Alcohol and Social Complexity in Ancient Western Asia." *Current Anthropology* 39: 297–322.

Johnson, G. A. 1975. "Locational Analysis and the Investigation of Uruk Local Exchange Systems." In *Ancient Civilizations and Trade*, ed. by J. A. Sabloff and C. C. Lamberg-Karlovsky, 285–339. Albuquerque: University of New Mexico Press.

———. 1976. "Early State Organization in Southwestern Iran." In *Proceedings of the Fourth Annual Symposium on Archaeological Research in Iran*, ed. by F. Bagherzadeh, 190–223. Tehran: Iranian Centre for Archaeological Research.

———. 1980. "Spatial Organization of Early Uruk Settlement Systems." In *L'archaéologie de l'Iraq du début de l'epoche néolitique a 333 avant notre ere*, ed. by M.-T. Barrelet, 233–64. Paris: Éditions du Centre National de la Recherche Scientifique.

———. 1987. "The Changing Organization of Uruk Administration on the Susiana Plain." In *The Archaeology of Western Iran*, ed. by F. Hole, 107–40. Washington, DC: Smithsonian Institution Press.

———. 1988–89. "Late Uruk in Greater Mesopotamia: Expansion or Collapse?" *Origini* 14: 595–611.

Kaldor, N. 1972. "The Irrelevance of Equilibrium Economics." *Economic Journal* 82: 1237–55.

Kantor, H. J. 1984. "The Ancestry of the Divine Boat (Sirsir?) of Early Dynastic and Akkadian Glyptic." *Journal of Near Eastern Studies* 43: 277–80.

Kasarda, J. D. 1974. "The Structural Implications of Social System Size: A Three Level Analysis." *American Sociological Review* 39: 19–28.

Kawami, T. S. 2001. "The Cattle of Uruk: Stamp Seals and Animal Husbandry in the Late Uruk/Jemdet Nasr Period." In *Proceedings of the XLV Rencontre Assyriologique Internationale, Part II, Yale University: Seals and Seal Impressions*, ed. by W. H. Hallo and I. J. Winter, 31–48. Bethesda, MD: CDL Press.

Keith, K. 1995. Review of G. Algaze's *The Uruk World System—The Dynamics of Expansion of Early Mesopotamian Civilization*. *American Journal of Archaeology* 99: 152–53.

Kolata, A. 1983. "Chan Chan and Cuzco: On the Nature of the Ancient Andean City." In *Civilization in the Ancient Americas: Essays in Honor of Gordon R. Willey*, ed. by R. M. Leventhal and A. Kolata, 345–72. Albuquerque: University of New Mexico Press.

Kohl, P. 1987a. "The Ancient Economy, Transferable Technologies and the Bronze Age World-system: A View from the Northeastern Frontier of the Ancient Near East." In *Centre and Periphery in the Ancient World*, ed. by M. Rowlands, M. T. Larsen, and K. Kristiansen, 13–24. Cambridge: Cambridge University Press.

———. 1987b. "The Use and Abuse of World Systems Theory: The Case of the Pristine West Asian State." In *Advances in Archaeological Method and Theory*, ed. by M. B. Schiffer, 11: 1–36. San Diego: Academic Press.

———. 2001. Review of Gil Stein's *Rethinking World-systems: Diasporas, Colonies, and Interaction in Uruk Mesopotamia*. *American Anthropologist* 103: 230–31.

Kohlmeyer, K. 1996. "Houses in Habuba Kabira South: Spatial Organization and Planning of Late Uruk Residential Architecture." In *Houses and Households in Ancient Mesopotamia*, ed. by K. R. Veenhof, 89–104. Istanbul: Nederlands Historisch-Archaeologisch Instituut Voor Het Nabije Oosten.

———. 1997. "Habuba Kabira." In *The Oxford Encyclopedia of Archaeology in the Near East*, ed. by E. Meyers, 446–48. New York: Oxford University Press.

Korotayev, A. 2005. "A Compact Macromodel of World Systems Evolution." *Journal of World-systems Research* 11: 79–93.

Kouchoukos, N. 1998. "Landscape and Social Change in Late Prehistoric Mesopotamia." Ph.D. diss., Yale University.

Kouchoukos, N., and F. Hole. 2003. "Changing Estimates of Susiana's Prehistoric Settlement." In *Yeki Bud, Yeki Nabud: Essays on the Archaeology of Iran in Honor of William M. Sumner*, ed. by N. Miller and K. Abdi, 53–60. Los Angeles: Cotsen Institute of Archaeology.

Kouchoukos, N., and T. Wilkinson. 2007. "Landscape Archaeology in Mesopotamia: Past, Present, and Future." In *Settlement and Society: Essays Dedicated to Robert McCormick Adams*, ed. by E. C. Stone, 1–18. Los Angeles: UCLA Cotsen Institute of Archaeology.

Kozbe, G., and M. Rothman. 2005. "Chronology and Function at Yarim Höyük, Part II." *Anatolica* 31: 111–44.

Kriger, C. E. 1993. "Textile Production and Gender in the Sokoto Caliphate." *Journal of African History* 34: 361–401.

———. 2006. *Cloth in West African History*. Lanham, MD: Altamira Press.

Krugman, P. 1991. "Increasing Returns in Economic Geography." *Journal of Political Economy* 99: 483–99.

———. 1995. *Development, Geography, and Economic Theory*. Cambridge: MIT Press.

———. 1996a. *The Self-organizing Economy*. Cambridge: Blackwell Publishers.

———. 1996b. "Confronting the Mystery of Urban Hierarchy." *Journal of the Japanese and International Economies* 10: 399–418.

———. 1998a . "What's New about the New Economic Geography." *Oxford Review of Economic Policy* 14: 7–17.

———. 1998b. "Ricardo's Difficult Idea: Why Intellectuals Don't Understand Comparative Advantage." In *The Economics and Politics of Free Trade, Volume 2: Freedom and Trade,* ed. by G. Cook, 22–36. London: Routledge.

———. n.d. "Networks and Increasing Returns: A Cautionary Tale." Http://web.mit.edu/krugman/www/metcalfe.htm.

Krugman, P., and A. J. Venables. 1995. "Globalization and the Inequality of Nations." *Quarterly Journal of Economics* 110: 857–80.

Kurtz, D. V. 1987. "The Economics of Urbanization and State Formation at Teotihuacan." *Current Anthropology* 28: 329–53.

Kuzucuoğlu, C. 2007. "Climatic and Environmental Trends during the Third Millennium B.C. in Upper Mesopotamia." In *Sociétés humaines et changement climatique a la fin du troisieme millénaire: Une crise a-t-elle en lieu en Haute Mésopotamie? Actes du colloque de Lyon, 5–8 décembre 2005*, ed. by C. Kuzucuoğlu and C. Marro, 459–80. Paris: De Boccard.

Lamberg-Karlovsky, C. C. 1995. Review of G. Algaze, *The Uruk World System.* *International History Review* 17: 767–68.

———. 1999. "Households, Land Tenure, and Communication Systems in the 6th–4th Millennia of Greater Mesopotamia." In *Urbanization and Land Ownership in the Ancient Near East,* ed. by M. Hudson and B. Levine, 167–201. Cambridge, MA: Peabody Museum of Archaeology and Ethnology.

———. 2001. "Comment." *Current Anthropology* 42: 220–21.

Landes, D. S. 1998. *The Wealth and Poverty of Nations.* New York: W. W. Norton.

Langbein, W. B. 1976. *Hydrology and Environmental Aspects of Erie Canal (1817–99).* Geological Survey Water-Supply Paper 2038. Washington, DC: U.S. GPO. Available at: Http://www.history.rochester.edu/canal/bib/langbein/.

Larsen, M. T. 1967. *Old Assyrian Caravan Procedures.* Istanbul: Nederlands Historisch-Archaeologisch Instituut Voor Het Nabije Oosten.

———. 1976. *The Old Assyrian City State and Its Colonies.* Copenhagen: Akademisk Forlag.

Lawler, A. 2006. "North versus South, Mesopotamian Style." *Science* 312: 1458–63.

Leemans, W. F. 1960. *Foreign Trade in the Old Babylonian Period.* Leiden: Brill.

Lenski, G. 1979. "Directions and Continuities in Societal Growth." In *Societal Growth,* ed. by A. Hawley, 5–18. New York: Free Press.

Levy, T. E. 1998. "Cult, Metallurgy, and Rank Societies—Chalcolithic Period." In *The Archaeology of Society in the Holy Land,* edited by T. E. Levy, 226–43. London: Leicester University Press.

Lévi-Strauss, C. 1964. *Tristes Tropiques.* New York: Atheneum.

Liverani, M. 1983. "Fragments of Possible Counting and Recording Devices." *Origini* 12: 511–21.

Liverani, M., and W. Heimpel. 1995. "Observations on Livestock Management in Babylonia." *Acta Sumerologica* 17: 127–44.

Lloyd, S., and F. Safar. 1943. "Tell Uqair: Excavations by the Iraq Government Directorate of Antiquities in 1940 and 1941." *Journal of Near Eastern Studies* 2: 131–58.

Lösch, A. [1940] 1954. *The Economics of Location,* translated by W. H. Woglom and W. F. Stolper. New Haven: Yale University Press.

Machiavelli, N. [1532] 1940. *The Prince,* translated by L. Ricci and E. R. P. Vincent. New York: Random House.

Maekawa, K. 1980. "Female Weavers and Their Children in Lagash—Presargonic and Ur III." *Acta Sumerologica* 2: 81–125.

Malecki, E. J. 1997. *Technology and Economic Development: The Dynamics of Local, Regional, and National Competitiveness.* Second edition. Essex: Longman.

Mann, M. 1986. *The Sources of Social Power.* Vol. 1. Cambridge: Cambridge University Press.

Marcus, J. 1983. "On the Nature of the Mesoamerican City." In *Prehistoric Settlement Patterns: Essays in Honor of Gordon R. Willey,* ed. by E. Z. Vogt and Richard M. Leventhal, 195–242. Albuquerque: University of New Mexico Press.

———. 1996. "Writing Systems." In *Encyclopedia of Cultural Anthropology,* ed. by D. Levinson and M. Ember, 4: 1387–91. New York: Henry Holt.

———. 1998. "The Peaks and Valleys of Ancient States: An Extension of the Dynamic Model." *Archaic States,* ed. by G. Feinman and J. Marcus, 59–94. Santa Fe: School of American Research Press.

Margueron, J. C. 1992. "Les bois dans l'architecture: Premier essai pour une estimation des besoins dans le bassin mésopotamienne." *Bulletin on Sumerian Agriculture* 6: 79–96.

Marshall, J. U. 1989. *The Structure of Urban Systems.* Toronto: University of Toronto Press.

Martin, R. 1999. "The New 'Geographical Turn in Economics: Some Critical Reflections." *Cambridge Journal of Economics* 23: 65–91.

Martin, R., and P. Sunley. 1996. "Paul Krugman's Geographical Economics and Its Implications for Regional Development Theory: A Critical Assessment." *Economic Geography* 72: 259–92.

Matthers, J., ed. 1981. *The River Qoueiq: Northern Syria and Its Catchment.* Oxford: British Archaeological Reports.

Matthews, R. J. 1994. Review of G. Algaze's *The Uruk World System—The Dynamics of Expansion of Early Mesopotamian Civilization. Bibliotheca Orientalis* 51: 665–71.

———. 1999. Review of Josef Bauer, Robert K. Englund, and Manfred Krebernik, *Mesopotamien Späturuk-Zeit. Bulletin of the Schools of Oriental and African Studies* 62: 549–50.

Matthews, R. J., ed. 2003. *Excavations at Tell Brak.* Vol. 4, *Exploring an Upper Mesopotamian Regional Centre, 1994–1996.* London: McDonald Institute for Archaeological Research.

McCormick, M. 2001. *Origins of the European Economy.* Cambridge: Cambridge University Press.

McCorriston, J. 1997. "The Fiber Revolution: Textile Extensification, Alienation, and Social Stratification in Ancient Mesopotamia." *Current Anthropology* 38: 517–49.

———. 1999. "Syrian Origins of Safflower Production: New Discoveries in the Agrarian Prehistory of the Habur Basin." *Proceedings of the International Symposium on the Origins of Agriculture, Aleppo, Syria,* ed. by A. B. Damania, J. Valkoun, G. Willcox, and C. O. Qualset, 39–50. Aleppo, Rome, and Davis, California: ICARDA, IPGRI, FAO, and GRCP.

———. 2001. "Comment." *Current Anthropology* 42: 221–22.

McGovern, P. E. 2003. *Ancient Wine: The Search for the Origins of Viniculture.* Princeton: Princeton University Press.

McNeill, W. H. 2000. "Information and Transportation Nets in World History." In *World System History*, ed. by R. A. Denemark, J. Friedman, B. K. Gills, and G. Modelski, 201–15. London: Routledge.

McNeill, J. R., and W. H. McNeill. 2003. *The Human Web.* W. W. Norton.

Meardon, S. J. 2001. "Modeling Agglomeration and Dispersion in City and Country: Gunnar Myrdal, François Perroux, and the New Economic Geography." *American Journal of Economics and Sociology* 60: 25–57.

Mokyr, J. 1990. *The Lever of Riches: Technological Creativity and Economic Progress.* New York: Oxford University Press.

———. 1996. "Evolution and Technological Change: A New Metaphor for Economic History." In *Technological Change*, ed. by R. Fox, 63–84. Amsterdam: Hardwood Academic Publishers.

———. 2000. "Evolutionary Phenomena in Technological Change." *In Technological Innovation as an Evolutionary Process*, ed. by J. Ziman, 52–65. Cambridge: Cambridge University Press.

Monroe, C. M. 2005. "Money and Trade." In *A Companion to the Ancient Near East*, ed. by D. C. Snell, 155–68. Malden, MA: Blackwell.

Moorey, P. R. S. 1994. *Ancient Mesopotamian Materials and Industries: The Archaeological Evidence.* Oxford: Clarendon Press

Moorey, P. R. S., and J. N. Postgate. 1992. "Some Wood Identifications from Mesopotamian Sites." *Bulletin on Sumerian Agriculture* 6: 197–99.

Mouck, T. 2004. "Ancient Mesopotamian Accounting and Human Cognitive Evolution." *Accounting Historians Journal* 31: 97–124.

Mudar, K. 1982. "Early Dynastic III Animal Utilization at Lagash: A Report on the Fauna from Tell Al-Hiba." *Journal of Near Eastern Studies* 41: 23–34.

Müller-Karpe, M. 1991. "Aspects of Early Metallurgy in Mesopotamia." In *Archaeometry '90*, ed. by E. Pernicka and G. A. Wagner, 105–16. Basel: Birkhäuser Verlag.

Myrdal, G. 1944. *An American Dilemma: The Negro Problem and Modern Democracy.* New York: Harper and Brothers.

———. 1957. *Economic Theory and Under-Developed Regions.* London: Duckworth.

———. 1970. *The Challenge of World Poverty: A World Anti-Poverty Program in Outline.* New York: Vintage.

Nissen, H.-J. 1976. "Zur Frage der Arbeitsorganistion in Babylonien während der Spät-uruk-Zeit." In *Wirschaft und Gessellschaft in Alten Vorderasien*, ed. by J. Harmatta and G. Komaróczy, 5–14. Budapest: Akadémiai Kiadó.

———. 1977. "Aspects of the Development of Early Cylinder Seals." *Seals and Sealings in the Ancient Near East*, ed. by McG. Gibson and R. Biggs, 15–24. Malibu: Undena.

———. 1986. "The Archaic Texts from Uruk." *World Archaeology* 17: 317–34.

———. 1988. *The Early History of the Ancient Near East.* Chicago: University of Chicago Press.

———. 1993. "The Early Uruk Period—A Sketch." In *Between the Rivers and Over the Mountains: Archaeologica Anatolica et Mesopotamica Alba Palmieri Dedicata,* ed. by M. Frangipane, H. Hauptmann, M. Liverani, P. Matthiae, and M. Mellink, 123–31. Rome: Dipartimento di Scienze Storiche Archeologiche e Antropologiche dell'Antichità, Università di Roma "La Sapienza."

———. 2000. "A Mesopotamian Hierarchy in Action in Ancient Uruk." In *Hierarchies in Action: Cui bono?* ed. by M. W. Diehl, 210–17. Carbondale: Center for Archaeological Investigations, Southern Illinois University.

———. 2001. "Cultural and Political Networks in the Ancient Near East during the Fourth and Third Millennia B.C." In *Uruk Mesopotamia and Its Neighbors,* ed. by M. Rothman, 149–80. Santa Fe: SAR Press.

———. 2002. "Uruk Key Site of the Period and Key site of the Problem." In *Artefacts of Complexity: Tracking the Uruk in the Near East,* ed. by J. N. Postgate, 1–16. Warminster: Aris and Phillips.

Nissen, H.-J., P. Damerow, and R. K. Englund. 1993. *Archaic Bookkeeping: Early Writing and Techniques of Economic Administration in the Ancient Near East.* Chicago: University of Chicago Press.

North, D. C. 1977. "Markets and Other Allocation Systems in History: The Challenge of Karl Polanyi." *Journal of European Economic History* 6: 703–16.

———. 1981. *Structure and Change in Economic History.* New York: Norton.

———. 1991. "Institutions." *Journal of Economic Perspectives* 5: 97–112.

North, D. C., and. R. P. Thomas. 1973. *The Rise of the Western World: A New Economic History.* Cambridge: Cambridge University Press.

O'Sullivan, A. 1996. *Urban Economics.* Third edition. Chicago: Irwin.

Oates, J. 1983. "Ubaid Mesopotamia Reconsidered." In *The Hilly Flanks and Beyond,* ed. by T. Cuyler Young, Jr. et al., 251–82. Studies in Ancient Oriental Civilization, 36. Chicago: Oriental Institute.

———. 2001. "Comment." *Current Anthropology* 42: 223–24.

———. 2002. "Tell Brak: The Fourth Millennium Sequence and Its Implications." In *Artefacts of Complexity: Tracking the Uruk in the Near East,* ed. by J. N. Postgate, 111–22. Warminster: Aris and Phillips.

Oates, J., and D. Oates. 1997. "An Open Gate: Cities of the Fourth Millennium B.C. (Tell Brak 1997)." *Cambridge Archaeological Journal* 7: 287–307.

Oates, J., A. McMahon, P. Karsgaard, S. Al Quntar, and J. Ur. 2007. "Early Mesopotamian Urbanism: A New View from the North." *Antiquity*: 81: 585–600.

Ochsenschlager, E. L. 1992. "Ethnographic Evidence for Wood, Boats, Bitumen, and Reeds in Southern Iraq." *Bulletin on Sumerian Agriculture* 6: 47–78.

———. 1993. "Village Weavers: Ethnoarchaeology at Al-Hiba." *Bulletin on Sumerian Agriculture* 7: 43–62.

———. 2004. *Iraq's Marsh Arabs in the Garden of Eden*. Philadelphia: University of Pennsylvania Press.

Otte, M. and M. R. Behm-Blancke. 1992. "Das Lithische Inventar." In *Hassek Höyük: Naturwissenschaftliche Untursuchungen und lithische Industrie*, ed. by M. R. Behm-Blancke, 165–78. Tübingen: Ernst Wasmuth Verlag.

Özbal, H., A. Adriaens, and B. Earl. 1999. "Hacınebi Metal Production and Exchange." *Paléorient* 25: 57–66.

Palmieri A., A. Hauptmann, and K. Hess. 1997. "The Metal Objects from the 'Royal' Tomb Dating to 3000 B.C. at Arslantepe (Malatya): A New Alloy (CU-AG)." *Arkeometri Sonuçları Toplantisi* 13: 115–22.

Parrot, A. 1948. *Tello*. Paris: Albin Michel.

Payne, S. 1988. "Animal Bones from Tell Rubeidah." In *Excavations at Tell Rubeidah*, ed. by R. G. Killick, 98–135. London: Aris & Phillips.

Pedde, F. 2000. "Metall." In *Uruk, Keinfunde IV: Metall- und Steinobjecte im Vorderasiatische Muzeum zu Berlin*, by S. Pedde, M. Heinz, and B. Müller-Neuhof, 1–103. Ausgrabungen in Uruk-Warka Endberichte, 21. Mainz am Rhein: Philipp von Zabern.

Pernicka, E., T. Rehren, and I. Schmitt-Strecker. 1998. "Late Uruk Silver Production by Cupellation at Habuba Kabira, Syria." *Der Anshnitt* 8: 119–30.

Perrin de Brichambaut, G., and C. C. Wallén. 1963. *A Study of Agroclimatology in Semi-arid and Arid Zones of the Near East*. Geneva: World Metereological Organization.

Petit-Maire, N., P. Sanlaville, and Z. W. Yan. 1995. "Oscillations de la limite nord du domaine des moussons africaine, indienne, et asiatique, au cours du dernier cycle climatique." *Bulletin de la Société Geologique de France* 166: 213–20.

Pirenne, H. 1936. *Economic and Social History of Medieval Europe*. London: Routledge and Kegan.

Pittman, H. 1993. "Pictures of an Administration: The Late Uruk Scribe at Work." In *Between the Rivers and Over the Mountains: Archaeologica Anatolica et Mesopotamica Alba Palmieri Dedicata*, ed. by M. Frangipane, H. Hauptmann, M. Liverani, P. Matthiae, and M. Mellink, 235–46. Rome: Università di Roma "La Sapienza."

———. 2001. "Mesopotamian Intraregional Relations Reflected through Glyptic Evidence in the Late Chalcolithic 1-5 Periods." In *Uruk Mesopotamia and Its Neighbors*, ed. by M. Rothman, 403–44. Santa Fe: SAR Press.

Polanyi, K. 1944. *The Great Transformation*. New York: Farrar & Rinehart, Inc.

———. 1957a. "Marketless Trading in Hammurabi's Time." In *Trade and Market in the Early Empires*, ed. by K. Polanyi, C. M. Arensberg, and H. W. Pearson, 10–26. New York: Free Press.

———. 1957b. "The Economy as Instituted Process." In *Trade and Market in the Early Empires*, ed. by K. Polanyi, C. M. Arensberg, and H. W. Pearson, 243–69. New York: Free Press.

———. 1977. *The Livelihood of Man*, ed. by H. W. Pearson. New York: Academic Press.

Pollock, S. 1990. "Archaeological Investigations on the Uruk Mound, Abu Salabikh, Iraq." *Iraq* 52: 85–93.

———. 1992. "Bureaucrats and Managers, Peasants and Pastoralists, Imperialists and Traders: Recent Research on the Uruk and Jemdet Nasr Period in Mesopotamia." *Journal of World Prehistory* 6: 297–336.

———. 1994. Review of G. Algaze's *The Uruk World System—The Dynamics of Expansion of Early Mesopotamian Civilization*. *Science* 264: 1481–82.

———. 1999. *Ancient Mesopotamia*. Cambridge: Cambridge University Press.

———. 2001. "The Uruk Period in Southern Mesopotamia." In *Uruk Mesopotamia and Its Neighbors*, ed. by M. Rothman, 191–232. Santa Fe: SAR Press.

Pollock, S., C. Steele, and M. Pope. 1991. "Investigations on the Uruk Mound, Abu Salabikh, 1990." *Iraq* 53: 59–68.

Postgate, J. N. 1972. "The Role of the Temple in the Mesopotamian Secular Community." In *Man, Settlement, and Urbanism*, ed. by P. J. Ucko, R. Tringham, and G. W. Dimbleby, 811–26. London: Duckworth.

———. 1975. "Some Old Babylonian Shepherds and Their Flocks." *Journal of Semitic Studies* 20: 1–21.

———. 1986. "The Transition from Uruk to Early Dynastic: Continuities and Discontinuities in the Record of Settlement." In *Gemdet Nasr: Period or Regional Style?* ed. by U. Finkbeiner and W. Röllig, 90–106. Weisbaden: Ludwig Reichert.

———. 1988. "A View from Down the Euphrates." In *Wirtschaft und Gesellschaft von Ebla*, ed. by H. Waetzoldt and H. Hauptmann, 111–20. Heidelberg: Orientverlag.

———. 1994. "How Many Sumerians per Hectare? Probing the Anatomy of an Early City." *Cambridge Archaeological Journal* 4: 47–65.

———. 1996. Review of G. Algaze's *The Uruk World System—The Dynamics of Expansion of Early Mesopotamian Civilization*. *Journal of the American Oriental Society* 116: 147–48.

Postgate, J. N., ed. 2002. *Artefacts of Complexity: Tracking the Uruk in the Near East*. Warminster: Aris and Phillips.

Potts, D. T. 1997. *Mesopotamian Civilization: The Material Foundations*. Ithaca: Cornell University Press.

Pournelle, J. 2003a. "The Littoral Foundations of the Uruk State: Using Satellite Photography toward a New Understanding of 5th/4th Millennium BCE Landscapes in the Warka Survey Area, Iraq." In *Chalcolithic and Early Bronze Age Hydrostrategies*, ed. by D. Gheorghiu, 5–24. Oxford: BAR International Series.

―――. 2003b. *Marshland of Cities: Deltaic Landscapes and the Evolution of Early Mesopotamian Civilization*. Ph.D. diss., University of California, San Diego.

―――. 2007. "KLM to Corona: A Bird's-eye View of Cultural Ecology and Early Mesopotamian Urbanization." In *Settlement and Society: Essays Dedicated to Robert McCormick Adams*, ed. by E. C. Stone, 29–62. Los Angeles: UCLA Cotsen Institute of Archaeology.

Powell, M. 1977. "Sumerian Merchants and the Problem of Profit." *Iraq* 39: 23–30.

―――. 1985. "Salt, Seed, and Yields in Sumerian Agriculture: A Critique of the Theory of Progressive Salinization." *Zeitschrift für Assyriologie* 75: 7–38.

―――. 1996. "Money in Mesopotamia." *Journal of the Economic and Social History of the Orient* 39: 224–42.

Pred, A. 1966. *The Spatial Dynamics of U.S, Industrial Growth*. Cambridge: MIT Press.

Reichart, G. J., M. den Hulk, H. J. Visser, C. H. van der Weijden, and W. J. Zachariasse. 1997. "A 225 KYR Record of Dust Supply, Paleoproductivity, and the Oxygen Minimum Zone from the Murray Ridge (Northern Arabian Sea)." *Paleogeography, Paleoclimatology, Paleoecology* 133: 149–69.

Renfrew, C., and J. F. Cherry, eds. 1986. *Peer Polity Interaction and Socio-political Change*. Cambridge: Cambridge University Press.

Renger, J. 1984. "Patterns of Non-Institutional Trade and Non-Commercial Exchange in Ancient Mesopotamia at the Beginning of the Second Millennium BC." In *Circulation of Goods in Non-Palatial Contexts in the Ancient Near East*, ed. by A. Archi, 31–123. Rome: Edizione Dell'Ateneo.

Ricardo, D. [1817] 1971. *On the Principles of Political Economy and Taxation*. Harmondsworth: Penguin.

Rothman, M. 1994. "Sealings As a Control Mechanism in Prehistory." In *Chiefdoms and Early States in the Near East: The Organizational Dynamics of Complexity*, ed. by G. Stein and M. Rothman, 103–20. Madison, WI: Prehistory Press.

―――. 2002. *Tepe Gawra: The Evolution of a Small Prehistoric Center in Northern Iraq*. Philadelphia: University of Pennsylvania Museum.

―――. 2004. "Studying the Development of Complex Society: Mesopotamia in the Late Fifth and Fourth Millennia BC. *Journal of Archaeological Research* 12: 75–119.

―――. 2005. "Sealing Function and Interaction at Tepe Gawra." In *Studi in Onore di Enrica Fiandra*, ed. by M. Perna, 341–55. Paris: De Boccard.

Rothman, M., ed. 2001. *Uruk Mesopotamia and its Neighbors*. Santa Fe: SAR Press.

Röttlander, R. C. A. 1990. "Lipid Analysis in the Identification of Vessel Contents." In *Organic Contents of Ancient Vessels: Materials Analysis and*

Archaeological Investigation, ed. by W. R. Biers and P. McGovern, 37–40. MASCA Research Papers in Science and Archaeology, 7. Philadelphia: University Museum of Archaeology and Anthropology.

Roualt, O., and M. G. Massetti-Roualt. 1993. *L'Euphrate e il tempo: Le Civilta del medio Euphrate e della Gezira siriana.* Milan: Electa.

Rupley, E. 2003. "¹⁴C AMS Determinations of the Fourth Millennium BC from Tell Brak." *Iraq* 65: 33–37.

Russell, K. W. 1988. *After Eden: The Behavioral Ecology of Early Food Production in the Near East and North Africa.* Oxford: British Archaeological Reports.

Ryder, M. L. 1983. *Sheep and Man.* London: Duckworth.

———. 1992. "The Interaction between Biological and Technological Change during the Development of Different Fleece Types in Sheep." *Anthropolozoologica* 16: 131–38.

———. 1993. "Sheep and Goat Husbandry with Particular Reference to Textile Fibre and Milk Production." *Bulletin on Sumerian Agriculture* 7: 9–32.

Safar, F., M. A. Mustafa, and S. Lloyd. 1981. *Eridu.* Baghdad: State Organization of Antiquities and Heritage.

Sahlins, M. 1972. *Stone Age Economics.* New York: Aldine.

Sallaberger, W., and J. Ur. 2004. "Tell Beydar/Nabada in Its Regional Setting." *Subartu* 12: 51–73.

Sanlaville, P. 1989. "Considerations sur l'evolution de la basse Mésopotamie au cours des derniers millénaires." *Paléorient* 15: 5–27.

———. 1992. "Sciences de la terre et archeologie: L'evolution de la Basse- Mésopotamie a l'Holocene." *Mémoires—Société géologique de France* 160: 11–18.

Sanlaville, P., and R. Dalongeville. 2005. "L'évolution des espaces littoraux du golfe Persique et du golfe d'Oman depuis la phase finale de la transgression post-glaciare." *Paléorient* 31: 9–28.

Santley, R. n.d. "Ranchoapan: The 'New Obsidian' City of the Tuxlas?" Http://www.laii.unm.edu/papers/research/santley.html.

Santone, L. 1997. "Transport Costs, Consumer Demand, and Patterns of Intraregional Exchange: A Perspective on Commodity Production and Distribution from Northern Belize." *Latin American Antiquity* 8: 71–88.

Sauren, H. 1966. *Topographie der Provinz Umma nach den Urkunden der Zeit der III. Dynastie von Ur: Kanale und Bewasserungsanlagen.* Bamberg: K. Urlaub.

Schmandt-Besserat, D. 1993. "Images of Ensiship." In *Between the Rivers and Over the Mountains: Archaeologica Anatolica et Mesopotamica Alba Palmieri Dedicata,* ed. by M. Frangipane, H. Hauptmann, M. Liverani, P. Matthiae, and M. Mellink, 201–20. Rome: Università di Roma "La Sapienza."

———. 2007. *When Writing Met Art: From Symbol to Story.* Austin: University of Texas Press.

Schoeninger, M., and K. Moore. 1992. "Bone Stable Isotope Studies in Archaeology." *Journal of World Prehistory* 6: 247–96.

Schwartz, G. M. 1994. "Before Ebla: Models of Pre-state Political Organization in Syria and Northern Mesopotamia." In *Chiefdoms and Early States in the Near East: The Organizational Dynamics of Complexity*, ed. by G. Stein and M. Rothman, 153–74. Madison, WI: Prehistory Press.

———. 2001. "Syria and the Uruk Expansion." In *Uruk Mesopotamia and Its Neighbors*, ed. by M. Rothman, 233–64. Santa Fe: SAR Press.

Schwartz, G. M., H. H. Curvers, F. A. Gerritsen, J. A. MacCormack, N. Miller, and J. A. Weber 2000. "Excavation and Survey in the Jabbul Plain, Western Syria: The Umm el-Marra Project 1996–1997." *American Journal of Archaeology* 104: 419–62.

Schwartz, M. 2002. "Early Evidence of Reed Boats from Southeast Anatolia." *Antiquity* 76: 617–18.

Schwartz, M., D. Hollander, and G. Stein. 1999. "Reconstructing Mesopotamian Exchange Networks in the Fourth Millennium BC: Geochemical and Archaeological Analyses of Bitumen Artifacts from Hacınebi Tepe, Turkey." *Paléorient* 25: 67–82.

Service, E. R. 1975. *Origins of the State and Civilization: The Process of Cultural Evolution*. New York: W. W. Norton.

Sharlach, T. 2004. *Provincial Taxation and the Ur III State*. Leiden: Brill.

Shennan, S. 1999. "Cost, Benefit and Value in the Organization of Early European Copper Production." *Antiquity* 73: 353–63.

Sherratt, A. 1997. "Comment." *Current Anthropology* 38: 539.

———. 2004. "Material Resources, Capital and Power: The Co-Evolution of Society and Culture." In *Archaeological Perspectives on Political Economies*, ed. by G. Feinman and L. M. Nicholas, 79–104. Salt Lake City: University of Utah Press.

Silver, M. 1995. *Economic Structures of Antiquity*. Westport, CT: Greenwood Press.

———. 2004. "Modern Ancients." In *Commerce and Monetary Systems in the Ancient World: Means of Transmission and Cultural Interaction*, ed. by R. Rollinger and C. Ulf, 65–87. Munich: Franz Steiner Verlag.

Sirocko, F., M. Sarnthein, H. Erienkeuzer, H. Lange, M. Arnold, and J. Duplessy. 1993. "Century-scale Events in Monsoonal Climate over the Past 24,000 Years." *Nature* 364: 322–24.

Smith, A. [1776] 1976. *The Wealth of Nations*. Oxford: Clarendon Press.

Smith, P. E. L., and T. C. Young Jr. 1972. "The Evolution of Early Agriculture and Culture in Greater Mesopotamia: A Trial Model." In *Population Growth: Anthropological Implications*, ed. by B. Spooner, 1–59. Cambridge: MIT Press.

Snell, D. 1977. "The Activities of Some Merchants of Umma." *Iraq* 29: 45–50.

————. 1991. "Marketless Trading in Our Time." *Journal of the Economic and Social History of the Orient* 34: 129–41.

Spencer, H. [1876, 1882] 1967. *The Evolution of Society: Selections from Herbert Spencer's Principles of Sociology*, ed. by R. L. Carneiro. Chicago: University of Chicago Press.

Spencer, C. S. 1997. "Evolutionary Approaches in Archaeology." *Journal of Archaeological Research* 5: 209–64.

Spufford, P. 2002. *Power and Profit*. New York: Thames and Hudson.

Staubwasser, M., and H. Weiss. 2006. "Holocene Climate and Cultural Evolution in Late Prehistoric—Early Historic West Asia." *Quaternary Research* 66: 372–87.

Stein, G. 1990. "Comment." *Current Anthropology* 31: 66–67.

————. 1999a. *Rethinking World-Systems: Diasporas, Colonies, and Interaction in Uruk Mesopotamia*. Tucson: University of Arizona Press.

————. 1999b. "Material Culture and Social Identity: The Evidence for a 4th Millennium BC Mesopotamian Uruk Colony at Hacınebi, Turkey." *Paléorient* 25: 11–22.

————. 2001. "Indigenous Social Complexity at Hacınebi (Turkey) and the Organization of Uruk Colonial Contact." In *Uruk Mesopotamia and Its Neighbors*, ed. by M. Rothman, 265–306. Santa Fe: SAR Press.

————. 2002. "The Uruk Expansion in Anatolia: A Mesopotamian Colony and Its Indigenous Host Community at Hacınebi, Turkey." In *Artefacts of Complexity: Tracking the Uruk in the Near East*, ed. by J. N. Postgate, 149–72. Warminster: Aris and Phillips.

————. 2005. "The Political Economy of Mesopotamian Colonial Encounters." In *The Archaeology of Colonial Encounters*, ed. by G. Stein, 143–72. Santa Fe: School of American Research Press.

Stein, G., and P. Wattenmaker. 1990. "The 1987 Tell Leilan Regional Survey: A Preliminary Report." In *Economy and Settlement in the Near East: Analyses of Ancient Sites and Materials*, ed. by N. Miller, 8–18. Philadelphia: MASCA.

Steinkeller, P. 1987. "The Administrative and Economic Organization of the Ur III State: The Core and the Periphery." In *The Organization of Power: Aspects of Bureaucracy in the Ancient Near East*, ed. by McG. Gibson and R. Biggs, 7–18. Chicago: Oriental Institute.

————. 1993. "Early Political Development in Mesopotamia and the Origins of the Sargonic Empire." In *Akkad, The First World Empire*, ed. by M. Liverani, 107–30. Padua: Sargon srl.

————. 1999. "Archaic City Seals and the Question of Early Babylonian Unity." In *Thorkild Jacobsen Memorial Volume*, ed. by Tzvi Abusch, 1–12. New Haven: American Oriental Society.

————. 2001. "New Light on the Hydrology and Topography of Southern Mesopotamia." *Zeitschrift für Assyriologie und Vorderasiatische Archäeologie* 91: 22–84.

———. 2004. "The Function of Written Documentation in the Administrative Praxis of Early Babylonia." In *Creating Economic Order: Record-Keeping, Standarization, and the Development of Accounting in the Ancient Near East*, ed. by M. Hudson and C. Wunsch, 65–88. Bethesda, MD: CDL Press.

Stevens, L. R., E. Ito, A. Schawalb, and H. E. Wright, Jr. 2006. "Timing of Atmospheric Precipitation in the Zagros Mountains Inferred from a Multi-proxy Record from Lake Mirabad, Iran." *Quaternary Research* 66: 494–500.

Stone, E. 1997. "City-states and Their Centers: The Mesopotamian Example." In *The Archaeology of City States*, ed. by D. L. Nichols and T. H. Charlton, 15–26. Washington, DC: Smithsonian Institution Press.

Strommenger, E. 1980. *Habuba Kabira: Eine Stadt vor 5000 Jahren*. Mainz am Rhein: Phillip von Zabern.

Stronach, D. 1994. "Village to Metropolis: Nineveh and the Beginnings of Urbanism in Northern Mesopotamia." In *Nuove Fondazioni nel Vicino Oriente Antico: Realtà e Ideologia*, ed. by S. Mazzoni, 85–114. Pisa: Giardini Editori.

Sumner, W. 1986. "Proto-Elamite Civilization in Fars." In *Gemdet Nasr: Period or Regional Style?* ed. by U. Finkbeiner and W. Röllig, 199–211. Wiesbaden: Ludwig Reichert.

Syracusano, G. 2004. "Preliminary Results of the Faunal Analysis from the Site of Zeytinlibahçe." In *Salvage Project of the Archaeological Heritage of the Ilisu and Carchemish Dam Reservoirs. Activities in 2001*, ed. by N. Tuna, J. Greenhalgh, and J. Velibeyoğlu, 49–54. Ankara: Middle Eastern Technical University.

Tengberg, M. 2005. "Les forets de la mer: Exploitation et evolution des mangroves en Arabie Orientale du Néolitique a l'époche Islamique." *Paléorient* 31: 39–45.

Thesiger, W. 1964. *The Marsh Arabs*. New York: E. P. Dutton.

Tiedemann, E. J., and K. A. Jakes. 2006. "An Exploration of Prehistoric Spinning Technology: Spinning Efficiency and Technology Transition." *Archaeometry* 48: 293–307.

Tilly, C. 1984. *Big Structures, Large Processes, Huge Comparisons*. New York: Russell Sage Foundation.

Tomé, K. 2005. "Note sur la exploitation des oiseaux 'aquatiques.'" *Paléorient* 31: 74–78.

Turkes, M. 1996. "Spatial and Temporal Analysis of Annual Rainfall Variations in Turkey." *International Journal of Climatology* 16: 1057–76.

Uchupi, E., S. A. Swift, and D. A. Ross. 1999. "Late Quaternary Stratigraphy, Paleoclimate and Neotectonism of the Persian (Arabian) Gulf Region." *Marine Geology* 160: 1–23.

Ur, J. 2002a. "Settlement and Landscape in Northern Mesopotamia: The Tell Hamoukar Survey, 2000–2001." *Akkadica* 123: 57–88.

———. 2002b. "Surface Collection and Offsite Studies at Tell Hamoukar, 1999." *Iraq* 64: 15–44.

Ur, J., P. Karsgaard, and J. Oates. 2007. "Early Urban Development in the Near East." *Science* 317: 11–88.

Vallet, R. 1996. "Habuba Kabire ou la naissance de l'urbanisme." *Paléorient* 22: 45–76.

———. 1998. "L'urbanisme colonial urukien, l'example de Djebel Aruda." *Subartu* 4: 53–87.

Van De Mieroop, M. 1993. "Sheep and Goat Herding According to the Old Babylonian Texts from Ur." *Bulletin on Sumerian Agriculture* 7: 161–182.

———. 1997. *The Ancient Mesopotamian City.* Oxford: Oxford University Press.

———. 2000. "Review of M. Hudson and B. A. Levine's Privatization in the Ancient Near East and Classical World." *Journal of Near Eastern Studies* 59: 40–43.

———. 2004. "Economic Theories and the Ancient Near East." In *Commerce and Monetary Systems in the Ancient World: Means of Transmission and Cultural Interaction*, ed. by R. Rollinger and C. Ulf, 54–64. Munich: Franz Steiner Verlag.

van Driel, G. 2002a. *Elusive Silver.* Leiden: Nederlands Instituut Voor Het Nabije Oosten.

———. 2002b. "Jebel Aruda: Variations on a Late Uruk Domestic Theme." In *Artefacts of Complexity: Tracking the Uruk in the Near East*, ed. by J. N. Postgate, 191–207. Warminster: Aris and Phillips.

van Driel, G., and C. van Driel-Murray. 1983. "Jebel Aruda, the 1982 Season of Excavations." *Akkadica* 33: 1–26.

van Neer, W., I. Zohar, and O. Lernau. 2005. "The Emergence of Fishing Communities in the Eastern Mediterranean Region: A Survey of Evidence from Pre- and Protohistoric Periods." *Paléorient* 31: 131–157.

van Soldt, W. H., ed. 2005. *Ethnicity in Ancient Mesopotamia: Papers Read at the 48th Rencontre Assyriologique Internationale Leiden, 1–4 July 2002.* Leiden: Nederlands Instituut voor het Nabije Oosten.

Vance, Jr., J. E. 1970. *The Geography of Wholesaling.* Englewood Cliffs, NJ: Prentice-Hall.

———. 1986. *Capturing the Horizon: The Historical Geography of Transportation.* New York: Harper & Row.

Veenhof, K. R. 1972. *Aspects of Old Assyrian Trade and Its Terminology.* Leiden: Brill.

Vila, E. 2006. "Data on Equids from Late Fourth and Third Millennium Sites in Northern Syria." In *Equids in Time and Space: Papers in Honour of Véra Eisenmann*, ed. by M. Mashkour, 101–23. Oxford: Oxbow.

von Haller, A. 1932. "Die Keramik der archäischen Schichten von Uruk." *Vorläufiger Bericht über die von der Deutschen Forschungsgemeinschaft in Uruk-Warka unternommenen Ausgrabungen* 4: 38–42.

von Wickede, A. 1990. *Prähistorische Stempel Glyptic in Vorderasien*. Munich: Profil Verlag.

Waetzoldt, H. 1972. *Untersuchungen zur neusumerischen Textilindustrie*. Rome: Centro per le Antichità e la Storia dell'Arte del Vicino Oriente.

———. 1992. "'Rohr' und dessen Verwendungsweisen anhand der neusumerischen Texte aus Umma." *Bulletin on Sumerian Agriculture* 6: 125–46.

Wallerstein, I. 1974. *The Modern World System*. Vol. 1. New York: Academic Press.

———. 1991. "World System versus World Systems: A Critique." *Critique of Anthropology* 11: 189–194.

Warburton, D. 2003. *Macroeconomics from the Beginning: The General Theory, Ancient Markets, and the Rate of Interest*. Neuchâtel: Recherches et Publications.

Wattenmaker, P., and G. Stein. 1986. "Early Pastoral Production in Southeast Anatolia: Faumal Remains from Kurban Höyük and Gritille Höyük." *Anatolica* 13: 90–96.

Weiss, H. 1986. "The Origins of Tell Leilan and the Conquest of Space in Third Millennium North Mesopotamia." In *The Origins of Cities in Dry-farming Syria and Mesopotamia in the Third Millennium B.C.*, ed. by H. Weiss, 71–108. Guilford, Conn.: Four Quarters Publishing.

———. 1989. "Comments." *Current Anthropology* 30: 597–98.

———. 1990. "Tell Leilan 1989: New Data for Mid-third Millennium Urbanization and State Formation." *Mitteilungen der Deutschen Orient-Gesellschaft* 122: 193–218.

———. 2003. "Ninevite V Periods and Processes." In *The Origins of North Mesopotamian Civilization: Ninevite 5 Chronology, Economy, Society*, ed. by H. Weiss and E. Rova, 593–624. Turnhout: Brepols.

Wells, P. S. 1980. *Culture Contact and Culture Change: Early Iron Age Central Europe and the Mediterranean World*. Cambridge: Cambridge University Press.

Wheatley, P. 1971. *The Pivot of the Four Quarters: A Preliminary Enquiry into the Origins and Character of the Ancient Chinese City*. Chicago: Aldine.

Wilcke, C. 2007. "Markt und Arbeit im alten Orient am Ende des 3. Jahrtausends v. Chr." In *Menschen und Märkte*, ed. by W. Reinhard and J. Stagl, 71–132. Vienna: Böhlau Verlag.

Wilkinson, T. J. 1990a. *Town and Country in Southeastern Anatolia*. Vol. 1,

Settlement and Land Use at Kurban Höyük and Other Sites in the Lower Karababa Basin. Chicago: Oriental Institute.

———. 1990b. "Early Channels and Landscape Development around Abu Salabikh: A Preliminary Report." *Iraq* 52: 75–84.

———. 1994. "The Structure and Dynamics of Dry Farming States in Upper Mesopotamia. *Current Anthropology* 35: 483–520.

———. 1995. "Late Assyrian Settlement Geography in Upper Mesopotamia." In *Neo Assyrian Geography*, ed. by M. Liverani, 139–59. Rome: Università di Roma "la Sapienza."

———. 2000a. "Archaeological Survey of the Tell Beydar Region, Syria 1997." In *Tell Beydar: Environmental and Technical Studies*, ed. by K. van Lerberghe and G. Voet, 1–37. Subartu, 6. Turnhout: Brepols, 2001.

———. 2000b. "Regional Approaches to Mesopotamian Archaeology: The Contribution of Archaeological Surveys." *Journal of Archaeological Research* 8: 219–67.

———. 2001. "Comment." *Current Anthropology* 42: 224–25.

———. 2003a. "Archaeological Survey and Long-Term Population Trends in Upper Mesopotamia and Iran." In *Yeki Bud, Yeki Nabud: Essays on the Archaeology of Iran in Honor of William M. Sumner*, ed. by N. Miller and K. Abdi, 39–52. Los Angeles: Cotsen Institute of Archaeology.

———. 2003b. *Archaeological Landscapes of the Ancient Near East.* Tucson: University of Arizona Press.

Wilkinson, T. J., and D. J. Tucker. 1995. *Settlement Development in the North Jazira, Iraq: A Study of the Archaeological Landscape.* London: British School of Archaeology in Iraq.

Winchester, S. 2001. *The Map That Changed the World.* New York: Harper Collins.

Winter, I. 2007. "Representing Abundance: The Visual Dimension of the Agrarian State." In *Settlement and Society: Essays Dedicated to Robert McCormick Adams*, ed. by Elizabeth C. Stone, 117–38. Los Angeles: UCLA Cotsen Institute of Archaeology.

Wittfogel, K. A. 1957. *Oriental Despotism, a Comparative Study of Total Power.* New Haven: Yale University Press.

Wright, G. A. 1969. *Obsidian Analyses and Prehistoric Near Eastern Trade, 7500–3500 BC.* Ann Arbor: University of Michigan, Museum of Anthropology.

Wright, H. T. 1969. *The Administration of Rural Production in an Early Mesopotamian Town.* Ann Arbor: Museum of Anthropology.

———. 1981a. "Conclusions." In *An Early Town on the Deh Luran Plain: Excavations at Tepe Farukhabad*, ed. by H. T. Wright, 262–79. Ann Arbor: University of Michigan, Museum of Anthropology.

———. 1981b. "The Southern Margins of Sumer: Archaeological Survey of the

Area of Eridu and Ur." In R. M. Adams, *Heartland of Cities: Surveys of Ancient Settlement and Land Use on the Central Floodplain of the Euphrates*, 295–346. Chicago: University of Chicago Press.

———. 1984. "Prestate Political Formations." In *On the Evolution of Complex Societies: Essays in Honor of Harry Hoijer*, ed. by T. Earle, 41–78. Malibu: Undena.

———. 1995. "Review of G. Algaze's *The Uruk World System—The Dynamics of Expansion of Early Mesopotamian Civilization*." *American Anthropologist* 97: 151–52.

———. 1998. "Uruk States in Southwestern Iran." In *Archaic States*, ed. by G. M. Feinman and J. Marcus, 173–98. Santa Fe: SAR Press.

———. 2001. "Cultural Action in the Uruk World." In *Uruk Mesopotamia and Its Neighbors*, ed. by M. Rothman, 123–48. Santa Fe: SAR Press.

———. 2006. "Early State Dynamics as Political Experiment." *Journal of Anthropological Research* 62: 305–19.

Wright, H. T., and E. Rupley. 2001. "Calibrated Radiocarbon Age Determination of Uruk Related Assemblages." In *Uruk Mesopotamia and its Neighbors*, ed. by M. Rothman, 85–122. Santa Fe: SAR Press.

Wright, H. T., and G. A. Johnson. 1975. "Population, Exchange, and Early State Formation in Southwestern Iran." *American Anthropologist* 77: 267–89.

Wright, H. T., N. Miller, and R. Redding. 1980. "Time and Process in an Uruk Rural Center." In *L'archéologie de l'Iraq du début de l'epoche néolitique à 333 avant notre ere*, ed. by M.-T. Barrelet, 265–84. Paris: Éditions du Centre National de la Recherche Scientifique.

Wright, Rita. 1989. "Comment." *Current Anthropology* 30: 599–600.

———. 1996. "Technology, Gender, and Class: Worlds of Difference in Ur III Mesopotamia." In *Gender and Archaeology,* ed. by R. Wright, 79–110. Philadelphia: University of Pennsylvania Press.

Wright, Robert. 2000. *Non-zero: The Logic of Human Destiny.* New York: Pantheon Books.

Yoffee, N. 1995. "Political Economy in Early Mesopotamian States." *Annual Review of Anthropology* 24: 281–311.

Young, G. 1977. *Return to the Marshes: Life with the Marsh Arabs of Iraq.* London: Collins.

Young, T. Cuyler Jr. 1995. Review of G. Algaze's *The Uruk World System—The Dynamics of Expansion of Early Mesopotamian Civilization. Bulletin of the American Schools of Oriental Research* 297: 84–5.

Zagarell, A. 1986. "Trade, Women, Class, and Society in Ancient Western Asia." *Current Anthropology* 27: 415–30.

Ziman, J. 2000. "Evolutionary Models for Technological Change." In *Technological Innovation as an Evolutionary Process,* ed. by J. Ziman, 3–12. Cambridge: Cambridge University Press.

Source List

Figures

1. Redrawn with modifications after Robert McC. Adams (1981).

2. Redrawn after Finkbeiner (1991), enclosure 12.

3. Redrawn after Finkbeiner (1991), enclosures 12–13.

4A. Redrawn after Amiet (1961), pl. 16, no. 266.

4B. Redrawn after Amiet (1961), pl. 44, no. 639.

4C. Redrawn after Amiet (1961), pl. 13 bis, g.

4D. Redrawn after Amiet (1961), pl. 40, no. 609.

4E. Redrawn after Amiet (1961), pl. 41, no. 618.

5. Redrawn after Algaze (2001a), fig. 1.

6. Photograph courtesy of Dr. Robert McC. Adams.

7A. Cylinder seal, redrawn after Amiet (1961), pl. 42, no. 629a.

7B. Gypsum trough, now at the British Museum but presumably from Warka, redrawn after Amiet (1961), pl. 42, no. 623.

8A. Redrawn after Amiet (1961), pl. 15, no. 260.

8B. Redrawn after Amiet (1961), pl. 13 bis, e.

8C. Redrawn after Amiet (1961), pl. 46, no. 655.

9. Photograph by and courtesy of Dr. Robert McC. Adams.

10. Photograph courtesy of Dr. Robert McC. Adams.

11A. Redrawn after Strommenger (1980), fig. 89.

11B. Redrawn after Van Driel and Van Driel-Murray (1983), map 1.

12. Photograph by and courtesy of Dr. Robert McC. Adams.

13. Photograph by and courtesy of Dr. Robert McC. Adams.

14A.   Redrawn after Amiet (1961), pl. 41, no. 620.

14B.   Redrawn after Amiet (1961), pl. 41, no. 621.

14C.   Redrawn after Amiet (1961), pl. 15, no. 255.

14D.   Redrawn after Delougaz and Kantor (1996), pl. 146e.

14E.   Redrawn after Amiet (1961), pl. 19, no. 319.

14F.   Redrawn after Amiet (1961), pl. 16, no. 275.

14G.   Redrawn after Delougaz and Kantor (1996), pl. 153f.

14H.   Redrawn after Delougaz and Kantor (1996), pl. 153b.

15.   Redrawn after Pittman (1993), fig. 7.

16.   Redrawn with modifications after Adams (1981), fig. 13.

17.   Redrawn with modifications after Adams (1981), fig. 12.

18.   Redrawn with modifications after Finkbeiner (1991), enclosure 23.

19.   Redrawn with modifications after Kouchoukos and Wilkinson (2007), fig. 10.

20.   Photograph by and courtesy of Dr. Geoffrey Emberling.

21.   Redrawn with modifications after Pournelle (2003b), fig. 58.

22A.   Redrawn after Amiet (1961), pl. 16, no. 266.

22B.   Redrawn after Amiet (1961), pl. 16, no. 276.

22C.   Redrawn after Amiet (1961), pl. 16, no. 273

22D.   Redrawn after Amiet (1961), pl. 16, no. 263.

22E.   Redrawn after Delougaz and Kantor (1996), pl. 152f.

22G.   Redrawn after Delougaz and Kantor (1996), pl. 149b.

22H.   Redrawn after Amiet (1961), pl. 16, no. 262.

23.   Photograph by Dr. Helene Kantor. Courtesy of the Oriental Institute of the University of Chicago.

24A–C. Redrawn after Delougaz and Kantor (1996), pls. 133a–133c

24D.   Redrawn after Frangipane and Palmieri (1983), fig. 69: 11

24E.   Redrawn after Frangipane and Palmieri (1983), fig. 70: 19

24F.   Redrawn after Frangipane and Palmieri (1983), fig. 71: 24.

25.   Photograph by Dr. Helene Kantor. Courtesy of the Oriental Institute of
        the University of Chicago.

26A.   A. Redrawn after Liverani (1983), fig. 1: 5.

26B.   Redrawn after Oates (2002), fig. 6 (bottom).

26C.   Redrawn after Englund (1998), fig. 53: W7227a.

Table

1.   Douglas White (UC, Irvine) kindly helped in the preparation of this
        chart.

Index

Adab, 113
Adams, Robert McCormick, 49, 92, 102, 103, 106, 114, 115, 155, 187nn2–3
agency, 152–54
agglomeration economies, 36
agricultural commodities, 20
agriculture, 41–43
Akkadian Empire, 19
Akkadian period, 20
Al-Hawa, Tell, 118, 120, 199
al-Hayyad, Tell, 165
Algaze, Guillermo, xiv–xvi, 121, 152
Anatolia, 19
animals, 141, 185n18. See also donkeys; livestock; transport, water vs. land pack, 67
Anu Ziggurat (Kullaba) area, 12, 13
Archaic Texts, 12, 41, 138, 177n1
    animals in, 48
    conventions of scribal administration in, 24
    kingly figures and, 190n1
    labor in, 129, 130
    metals in, 93
    from Umma, 112
    wool textiles in, 81, 85, 87, 88, 91, 94, 130
Arslan Tepe, 133–37
art, 23–24
Assyrian trade. See Old Assyrian trade

backward linkages, 38, 131. See also forward linkages
Badler, Virginia, 183n5
Bairoch, Paul, 53–54, 183n3
bala (tax) payments, 56, 58

Balanced Silver Accounts, 21
barley, 58
beveled rim bowls, 131, 132
Beydar, Tell, 119
boat texts, 58–59
boats, 58–60. See also transport, water vs. land
Brak, 117–18, 120, 121, 146
Brak, Tell, 70, 117, 119, 136
"buffer zones," 114
burial practice, Uruk period, 161

canals, 124, 147
captives. See slaves
cargo texts, 58, 59
central place models, 25–27
Chalcolithic. See Late Chalcolithic sites and societies
Chicago, 2
Chogha Mish, 114
Christaller, W., 25, 179n3
chronology, 163–64
Cioffi-Revilla, Claudio, 152–53
circular and cumulative causation, 37–40
cities, 160. See also urbanism
    evolution of systems of, 27
    ideological and administrative roles, 14–15
clay, seal impressions on. See sealings
clay sickle, 75
Clinton, DeWitt, 178n1
cloth production, 96
"collective action problem," 152
colonial process, Middle and Late Uruk, 73. See also Uruk, outposts

combing wool, 89–90
commerce. *See* trade
commodities, 17. *See also* exports; imports; trade
  prices, 21–22, 35–36
  production and distribution, 16, 17, 40
communication
  interpersonal, 126, 127, 138–39
  technologies of, 15, 16, 140, 188n2 (*see also see also* synergies of civilization, technologies of the intellect)
  written, 133–39
comparative advantage, 29–30, 35, 63
competition, 63, 123–24, 149
competitive advantage, 35, 36, 63, 139, 150
competitive emulation, 65
copper ores, 76
cows, 46, 48–49
created landscape(s), 1–3, 128, 150
Crone, Patricia, 149
Cronon, William, 1–2, 40, 150
crowding, 29
crucibles, 76
cumulative causation theory, 37–39. *See also* circular and cumulative causation
cumulative process, 180n6
cuneiform archives, 12. *See also* Archaic Texts

dairy products, 48–49
demographics, 124
Dercksen, J., 55
developmental inequalities, 36
developmental rates, differentiation in regional, 3, 16, 36
developmental sequences of southern and northern Mesopotamia, divergent, 144
Dewar, Robert, 108
differentiation, 30–31. *See also* developmental rates
  intrasite, 3
  in regional developmental rates, 3, 16, 36
disease (in early cities), 29
Dittmann, Rene, 131–32, 135, 154
diversification, 36
  urban growth as, 30–32
donkeys, 183n3
  domestication, 66–68
  transport using, 55–57, 66–68, 141–42
Drehem. *See* Puzrish Dagan
Drennan, Robert, 53, 183n3

Eanna area, 12, 13
Early Uruk problem, 164–65
economic activity, 25–27
economic behavior and processes, 17–18. *See also* wealth-maximizing behaviors
economic competition, 149. *See also* competition
economic differentiation, 31. *See also* differentiation
economic growth, 30–34 *See also* urban growth
economic innovations, 123–24
economic specialization, 140, 190n1
economics, 15. *See also* trade
economies
  human, compared with biological ecosystems, 31
  of scale, 16, 124
ecosystems, 41
Emberling, Geoffrey, 120
emulation, 123
encumbered workers, 129–31. *See also* slaves
Englund, Robert, 129, 138, 177n1, 181n7, 185n19
environmental advantages of southern Mesopotamia promoting urbanism, 40–49
environmental factors, 148. *See also* paleoenvironment
Eridu, 106
Erie Canal, 2
Euphrates, 94, 116
exaptation, 66, 182n1
excavation, 11, 98, 159–61
exchange, 123, 178n3. *See also* trade
exotics, 98–99
exports (Uruk period), 96
extensification, 79

Farber, Howard, 21–22
Farukhabad, 191n4
Feinman, Gary, 28
Fernandez-Armesto, Felipe, 147
"fiber revolution," 161
fish, 161
Flannery, Kent, 109–10
flax vs. wool, 78–80, 86
flint, 73–75
forward linkages, 38. *See also* backward linkages
Foster, Ben, 20

Fox, Edward Whiting, 145, 148
Frangipane, Marcella, 141
Frankfort, Henry, 23
fulling wool, 81, 85, 86. *See also* woolen
    textile industry

geographical advantages of southern Meso-
    potamia promoting urbanism, 50–62
geography, importance in history, 145, 148
geomorphical processes in Upper and
    southern Mesopotamia, 101–2
Gibson, McGuire, 112
Girsu (Tello), 60, 61
glyptic, 133–35, 154. *See also* sealings
Godin, 97, 183n5
Goody, Jack, xv, 128
Gould, Stephen Jay, 182n1
grain, 53, 56–58, 181n6
grasses, C4 salinity resistant, 43
"great leap forward" of Sumerian societies,
    152
growth, urban. *See* urban growth
Gunder Frank, Andre, 23

Habuba Kabira-süd, 70, 158
Habuba Kabira-süd/Tell Qannas settle-
    ment, 71–72
Hacinebi Tepe, 69, 76, 189n6
Hamoukar, 118, 120, 121
Harrapan civilization, 189n1
Hassek Höyük, 74
Hawa. *See* Al-Hawa
Hawley, Amos, 116, 121, 140
Hole, Frank, 154
Holstrom, J. E., 182n3
households and property, 157–59

ideational technologies. *See* "technologies
    of the intellect"
import substitution, 38, 65–66
import substitution process, multiplier
    effects of, 73
    flint, 73–75
    metals, 74, 76–77
    textiles, 77–92
imports, 93–98
information, xv
innovation, 39, 123–26. *See also* techno-
    logical innovation
interpersonal interaction. *See* communica-
    tion, interpersonal

Iraq, 43
irrigation, 147
Isin-Larsa period, 184n15

Jacobs, Jane, 30–32, 36–38, 64
Jagh Jagh River, 117
Jebel Aruda, 70–71, 158
Jemdet Nasr period, 114
Johnson, Gregory, 114, 161
Jokha, Tell. *See* Umma

Kantor, Helene, 23
Kasarda, John, 139
Khabur area, xvi, 4–5, 117–22
kingship, 153, 190n1
Kouchoukos, Nicholas, 108, 109
Krugman, Paul, 2–3, 27, 30, 34–36, 38, 39
Kültepe (Kanesh), 20, 55, 181n5

labor, xv, 91–92. *See also* woolen textile
    industry
    division of, 33, 34, 36, 82, 124, 190n1
    encumbered, 129–31
    shift in perception (and exploitation) of,
        128–31
labor flexibility, 124
labor organization, 40
"labor revolution," 128, 138
labor scenes, depiction of, 130
labor texts, 58, 60
laborers, 128, 129
Lagash (Tell al-Hiba), 159
lagoons, 44, 45
Lamberg-Karlovsky, Carl, 6
landscapes, natural vs. created, 1–3, 128,
    144, 150
Late Chalcolithic sites and societies, 3–6,
    133–37
Late Ubaid settlements in southern Meso-
    potamia, 3
Lenski, Gerhard, 127
Lévi-Strauss, Claude, 138, 189n5
linen, 82. *See also* flax vs. wool
littoral resources (Persian Gulf), 161
Liverani, Mario, 24
livestock, 46–49, 180. *See also* sheep
    herds
location theory, 34
locational theories, 25
    assumptions of, 25–27
luxury goods, 17

Machiavelli, Niccolò, 69
macrohistorical research, xiii, xiv
Malthus, Thomas, 31
Malthusian equilibrium, 31, 32, 63
Malthusian trap, 32
Mann, Michael, xv, 128
Marcus, Joyce, 109–10, 189n4
Margueron, Jean Claude, 97–98
market effects, 36
marketless trade, 19
markets, price-making, 20, 21
Marshall, Alfred, 179nn1–2
marshes, 44–46, 48, 49
Marx, Karl, 23
Matthews, Roger, 177n1
McCorriston, Joy, 43, 77, 79, 80, 161
McNeill, William, 29, 92, 162
Mesopotamia, southern vs. northern, 120, 144
metal-processing activities, 183
Metcalfe, Robert, 188n2
microhistorical research, xiii
milk production, 48–49
Mokyr, Joel, 127, 148
Moorey, Roger, 183n7
mortality (in early cities), 29
mortuary evidence, 162–63
multiplier effects. *See* import substitution process; trade
Myrdal, Gunnar, 30, 37–38

"natural environment," 40
natural landscape(s), 1–3, 144, 150. *See also* created landscape(s)
"new economic geography," 33–36
New York City, 2–3, 178n1
Nineveh, 118
Ninevite V period, 121
Nippur-Adab survey area
    demographic trends, 110
    Early-Middle Uruk period settlement patterns in, 103, 104, 106, 155
    Late Uruk period settlement patterns in, 103, 105, 106, 113, 155
Nissen, Hans-J., 12, 16, 103, 131, 135, 163, 164, 187n2

Oates, David, 77
Oates, Joan, 3, 77
obsidian blades, 75

Old Assyrian trade, 19–20, 55, 56, 67. *See also* trade
organizational efficiencies, 16

paleoenvironment, 154–55
paleozoology, 161–62
pasturing sheep, 87, 88. *See also* woolen textile industry
path-dependent processes, 39
Persian Gulf, 43–44
pictorial representations, 12, 14
plains across the north, 145
plucking wool, 88–89
Polanyi, Karl, 18–20, 23
political fragmentation, 149
Pollack, Susan, 116
population density and dispersion, 124, 126, 127
Porters, 182n2
Postgate, Nicholas, 87, 187n2
Pournelle, Jennifer, 49, 111, 116, 161, 188n8
power, xv
power, technologies of, 128. *See also* synergies of civilization, technologies of the intellect
precipitation. *See* rainfall
Pred, Allen, 37
prestate vs. state societies, 23
prestige goods economies, 17
"priest-king," 132, 190n1
property, 157–59
protocuneiform tablets, 12
Puzrish Dagan (Drehem), 55, 56, 82, 84–85, 185n16

rainfall, 43, 44
Ratzel, Frederick, 180n5
reckoning systems/devices, 12
record keeping, 133–39
reed hut, 47
religious sites, 115
Renfrew, Colin, 123
Ricardo, David, 15, 29, 31, 34, 63
Riemchengebäude, 95–96
rivers, 147
roofing timber, 97–98
Russell, Kenneth, 88

sail barge, 60. *See also* boats
Samsat, 118–20

Santone, Lenore, 54
Sauren, Herbert, 147
Schmandt-Besserat, Denise, 135
scribes, 138, 139. *See also* writing
seal, 133–36
sealings, 133–36
settlement patterns, fourth millennium
   in southern Mesopotamia, 102–17
   in Upper Mesopotamia, 117–22
Sharlach, Tonia, 55–60
sheep herds, 87–90, 184n9. *See also* woolen
   textile industry
Sherratt, Andrew, 98
silver, 19–21
slaves, 114, 129. *See also* encumbered
   workers
Smith, Adam, 15, 62, 69, 124, 140, 143, 146
Snell, D., 21, 179n2
social change, levels of analysis of, xiii–xiv
social differentiation, 31. *See also*
   differentiation
social evolution, (trans)regional patterns
   of interaction and, 143
social innovations, 123–24
social relations, institutions that structured,
   14
socioeconomic phenomena, 17–18. *See also*
   economic behavior and processes
specialization, 39. *See also under* urban
   growth
Spencer, Charles, 182n1
Spencer, Herbert, 30
spinning wool, 90
standardization, 33
state formation, pristine, 28
Stein, Gil, 68
Steinkeller, Piotr, 55, 60, 61, 114–15
Stronach, David, 118
"Sumerian" civilization, 177n1
Sumerian takeoff, 5, 144, 150
   conceptual problems concerning, 14–24
   material limits of the evidence, 11–14
   methodological problems, 24–27
   necessary conditions for, 66
supply and demand, 18, 20, 22
survey, 159
Susa, 19, 97, 114
Susiana Plain, 3, 114, 163
synergies of civilization, 123–24, 126–27,
   150

propinquity and its consequences,
   123–27
technologies of the intellect, 127–39

tartaric acid, 97
taxes, 56, 58, 185n16
technological innovation, 123, 126–27
technological parity of Mesopotamian and
   peripheral polities, xv–xvi
"technologies of the intellect," 128. *See*
   also under synergies of civilization
technology(ies), xv–xvi, 39. *See also*
   under communication; synergies of
   civilization
   of the mind, 128
Tello. *See* Girsu
textiles and textile production. *See also*
   import substitution process, textiles;
   woolen textile industry
   centrality to urban process, 92
   iconography, 81, 83, 84, 91
   materials used for, 82
   sources of evidence regarding, 81
textual evidence, 12
Tigris, 111
Tigris-Euphrates rivers. *See also* urbanism,
   advantages of
   alluvial lowlands, 3, 5
Tigris-Euphrates watershed, 116
Tilly, Charles, xiii, xiv
timber, roofing, 97–98
"Titles and Professions List," 190n1
towns, 160
trade, 15–20, 32, 149–50, 155–57
   cross-cultural, 36, 99 (*see also* imports;
   urbanism, in comparative perspective)
   evidence for, 93–99
   factors enhancing foreign, 66
   as fundamental agent of change, 40, 156
   terminology, 178n3
trade-fueled diversification, 33
transport, 15, 16, 36–37, 145–46
   importance, 144
   water vs. land, 53–55, 57–59, 61–62
   (*see also* urbanism, advantages of,
   geographical)
transport costs, 34

Ubaid period, 156, 157
Umm al-Aqarib, 114, 188n6

Umma (Tell Jokha), 20, 60, 61, 112, 114,
  159, 188n6
Ur, 106
Ur III Empire, 55, 56, 62, 147
Ur III period, 184n15
urban economies, growth of early Mesopotamian, 65–68. *See also* Sumerian
  takeoff
  stages, 64–66
urban growth, modeling the dynamics of,
  28–30
  growth as diversification, 30–32
  growth as specialization, 33–37
  growth institutionalized, 37–39
urban revolution revisited, 140–42
urban-rural hierarchies, 160
urban temples, 19
urbanism, 40
  advantages of
    comparative and competitive, 63
    environmental, 40–49
    geographical, 50–62
  in comparative perspective, 102–9 (*see
    also* Warka, primacy of)
    aborted in Upper Mesopotamia,
      117–22
    evidentiary biases, 100–102
    importance of location, 116 (*see also*
      Warka, primacy of)
  early, in alluvial Mesopotamia, 102–9
Uruk. *See also* Warka
  art, 23–24, 83
  outposts, 69–74 (*see also* import substi-
    tution process)
  "Uruk expansion," 68–73, 149
Uruk period, xiv–xv, 3, 11, 124, 149. *See
  also specific topics*
  Early-Middle Uruk period settlement
    pattern, 102, 103, 167–71
  Late Uruk period settlement pattern,
    103, 106, 173–76
  Late Uruk period sites and waterways,
    124
Uruk settlements, intrusive, 68
  types of, 68–69
Uruk-Warka, Late Uruk occupation of,
  106, 107
"Uruk world system," xv–xvi

Van De Mieroop, Marc, 14, 28, 185n18

Waetzoldt, H., 57, 82–83, 86, 90, 91, 184n13
wages, 21–22
warfare, 149
Warka, 11–12, 124, 162, 163. *See also* Uruk;
  Uruk-Warka
  primacy of, 109–17
Warka survey area, 124
  demographic trends, 110
  Early-Middle Uruk period settlement
    patterns in, 103–4, 106, 155
  Late Uruk period settlement patterns in,
    103, 105, 106, 112, 113, 155
water transport, 144–47. *See also* transport,
  water vs. land
wealth-maximizing behaviors, 18–19
weather. *See* rainfall
Weber, Max, 6
White, Douglas, 189n3
Wilcke, Claus, 179n1
Wilkinson, Tony, 3, 108, 109
Winchester, Simon, 54
wine, 96–97, 182n2, 186n5. *See also* tartaric
  acid
Wittfogel, Karl, 147
wool shearing, 185n20
woolen textile industry, 82, 86–92, 94.
  See also import substitution process,
  textiles; textiles
  factors accounting for takeoff of, 80–81
wooly sheep, introduction into Mesopotamia, 184n9
workers. *See also* laborers
  encumbered, 129–31
world-historical analysis, xiii
world-systemic studies, xiii, xiv
Wright, Henry T., xvi, 3, 6, 106, 117, 124,
  126, 156, 161, 191n4
Wright, Rita, 94
Wright, Robert, 123
writing, 135–39. *See also* record keeping

Yarim Tepe, 69

Zeytinlibahçe Höyük, 141–42
"Zipf's Law," 112